By the same author

Violence and Responsibility

The value of life

John Harris

London and New York

First published 1985
by Routledge

Reprinted 1991
by Routledge
2 Park Square, Milton Park, Abingdon, Oxon, OX14 4RN
270 Madison Ave, New York NY 10016

Reprinted 1992 (twice), 1994, 1997

Transferred to Digital Printing 2009

© *John Harris 1985*

Library of Congress Cataloguing in Publication Data

Harris, John, 1945–

The value of life.
Bibliography: p.
Includes index,
1. Medical ethics. 2. Bioethics. 3. Social
ethics. I. Title. [DNLM: 1. Ethics, Medical.
W 50 H314v]
R724.H24   1985   174'.2   84–18169

British Library Cataloguing in Publication Data

A catalogue record for this book is available from the British Library

ISBN 0–415–01032–9

Publisher's Note
The publisher has gone to great lengths to ensure the quality of this reprint
but points out that some imperfections in the original may be apparent.

For Sita

ALGERNON   My dear Aunt Augusta, I mean he was found out! The doctors found out that Bunbury could not live, that is what I mean—so Bunbury died.

LADY BRACKNELL   He seems to have had great confidence in the opinion of his physicians. I am glad, however, that he made up his mind at the last to some definite course of action, and acted under proper medical advice.

Oscar Wilde
The Importance of Being Earnest

Contents

Preface

Not very long ago medical ethics consisted of two supremely important commandments. They were: do not advertise; and avoid sexual relations with your patients. At about the same time as doctors were doing their best to obey these commandments, moral philosophers were more concerned with the meaning of words than with the meaning of life. Now, not just doctors but all health care professionals are interested in ethical questions as they relate to medical practice, and moral philosophers have once again become interested in and committed to trying to find answers to the most fundamental and substantial moral questions, rather than remaining content merely to clarify or otherwise analyse the questions.

In this way the interests of health professionals and moral philosophers have converged on the same range of issues. This book is an attempt by a philosopher to grapple with and to try to answer some of the most perplexing ethical questions that are raised by medical practice very broadly conceived.

The table of contents of this book indicates the range of problems that we will be examining, and the introduction says something about how this will be done and the ways in which the various issues lead into one another. Here I want primarily to put the reader on guard. The sorts of questions with which we will be dealing, many of them literally matters of life and death, are not of the sort about which it is easy to be dispassionate or indifferent. And I have not tried to be either. On the contrary, because the issues are so important and so pressing, the task of finding answers or solutions is equally so. I have accordingly tried to argue towards conclusions, and where this has proved possible I have presented the arguments, and the reasons for accepting those ideas, as forcefully and convincingly as I can. Where I cannot see the way so clearly I have indicated why this is so.

Those who expect philosophers to be dispassionate and impartial will consequently be disappointed. About matters so vital it is not possible to come to a conclusion, and then think it a matter of indifference that others might ignore it, or the good reasons for accepting it. Of course I hope to convince; that is the point of moral argument, and indeed the point of attempting to grapple with the problems in the first place. But where I fail to convince, I will be almost as pleased if the arguments I produce will provoke others into finding better arguments towards more sound conclusions. It is only in this way, by moral argument, that we may hope to improve the ways in which we decide moral questions and so have a chance of making the world a better place.

Those who are looking for guidance, in the sense of rules or rubrics to apply to situations or cases, will find none. Rather than try to show how our familiar and comfortable moral beliefs apply to new situations, I have tried to show how the new situations and discoveries of medical science and practice challenge our basic beliefs, and force us to think the problems through afresh.

A few words need to be said about *rights*. It will soon become apparent that I do not accept that there are any 'absolute' or 'natural' rights. Indeed, I think that generally the use of the word 'right' more often serves to obscure the rights and wrongs of an issue than to elucidate them; but the terms 'right' and 'rights' are so entrenched in normal usage that it is impossible entirely to abjure their employment. I should make it clear, however, that as I use the term, 'rights' are attributable only as the *conclusion* of a moral argument – not as one of its *premises*. So that when it is said that someone has a right to something, that just means that in all the circumstances of the case she should not be hindered in or prevented from doing or achieving that something. And if it is asked why she should not be hindered, the answer is *not* 'because she possesses something called a right which has been independently established or "discovered",' but simply because there are good moral reasons why it is wrong to hinder her.

Finally, readers will note that I do not assume that all health care professionals, let alone all patients, are men. I accordingly make what I hope is random use of the pronouns 'he' and 'she', despite the price to be paid in terms of loss of elegance and violation of traditional usage. But then violation, or at least questioning, of traditional practices is one of the purposes of this book.

Acknowledgments

I am grateful to the many people who have influenced this book. I have discussed the problems with which it deals with my students at Manchester, and with colleagues and students at other universities and colleges. Parts of the book have been given as papers or lectures to gatherings of people working in all branches of health care over the past eighteen months. In each of these contexts I have profited a great deal from the comments and questions, and this has shaped the book in all sorts of ways.

Raanan Gillon, Rodney Harris, Harry Lesser, Tom Sorrel and Hillel Steiner have each responded in detail to particular chapters, and the book is greatly improved as a result of their help.

Others with whom I have discussed these issues recently, and from whose help I have greatly benefited, are: Tony Ellis, Gavin Fairbairn, James Grant, Tony Howell, Bob Johnson, Richard Lindley, Mary Lobjoit, Judy Sebba, Simon Winner and Crispin Wright.

Thanks are due to my colleagues at Manchester University who granted me a term's study leave to work on this book and especially to Bernard Curtis who shouldered many of my responsibilities during my absence, and whose help and co-operation have been particularly important.

Parts of Chapters 2, 3, and 6 have appeared in previously published papers although they have been re-worked and re-thought for this book. The places in which they originally appeared were: 'Ethical problems in the Management of Some Severely Handicapped Children', *Journal of Medical Ethics*, vol. 7, no. 3, September 1981; 'Must Doctors Save Their Patients?', *Journal of Medical Ethics*, vol. 9, no. 4, December 1983; and 'In Vitro Fertilization: The Ethical Issues', *Philosophical Quarterly*, vol. 33, no. 132, July 1983; 'Full Humans and Empty Morality', *Philosophical Quarterly*, April 1985.

I have a special debt to Ronald Dworkin and to Jonathan Glover, who have been continuing sources of support and encouragement, and from whose philosophical example I hope I have learnt.

It remains only to acknowledge my own rather erratic typing skills which, flattered greatly by an electronic typewriter, are responsible for the completed script.

Introduction

This book, like the practice of medicine itself, is about the value of life. Health care is one of the clearest and most visible expressions of a society's attitude to the value of life. It is moreover one of the most important dimensions of the way in which we, as individuals and as members of society, demonstrate the value that we place on one another's lives and display the respect that we believe we owe to each other.

We do this in a number of ways. Firstly by the extent to which we show ourselves prepared to save the lives of others if we can, and by the extent we show ourselves prepared to pay the costs of so doing. Secondly by the way in which we sometimes select among the others whom we are prepared to save, or whom we judge worth saving. Sometimes this selection is made under the duress exerted by scarce resources; where we literally do not have, at a given moment, the ability to save all whose lives are at risk. Here we must choose, and our choice sometimes reflects the differential value that we place on the candidates for rescue. At other times we choose to save some and not others, where it is not the case that we are unable to save all those at risk. This happens right across the spectrum of health care, where for example decisions are taken not to resuscitate very old people or terminally ill patients on the one hand, and where, on the other, severely handicapped babies are sometimes given neither food nor treatment for dangerous infections, sometimes in the hope and certainly with the knowledge that they will not survive. All of these practices, and many others that we shall consider in the course of this book, show that we do in fact place very different value on the lives of other individuals. To see whether this is justified will be one of our tasks.

To discuss the value of life of course begs one of the most

fundamental questions. That is, what sorts of lives have value at all, and in virtue of what do they have value? In questions arising out of the practice of medicine, we tend to assume that it is not lettuces and chickens whose lives are in question, but only human beings. This may be a rash assumption since health care depends at many points upon research done upon animals, and even plants. Clearly it is taken for granted that animals and plants do not count morally, but the basis for this assumption is usually left unexamined. Even if our concern is focussed exclusively upon human beings, problems remain. When does human life begin? Is the human egg valuable at the moment of conception? Is it as valuable as the mature adult in the fullness of her powers, and is her life in turn more worth saving than that of the 90-year-old in the grip of senile dementia?

Our interest in the value of life is not of course simply a question of life and death. We show how we value others as much by the way we treat them as by the price we are prepared to pay, or the efforts we are prepared to make, to save their lives. Our concern for others is manifested in the way, and to the extent, that we are prepared to show to them both concern and respect. These are rather different ideas, as we shall see when discussing 'respect for persons' in more detail in Chapters 10 and 11. For the moment it is sufficient to note that our *concern* for others is manifested in the way we care for their health, safety and general welfare. In respect of these things most people's needs are remarkably similar, although of course each individual's personal circumstances will make the task of meeting these needs in particular cases more or less difficult, costly and complex. Our *respect*, on the other hand, is for others as individuals, with their own and unique conceptions of themselves, of what their lives are about, and of what they want for themselves. If we are to respect others, we must give priority not to what we want for them or think they ought to want, but to what they in fact want, or want to do. There is obvious scope here for some tension between these two demands to show both concern for another's welfare and to respect their wishes. For people are apt to develop preferences for things and simply to choose to do things which are manifestly not conducive to their own health, safety or general welfare.

Many classic and traditional dilemmas of medical ethics have arisen out of this tension. The problem of confidentiality, for example, is very often one of whether to keep secret information about a patient and thus respect her autonomy, or to reveal it to protect her own or another's welfare. Similarly, the many dilemmas concerning whether or not to tell patients the truth about their condition, or about how much of the truth to tell them, are problems because respecting their wish, or their supposed right to know, is perceived as damaging to their health or some other dimension of their welfare.

Many of our attitudes to and judgments about these dilemmas are prompted by our most basic beliefs and most fundamental values. These we are likely to have acquired unself-consciously, and to have preserved uncritically until we need to use them. Although these beliefs and values form the basis of our morality, they seldom themselves become the subject of critical examination and evaluation, although the decisions which they generate may well be discussed, reviewed and criticised in detail.

Since Socrates, one of the principal concerns of philosophy, and perhaps its chief claim to be considered seriously by non-philosophers, has been its preoccupation with the justification of the most fundamental beliefs and values. For if these cannot be justified, or if the justifications given for them are defective, or otherwise open to criticism, then the decisions based on them will be left without adequate support. Moreover, if these basic beliefs are themselves unclear, either in content or in scope, they can be worse than useless as guides to conduct. One of the other major preoccupations of philosophy has been the analysis and clarification of concepts and the relations between concepts and hence has been to make both clearer and more substantial the components from which our basic beliefs and values are constructed.

In attempting to resolve the moral dilemmas posed by medical practice, we will be sharing these preoccupations and concerns. For the resolution of moral dilemmas both requires and presupposes a willingness and an ability to question and challenge basic beliefs, and to show whether or not they can be justified. And this activity in turn requires that we understand the concepts used to frame these beliefs, and are clear as to what they mean and imply. Both these activities are essentially philosophical. That does not of course mean that only people who self-consciously regard themselves as philosophers, or who are professional philosophers, can undertake them. Philosophy, unlike medicine, has never been the exclusive preserve of professionals, and one of the tasks of this book is to show how the resolution of the dilemmas of medical practice raises important issues of personal morality and of public policy in which we all have an interest.

I should emphasise here that our interest in all these problems and dilemmas will be an interest in their resolution. We shall not merely be attempting to rehearse the considerations relevant to resolving the various problems, but in actually trying to do so. The problems are so important and so pressing that it would be difficult to take them seriously without wanting not merely to know how to go about solving them but actually to do so. Just as the proper business of medicine is not merely to understand the nature and causes of illness but to try to prevent or cure it, so the proper business of medical ethics is not merely to understand the nature of the moral problems raised by medical practice but to try to resolve them.

Many people are sceptical about the possibility of doing this, and particularly perhaps about the value of attempts by philosophers to do this. This scepticism is partly occasioned by a belief that medical ethics is properly the concern and perhaps even the preserve of those professionally involved in health care. It is also perhaps a product of the belief that ultimately morality is a personal matter, in that even if it is not the case that one person's moral beliefs are as good as another's, it is at any rate impossible to *demonstrate* that they are not.

Neither scepticism about the possibility of resolving the dilemmas posed by medical practice nor that about the contribution of 'lay' people is justified. All moral issues, particularly ones so important as those which arise in health care, are of public importance; and anyone who is prepared to think critically and seriously about them can contribute to their resolution. I will argue this point in more detail in Chapter 3. Nor is scepticism about the possibility of progress in moral argument any more justified. While it is true that there are many different moral outlooks and perspectives, and perhaps equally many and various ethical theories, all presuppose the possibility of moral argument. Indeed, all people who think that it is possible either to do wrong, or for that matter to do what's right, depend upon and use moral argument. This reveals a very important fact about the nature of morality and hence about the nature of ethics. It is simply that if something is right or wrong, morally right or wrong, there must be some reason why this is so. And reasons can always be scrutinised for their adequacy.

Indeed, someone can only claim that their actions or decisions stem from moral conviction or are dictated by moral considerations—are in short part of an attempt to live by ethical standards, if they can say why those actions and decisions are *right*, if they can show how they are *justified*. To have a moral belief is, whatever else it is, to believe that the world[1] will be a better place if certain things happen and others do not, and that it will be a worse place if the reverse is true. Such a judgment would be incoherent if the maker of that judgment could not say why it would be better or worse in these and these circumstances. And it is the reasons that are given in support or defence of a moral position that make rational debate about ethics possible.

For reasons may be weak or strong, better or worse, defective or compelling, in a number of ways. It is not possible to produce an exhaustive account of the ways in which reasons given in defence of a moral position or judgment may be legitimately criticised. Or, how other and different reasons may be best defended. The argument of this book just consists in the provision of reasons for holding the views it defends and of reasons for rejecting the positions it criticises. The best way to see what such reasons might be and to see if they are sound is to see them in action!

I have said that this book is about the value of life. I shall endeavour to present and defend an argument about how we are to understand just what it is to value life and about what is involved in respecting the lives of those we conclude do have valuable lives. This argument will gradually unfold as particular moral dilemmas posed by medical practice are considered. I have tried to deal with the major issues of medical ethics in a way that allows this argument to proceed logically and progressively; so that the problems raised in the attempt to resolve each successive issue both lead into, and show the need for, the next stage in the discussion. As the argument progresses, very many definite and specific theses will be advanced and claims made. In support of these I offer in each case reasons for accepting the thesis or believing the claims. Only those who can find better reasons for better conclusions will be entitled to reject them.

One final point needs to be made about my method of proceeding. It is that although on all occasions our point of departure will be one of the central dilemmas of medical ethics, we may have to stray some way from medical practice in our attempt to resolve it. Sometimes this will involve our considering imaginary and perhaps even extraordinary, or extraordinarily unlikely, cases and possibilities. The point of doing so will be to assess our basic beliefs and values by 'testing them to destruction' on extreme and extremely disturbing possibilities. It is sometimes only such possibilities that provide a shock sufficient to allow us to see just how committed to our values and beliefs we are, or to make us see the need to change or revise them.

1 Beings, human beings and persons

The ultimate question for medical ethics, indeed, for any ethics, is also in a sense the very first question that arises when we begin to grapple with moral problems. The question is simply: what makes human life valuable and, in particular, what makes it more valuable than other forms of life? There is of course no doubt that we do value human life supremely, we think it important to save a person rather than a dog where we cannot save both, and we think it right to do so. We do not regard a preference for human life as a mere prejudice in favour of our own species. But what is the basis of this belief, what justifies it and what, if anything, makes it more than mere prejudice in favour of ourselves and our own kind?

This question—what makes human life valuable—may seem excessively abstract, a purely philosophical question, interesting perhaps, but too difficult and controversial to be of help in solving the practical problems that every day face health care professionals. Ironically, many of the day-to-day decisions taken in medical practice presuppose particular answers to this question. Abortion, for example, could be permissible only in cases where there is no danger to the mother and where the foetus is normal on the assumption that it is somehow less valuable than adults, and so lacks the protections and rights that adults have. Most people would not, I suppose, think that mentally or physically handicapped individuals are somehow less valuable than others, and yet anyone who thinks that the detection of handicap in the foetus is a good reason for abortion, must accept that such an individual is, or will become, less valuable than one without such handicap, less valuable because less worth saving or less entitled to life. The same issue of value arises at the other end of the continuum, where questions are raised as to whether we should continue to devote resources to the rescue and resuscitation of the aged or the terminally ill, or those in a permanent coma, and so on. If we decide against resuscitation, or divert resources to more 'worthwhile' cases, or types of cases, we are treating these lives as less valuable, less worthy of preservation than the others whom we choose to help.

The new techniques of *in vitro* embryology, which make possible the growing of embryos to provide tailor-made human tissue,[1] give us further reasons for being clear about the relative value of the embryo and the adult. Many people think the answer to this question could be settled if we could be sure about the answer to the related question 'when does life begin?', and, returning to the other end of the continuum, that our problems about the management of those in a persistent vegetative state would be resolved if we had an adequate definition of death. I shall argue that both these questions are misconceived even if they could be given determinate answers, and that what we need to know is not when life begins, but rather when life begins to matter morally. And the correlated question is not 'when does life end?' but rather 'when does life cease to matter morally?' In short, when does life begin to have that special value we believe attaches to human life and when does it cease to have that value?

What do we mean by 'value'?

When we ask what makes human life valuable we are not concerned with what might make for differences in value between individuals, but with what makes individuals of a particular kind more valuable than others. So, we are not concerned with any of the sorts of considerations that might figure in a balloon debate, where reasons are given why each person in the balloon is more worthy and valuable than the others and so should be the last person to be thrown out to prevent a crash.[2] Rather we are interested in why and whether people have a particular significance and value simply because they are people and have whatever it takes to be a person, and are not quite different sorts of beings, animals or plants perhaps, which do not have what it takes.

To put this point another way, to believe that people are valuable in this sense is to accept that they should be treated as equals, that is *as if they had equal value*, quite irrespective of any reasons we might have for showing preferences between them for particular purposes. This is sometimes expressed as the view that there are basic human rights possessed by all people in virtue of their humanity, or as a belief in equal rights, or as the view that all people should be treated as equals.[3] It is the assumption behind a belief in equality before the law, and it underlies the view that all are equally entitled to the care and protection of the state, including its medical care and protection. So, to hold that life is valuable in this sense is to believe that the individual whose life is valuable is entitled to the same concern, respect and protection as that accorded to any other individual.

When we ask what makes human life valuable we are trying to identify those features, whatever they are, which both incline us and entitle us to value ourselves and one another, and which license our belief that we are more valuable (and not just to ourselves) than animals, fish or plants. We are looking for the basis of the belief that it is morally right to choose to save the life of a person rather than that of a dog where both cannot be saved, and our belief that this is not merely a form of prejudice in favour of our own species but is capable of justification. So the features we are looking for, although they will be possessed by normal adult human beings, will not simply catalogue the differences between such beings and other creatures. Rather they will point to features which have moral relevance, which justify our preference for ourselves and our belief that it is right to treat people as the equals of one another and as the superiors of other creatures.

Humans and persons

In identifying the things that make human life valuable we will be pointing to the features that would make the existence of any being who possessed them valuable. It is important to have a word for such beings which is not simply anthropocentric or species-specific. I shall use the term *person* to stand for any being who has what it takes to be valuable in the sense described, whatever they are otherwise like. Although in normal use 'person' is just another (and usefully gender-neutral) term for 'human being', as I shall use it from now on it will also be species-neutral as well. This does not put as great a strain on our normal understanding of the word as may be imagined. For example, the question of whether or not there are people on other planets is a real one. If there are, we need not expect them to be human people (it would be bizarre if they were!), nor need we expect them to look or sound or smell (or anything else) like us. They might not even be organic, but might perhaps reproduce by mechanical construction rather than by genetic reproduction. But if we are able to answer the question in the affirmative, we will be distinguishing between people on other worlds and animals, plants or machines on those worlds. We will be deciding whether an appropriate response to them would be to have them for dinner in one sense or in the other. And if the people who we find (or who find us) turn out to be technologically very much our superiors, we may hope to persuade them that we are also people, not just like them maybe, but enough like them to be valuable, and to warrant being accorded the same concern, respect and protection as they would show to each other. And, if the boot is on the other foot, to warrant our according to them the same concern, respect and protection as we accord to one another. But in what respects must we be like them or they like us?

If we can answer this question, we will have sketched a concept of the person, and of what makes such creatures valuable, which we can apply to the dilemmas which face us every day and do not merely await us in some science fictional future. To begin our attempt to arrive at such an account we will start at the beginning.

I When does life begin?

Many people have supposed that the answer to the question 'when does life begin to matter morally?' is the same as the answer to the question 'when does human life begin?' The moment of conception may seem to be the obvious answer to the question of when life begins. Over any rival candidates it seems to have the decided edge that it is an identifiable event from which point the egg begins the continuous process that leads to maturity. But of course the egg is alive well before conception and indeed it undergoes a process of development and maturation without which conception is impossible. The sperm, too, is alive and wriggling. Life is a continuous process that proceeds uninterrupted from generation to generation continuously (or at least sporadically) evolving. It is not, then, life that begins at conception. But if not life, is it not at least the new *individual* that begins at conception?

A number of 'things' may begin at conception. Fertilisation can result not in an embryo but in a tumour which can threaten the mother's life. This tumour, called a hydatidiform mole, would not presumably be invested with all the rights and protections that many believe spring fully armed into existence at fertilisation.

Even when fertilisation is, so to speak, on the right tracks, it does not result in an individual even of any kind. The fertilised egg becomes a cell mass which eventually divides into two major components:

> the embryoblast and the trophoblast. The embryoblast becomes the foetus and the trophoblast becomes the extraembryonic membranes, the placenta and the umbilical cord. The trophoblastic derivatives are alive, are human, and have the same genetic composition as the foetus and are discarded at birth.[4]

A further complication is that the fertilised egg cannot be considered a new individual because it may well become two individuals. The fertilised egg may split to form twins and this can happen as late as two weeks after fertilisation.

Life, then, is a continuum and the emergence of the individual occurs gradually. At this point it is commonly argued that if life does not begin at conception and if it cannot be said that a new individual human being begins there, at least the potential for a new human being is then present complete with its full genetic make-up and with all its uniqueness and individuality. And since the fertilised egg is potentially a human being we must invest it with all the same rights and protections that are possessed by actual human beings. This we may call 'the potentiality argument'.

The potentiality argument

There are two sorts of difficulty with the potentiality argument which are jointly and severally fatal to it. The first is that the bare fact that something will become X (even if it will inevitably become X, which is far from being the case with the fertilised egg and the adult human being) is not a good reason for treating it now as if it were in fact X. We will all inevitably die, but that is, I suppose, an inadequate reason for treating us now as if we were dead.

The second difficulty is that it is not only the fertilised egg that is potentially a human being. The unfertilised egg and the sperm are equally potentially new human beings. To say that a fertilised egg is potentially a human being is just to say that if certain things happen to it (like implantation), and certain other things do not (like spontaneous abortion), it will eventually become a human being. But the same is also true of the unfertilised egg and the sperm. If certain things happen to the egg (like meeting a sperm) and certain things happen to the sperm (like meeting an egg) and thereafter certain other things do not (like meeting a contraceptive), then they will eventually become a new human being.

It is sometimes objected that it is only the fertilised egg that has all the necessary potential present in one place, so to speak, and it is this that is crucial. It is only when the egg has been fertilised, so the argument goes, that a new unique entity exists that itself has all the potential necessary to become a new human being. This seems plausible enough until we remember that something had the potential to become that fertilised egg; and whatever had that potential, had also the potential to become whatever it is that the fertilised egg has the potential to become!

If then we ignore the first difficulty with the potentiality argument, and concede that we are somehow morally required to actualise all human potential, we are all in for a highly exhausting time. And it is clear that if we put the maximal effort into procreation that this imperative demands, our endeavours will ultimately be self-defeating.

All that can safely be said of the fertilised egg is that it is live human tissue. Life itself does not begin at fertilisation, for the egg and the sperm are alive also. Life continues, and so what we need is not an account of when life begins but of when life begins to matter morally. Clifford Grobstein's answer to this question has been influential, and it is worth looking at what he proposes.

When does self begin?

Grobstein argues that what matters is not the beginning of life, nor yet of human life, but of *self*. Self for Grobstein is personhood, that which makes us 'characteristically human', that which has an 'inner' life. A self will have a sense of self, and this means in effect self-awareness. 'Self is not just sensation, it is sensation within a bounded object that is the physical equivalent of the discreteness of the feeling of self.'[5] This is a fairly minimal conception of self, as we shall see, and Grobstein offers three criteria of recognition of the presence of self. First, a self will exhibit 'behaviour diagnostic of a rudimentary self-state',[6] and this behaviour would be some minimal response to external change. The example offered of such a response is the stimulation of an embryo by stroking its skin with hairs, and the response 'was a slow and weak turning of the head away from the stimulus'.[7]

The second criterion is the possession of 'non-behavioural

functional processes'.[8] An example of such a process is the nervous system, and the criterion is that 'the self be capable of being recognised as a self by others'.[9] The first two criteria are very rudimentary and do not in fact distinguish persons from animals, or even the human foetus from that of most animals. For these reasons, Grobstein is forced to place all the burden of recognition of self in this third criterion:

> The question is to determine when in development the embryo or fetus is generally recognizable as human and evokes empathy as another self. Prior to that point, assumption of the presence of an inner self requires some objective evidence of its existence. Subsequent to that point the burden of proof shifts. A self is to be assumed unless there is strong evidence to the contrary. The question thus becomes the stage at which the embryo or fetus can first be generally recognized as human, generating empathy as a person or a person to be.[10]

By showing us diagrams of more and more humanoid foetuses Grobstein is able to persuade us that the stage in question is at the end of the first trimester of pregnancy, and that this point happily coincides with 'the time at which it has been traditional to change the term embryo to fetus as the designation for the developing human'.[11]

This recognition of self by others is necessary, Grobstein believes, to get over the problem familiar in philosophy as the problem of other minds:

> Although we directly know the experience of self only individually—as an internal state—we infer it in others and they in us. In the process, the sense of self is affirmed and reinforced. In that sense the self is partly a product of social interaction. In particular the social status of personhood is accorded through recognition and acceptance by others. Recognition and empathy registered by observers are especially important criteria for assessing levels of selfness when policy issues are at stake.[12]

While Grobstein is doubtless right to see the sense of self as partly the product of social interaction, he has no reason to suppose that recognising a foetus (or anything) as distinctly humanoid is any evidence at all of the presence of the requisite inner qualities. What reason is there to suppose that we feel empathy only in the presence of self-awareness? Why should we not assume that the empathy evoked by the sight of the 3-month-old foetus is just the soggy sentimentality classically evoked by proximity to dependent sentient creatures, like puppies?

II When does life begin to matter morally?

Grobstein (and all of us) needs a way of recognising others as persons rather than animals, machines or collections of living human cells. If the social and moral status of person is 'accorded through recognition and acceptance by others', it is so accorded we may hope with justification. People are not people because they are accepted, but rather they are accepted because they are people. The question must be, what should lead us to accept the embryo or the foetus or the neonate or the child or anything at all as having that range of qualities that make them persons. In virtue of what are we morally required to accept something/someone as a person, and consequently morally required to refrain from treating them in ways that we may not treat people?

There seem to me to be two different strategies that might be adopted in attempting to discover just what it is that entitles an individual to be considered a person. Although each strategy is distinct, they each seem to point towards the same sort of answer. While no answer to such a profound and difficult question is likely to be entirely satisfying or uncontroversial, the convergence of these two strategies upon one sort of answer is encouraging.

Strategy 1: what is a person?
The first strategy involves looking at what it is that's so different about a person that justifies our valuing such a creature above others. This strategy treats as unproblematic the question of what it is that makes the lives of people valuable, and concentrates on examining which of the differences between people and other creatures seem to be relevant to the question of their differential value. This is the strategy adopted by Grobstein and, as we have seen, the features to which he points do not in fact distinguish persons and animals. If we look at creatures we are sure are persons if any are—normal adult human beings—and can find features of their lives or capacities which, unlike differences of the 'featherless biped' type, incline us to judge their lives of more significance and value than lives which lack such features, we might come close to a concept of the person.

What features, for example, do we possess, that, if we were to encounter similar or related features in beings from other worlds, would incline us to accept that there were after all *people* on other planets and that we had at last made contact with them?

This strategy for identifying the defining characteristics of a person by pointing to features that could in principle be possesed by beings other than humans has a distinguished history. John Locke, in the second half of the seventeenth century, produced an elegant account, although it must be admitted that he was not looking for beings from other worlds. What he was thinking about, however, was how to distinguish persons from other creatures in a way that made sense of the difference in value that we place upon them.

> ... we must consider what *person* stands for; which, I think, is a thinking intelligent being, that has reason and reflection, and can consider itself, the same thinking thing, in different times and places; which it does only by that consciousness which is inseparable from thinking and seems to me essential to it; it being impossible for any one to perceive without perceiving that he does perceive.[13]

This account, making a combination of rationality and self-consciousness the distinguishing features of a person has much to recommend it. The rationality required is of a fairly low order, just sufficient for the individual to 'consider itself the same thinking thing in different times and places'; and for Locke self-consciousness is simply the awareness of that reasoning process.

Certainly, Locke has gone far enough to distinguish persons from other creatures, animals and so on; he has isolated features of the person that we value having, and which make the whole business of valuing other things possible. For valuing is a conscious process and to value something is both to know what we value and to be conscious of our attitude towards it. Any rival account of what it is to be a person would have to isolate features that were similarly valued by us and which were of the sort to account for the peculiar status that we give to creatures possessing such features.

Before taking the concept of the person further we must examine the second strategy, which involves asking just what it is that makes life valuable.

Strategy 2: what is valuable?

Instead of concentrating on the differences between people and other sorts of being, we might try to investigate the issue of just what it is that makes existence valuable.

Here, our question is so difficult and so profound as to be almost absurd. Like the question of the meaning of life, that of the value of life, when put in such broad terms, seems unanswerable. Not because there is no answer, but rather because there are so many answers! There are likely to be, and perhaps are, as many accounts of what makes life valuable as there are valuable lives. Even if we felt confident that we could give a very general account of what makes life valuable for human beings, perhaps by singling out the most important or most frequently occurring features from the lists of what they value of a large cross-section of people, we would have no reason to suppose that we had arrived at a satisfactory account. For one thing, people's reasons for valuing life might well change over time; but more importantly, there would be no reason to suppose that our list bore any relation at all to the account that might be given of the value of life by non-human people, people on other worlds.

This problem need not, however, bring our investigation to a halt before it has taken off, for the point of the question lies not so much in our arriving at a satisfactory account of the value of life, but rather in our discovering a way of knowing when we are confronted with valuable lives. Our interest is in knowing which other beings have valuable lives, and there may be good reasons for being much surer of this than of the value of any of the features that are supposed to make life valuable![14] If there are, as there may well be, as many accounts of what it is that makes life valuable as there are valuable lives these accounts in a sense cancel each other out.[15] What matters is not the *content* of each account, but rather that the individual in question has the capacity to give such an account.

The point is this: if we allow that the value of life for each individual consists simply in those reasons, *whatever they are*, that each person has for finding their own life valuable and for wanting to go on living, then we do not need to know what the reasons are. All we need to know is that particular individuals have their own reasons, or rather, simply, that they value their own lives.

Valuable lives should not be ended

Each of us will have our own reasons for valuing our own lives and each of us is able to appreciate that the same is true of others, that they too value their own lives. What we have in common is our *capacity* to value our own lives and those of others, however different our *reasons* for doing so may be or may seem to be. I believe those rather simple, even formal features of what it takes to be a person—that persons are beings capable of valuing their own lives—can tell us a good deal about what it is to treat someone as a person. They can tell us how to recognise other beings as people, and they also tell us why it's wrong to kill such creatures against their will. They are people because they are capable of valuing life, and it's wrong to kill them because they do value life.

The wrongness of killing another person is, on this view, chiefly the wrongness of permanently depriving her of whatever it is that makes it possible for her to value her own life. So that although each person may find different and unique value in their own life, each is equally wronged by being deprived of a life, the continuation of which they value. We can thus see what's wrong with prematurely ending such a life without in any way sharing the values that make it worthwhile. If we discover persons on other worlds, we may recognise them as persons and appreciate the wrongness of killing them, without any understanding of 'what makes them tick' or of what they could possibly value; so long as it was clear that they are capable of valuing their own existence.

It is important to be clear that it is the *capacity* to value one's own life that is crucial, for of course those with the capacity to value their own lives may not in fact do so. This does not make them any the less persons, for only someone with the capacity to value their own life could disvalue it. But where people do not in fact value their own lives or do not want their lives to continue, then of course it will not be wrong for them to kill themselves, or for others to help them do so, or for others to kill them at their request. So that on this conception of the person neither suicide, nor aiding suicide, nor voluntary euthanasia will be wrong, for individuals by wishing to die show that they do not value life, or that they value death more. To frustrate the wish to die will on this view be as bad as frustrating the wish to live, for in each case we would be negating the value that the individuals themselves put on their lives.[16]

The convergence of the two strategies

We can now see how the two strategies for finding out what it takes to be a person converge. For, if we ask what it takes to be the sort of being that has the capacity to value its own existence, we find features very like those identified by John Locke—features which not only characterise the person, but distinguish persons from other creatures like plants, fish or animals.

In order to value its own life a being would have to be *aware*
that it has a life to value. This would at the very least require
something like Locke's conception of *self-consciousness*, which involves a person's being able to 'consider itself as itself in different
times and places'. Self-consciousness is not simple awareness,
rather it is awareness of awareness. To value its own life, a being
would have to be aware of itself as an independent centre of
consciousness, existing over time with a future that it was capable
of envisaging and wishing to experience. Only if it could envisage
the future could a being want life to go on, and so value its
continued existence. The capacity to value existence in this sense
is a fairly low-level capacity; it does not require rationality in any
very sophisticated sense of that term, merely the ability to want
to experience the future, or to want not to experience it and the
awareness of those wants.

The concept of the person

We have at last arrived at a concept of the person. On the account
that has emerged, a person will be any being capable of valuing
its own existence. Apart from the advantage of its simplicity, this
account has two other major advantages. The first is that it is
value- and species-neutral. It does not imply that any particular
kind of being or any particular mode of existence is more valuable
than any other, so long as the individual in question can value its
mode of existence. Once this threshold is crossed, no individual
is more of a person or more valuable than any other. This concept
of the person sets out to identify which individuals and which
forms of life have the sort of value and importance that makes
appropriate and justifies our according to them the same concern,
respect and protections as we grant to one another. And it tries
to do so without begging any questions as to the sort of creatures
that will be found to qualify.

The second advantage is that it is capable of performing the
two tasks we require of a concept of the person. These are that it
should give us some grasp of why persons are valuable and make
intelligible the moral difference between persons and other
beings. The second task is that it should enable us, in principle,
to tell persons from non-persons.

On this concept of the person, the moral difference between
persons and non-persons lies in the value that people give to their
own lives. The reasons it is wrong to kill a person is that to do so

robs that individual of something they value, and of the very thing that makes possible valuing anything at all. To kill a person not only frustrates their wishes for their own futures, but frustrates every wish a person has. Creatures that cannot value their own existence cannot be wronged in this way, for their death deprives them of nothing that they can value.

Of course non-persons can be harmed in other ways, by being subjected to pain for example, and there are good reasons for avoiding subjecting any sentient creatures to pain if this can be avoided.[17]

The idea that persons are beings capable of valuing their own existence also gives us a way, at least in principle, of recognising persons when we confront them, although in particular cases this may be no easy matter.

III How do we recognise persons?

Usually this is simplicity itself. If we want to know whether or not someone values their own existence we can ask them; and their ability to answer or even to entertain the question will show that they have the requisite capacity. We could say, then, that language is the hallmark of self-consciousness. Any creature with even the most rudimentary form of language will be able to let us know that it values life and wants to go on living. Moreover, language is the only vehicle we know of for self-consciousness. With language we can display, through commentary, that awareness of our awareness that is self-consciousness. It is apt that our thoughtful self-monitoring process is sometimes called the 'internal soliloquy'.

The problem is of course to tell whether creatures that do not have or do not appear to have language are or are not self-conscious and so capable of valuing life. If they have language they can value life, but could they do so without language?

Animal psychologists[18] have developed tests which do indicate that some creatures have developed a rudimentary self-awareness. Normally animals do not recognise their own reflections in mirrors, responding to those reflections as if to other members of their own species, by hostile display. However, some chimpanzees and orang-utans seem to become aware after a while that the mirror image is of themselves, using it to inspect inaccessible parts of their bodies. A simple test has been devised to see

whether monkeys understand that the mirror image is of themselves. By painting a red patch on both the wrist and the forehead
of the monkey, experimenters were able to tell the sheep from the
goats. Some monkeys showed no interest in the reflections,
although they were interested in the patches on their wrists, while
chimps and orang-utans immediately scratched their own fore-
heads rather than the reflected ones.

While it is difficult to resist the conclusion that this demonstrates some degree of awareness of self in those chimps that
recognise that the reflection is of themselves, it does not seem
enough to attribute to them the sort of self-consciousness that
would enable them to value their own lives. They would, for
example, need no conception of themselves as existing over time
with a future that they wished to experience in order to recognise
that a reflection in a mirror was of themselves.

Much more convincing in terms of discovering other species
capable of valuing their own lives are the numerous attempts that
have been made since 1966 to teach chimpanzees a natural language. The first, and still one of the most successful, of such
attempts was made by two American psychologists, R. Allen and
Beatrice Gardner, with an infant female chimpanzee called
Washoe [19] The Gardners thought a gestural language much more
likely to succeed than a 'spoken' one and embarked on a long
programme teaching Washoe American Sign Language or 'Ames-
lan' which is used by many deaf people in the United States.
After five years Washoe had a vocabulary of about 160 words
which she could combine into relatively complex sentences.
Although controversy still surrounds the claim that Washoe can
speak, I think she clearly can and is therefore equally clearly a
person. If, for the sake of argument, this is correct, does it re-
inforce the possiblity that the monkeys exhibiting an awareness
of self but which do not have language, are also persons? This is
an important question because of the parallel with human beings.

We know that almost all human beings will naturally develop
the capacity for language and equally naturally will develop into
persons. Should we, in human beings, take the first signs of
self-awareness (that might be revealed in the same way as it has
been in monkeys) as signs that self-consciousness is also established and all that is required is a language to express that self-
consciousness? It seems to me doubtful that signs of self-awareness are also signs of the sort of self-consciousness that enables
persons to value their own lives. This is because it seems probable

that thoughts as complex as the idea of a future that one wishes to live to experience require a vehicle of thought, language, in which they can occur. However, it is difficult to know how this could be established and, because so much is at stake, it seems highly desirable to err on the safe side. For this reason in the cases of beings that we know are of a kind capable of being persons, like humans and perhaps chimpanzees, we should perhaps take the capacity to exhibit self-awareness of the rather primitive sort we have noted to be the first signs of personhood. For other sorts of being where we have no independent evidence that they have any capacities of the requisite sort, we can be more cautious and look for evidence of the ability to use language.

So, the presence of language is definitive evidence that the beings who possess it are persons.[20] And where self-awareness is exhibited by beings of the kind we know to be capable of valuing their own lives we should, for safety's sake, take this as evidence that they are, or are starting to be, self-conscious and able to value their existence.

There's value in numbers

Precisely because each person's life is individually valuable, two lives are more valuable than one. So that in cases where we have to choose between lives where we cannot save all at risk, we should choose to save as many lives as we can. It is sometimes thought[21] that such policies disvalue the individual because the 'loss of each life is the loss of a whole world' but precisely because of this the opposite is the case. If a whole world is lost when one person dies, then two whole worlds are lost when two die and so on. If I do not always try to avoid shortening the life of another person who values their life, or, if I do not always help to prolong life if I can and similarly, always try to save as many lives as I can or try to kill as few people as possible (if circumstances leave me no better choice), then I have effectively discounted the value of each and every extra life that I could have saved or could have refrained from killing. To believe that where I could save two lives rather than one, that I would have no moral reason for so doing, I would have to believe that the life of the additional person adds nothing of value to the calculation I must make. If I think that the presence of an additional person gives me no additional reason to rescue a group of three rather than a group of two where I cannot save both, I must, presumably, judge the

presence of the extra life at risk to have added nothing of value
to the balance. To make such a judgment would entirely discount
the value of the extra life. If we ask what reason there could be
for valuing at zero the extra life, there seems to be no answer, and
there is none because the presence of that extra life does add
something, it adds a valuable life, a life that is worth saving.

We can thus see that a policy of maximising the numbers of
lives that we try to save, so far from being anti-individualistic, in
the sense that it is prepared to sacrifice individuals to groups, is
in fact the only policy that can plausibly claim to value individuals! This is because it values each and every individual whether
or not they happen to find themselves alone at risk, or happen to
be in the company of others. To believe otherwise would involve
regarding someone's life as valuable if she happened to be the
only person in danger, but suddenly of no value if in danger
accompanied by others, where a new individual provides an alternative and mutually exclusive opportunity for rescue.

We will examine later, in Chapter 5, arguments that point towards a different sort of calculus where rival groups of lives are
at stake.

IV Persons and full human beings

Having established a concept of the person and one which will be
of considerable use to us in the ensuing discussion, we should
consider some arguments for disestablishing such a concept. One
powerful objector to any use of the term 'person' is Mary Warnock. Replying to an earlier essay of mine on the ethics of *in vitro*
fertilisation, Mrs Warnock suggested that:

> we would do better to remove the concept 'person' altogether from
> the debate. It is both confusing and redundant. Since it is a word
> both in legal and in common use its deployment ... lends a spurious
> exactitude to the argument, as if something had been settled by
> deciding when to call someone a person. But nothing has. The
> question 'is he a person?' is only another way of asking 'may I do
> what I like with him?'[22]

Of course Warnock is right to say that nothing is settled by
deciding simply what to call someone, however, as I hope is now
clear, something might be settled by the arguments for calling an
individual a person where 'person' is used not simply to name a

natural kind, like 'human being', but plays precisely the role that Warnock identifies, where 'person' is used to identify beings whose existence has a particular value and importance. Now Warnock 'would rather ask whether the object of treatment was a full human being than whether or not he was a person'. The reason for Warnock's preference for the term 'full human being' cannot stem from a wish to avoid spurious exactitude, for 'human' shares this trait with 'person'. The use of such terms becomes non-spurious, as Warnock rightly suggests, only when we explain why those properly so called are in some sense valuable. For Warnock it is not humans *per se* that are valuable, but full human beings. However, Warnock makes it a point of principle to decline to give an account of what it is about human beings that makes them valuable, or indeed even of what might make them more valuable than other species and so is unable to say what is so good about plenitude. If humanness has no moral content then it cannot be better to be full rather than empty.

Warnock is adamant in rejecting the whole idea of finding some moral basis for our preference for human beings and hence for full ones:

> I would argue, on the other hand, that the concept of 'speciesism' as a form of prejudice is absurd. Far from being arbitrary it is a supremely important moral principle. If someone did *not* prefer to save a human rather than a dog or a fly we would think him in need of justification ... To live in a universe in which we were genuinely species indifferent would be impossible, or if not impossible, in the highest degree undesirable. I do not therefore regard a preference for humanity as 'arbitrary', nor do I see it as standing in need of further justification than that we ourselves are human.[23]

Now, while it might be undesirable or even perhaps impossible to live in a universe in which we were genuinely gender or race, religion or nationality indifferent, it does not follow that it would not be 'culpable injustice' to accord members of our own sex, or race or religion or nationality[24] a 'privileged position with regard to resources or care'.[25] What would make such discrimination culpable is not the simple fact that all such beings are members of the same species, but rather that there are no morally relevant differences between such beings. Quite apart from its complacency, we should be warned against a view that asserts that species preference stands in need of no further justification 'than that we ourselves are human', if only because the same impenetrable preference has been asserted for race, gender and nationality with familiarly disastrous consequences.

Of course Warnock is right to say that 'if someone did not prefer to save a human rather than a dog or a fly we should think him in need of justification' but this is not simply because humans are *our kind of being*, and dogs and flies are not; but rather that we believe, and believe we can show, that humans are more valuable than dogs and flies. We can, as we have seen, point to relevant differences between such beings and persons which support our preference—differences, moreover, which are species-neutral in the sense that they do not merely describe and value features possessed uniquely by adult human beings (the featherless biped syndrome) but rather point to features that should lead us to value any sort of beings who possessed them. If there were no moral requirement that we should point to relevant moral differences, arguments similar to Warnock's would justify our saving, as a matter of public policy, 'our kind of beings' if they are men rather than women or whites rather than blacks or Gentiles rather than Jews.

Having raised membership of the human species to the level of an ultimate, or at least a 'supremely important moral principle', Warnock surprisingly abandons this line altogether. She poses the question left unanswered by her defence of humanity thus: 'how do we decide whether an embryo or fertilised egg is *sufficiently* human to warrant protection?'[26] But she does not answer it. Rather she makes the answer to the question of what we may do to or with the embryo turn not on its degree of humanity but on how other people, or rather other humans, feel about it. Warnock's thought here is that if people's moral feelings are outraged by something, they may be entitled to be protected from such outrage and that this protection is required by morality. Warnock, however, nowhere tells us how to distinguish outrage to *moral* feelings from outrage to less creditable feelings, nor just how much weight to give to this feeling of outrage. She concludes by narrowing the discussion, again without argument, so that the feelings relevant to the moral status of the embryo are those of its mother alone. Although her discussion of these matters is a long one, her conclusions are summarised in the following passage:

> I believe that the relationship between [the mother] and the egg or the foetus or the spare embryo is such that they should be used only with her consent. If she objects to their use for experimenta-

tion then her objection should be respected and the material not used. That she may be able to give no good reasons for her attitude makes no difference. The matter turns not on her reasons but on her feelings ... I believe it is to offend against the concept of morality itself to refuse to take moral feelings or sentiments into account in decision making.[27]

The crucial feature of Warnock's solution to the problem of the moral status or value of the embryo is that she has absolutely nothing to say about its moral status or value. Despite its humanity, the question of how full or empty the embryo is of it is not considered. Instead its value is made to depend on its evoking the right sort of feeling response in mothers. This has echoes of Grobstein's account in which acceptance as a person depends upon the embryo being felt to be a person by adults. A further problem with Warnock's account is that of how the status of the embryo is to be assessed if it does not in fact evoke such a response from its mother or has no mother from whom to evoke such a response. Even if we accept Warnock's argument we cannot know what to do about unclaimed embryos nor about embryos that, for example, can be kept alive only at the cost of their mother's life, unless we have an account of what it is that makes life valuable and know where embryos fit into such an account. If the account given here is unacceptable, still some such account is required.

V Once a person always a person?

Persons are beings with the capacity for valuing their own existence. In the case of human beings, they become persons when the capacity to value their own lives develops and will cease to be persons when they have lost that capacity. It is obviously crucially important to be clear about when it is correct to say that an individual has lost the capacity to value existence.

Firstly, it is worth repeating that an individual has not lost the capacity to value life when they do not in fact value it or positively disvalue it. One cannot disvalue something without being also capable of valuing it, for to disvalue it is to value it at zero.

If an individual is asleep or unconscious they may not be able to value life at that time, but they have not necessarily lost the capacity to value life. It is a fact about human capacities and powers that it is correct to attribute them to individuals at times when they are not exercising those capacities or powers. It is true of me that I can speak French and remains true of me while I am asleep or unconscious and even if I do not speak a word of it for years on end. If you say 'John Harris can speak French', your remark is not true if I happen to be awake when you make it but false if I happen to be asleep. It remains true of me until I have permanently lost the capacity to speak French. And the same is true of all other powers, capacities and abilities, including the capacity to value one's own life.

But isn't the capacity for valuing existence just the potential for valuing it, and doesn't it then fall victim of the defects of the potentiality argument that we have already rehearsed? No, because to have the potential for a given capacity it must be the case that one lacks that capacity but might develop it under certain circumstances. I don't have the potential to speak French, I can speak French. I have, maybe, the potential to speak Russian and we could then see if I were capable of fulfilling my potential. But I don't have to fulful my potential to speak French, I already *can* speak it. I don't need to acquire the capacity, merely to exercise an existing capacity. I only have the potential if I lack the capacity. This may seem like a linguistic quibble but it is not and this is made clearer if we remember how the defects of the potentiality argument were revealed. We saw that if someone had the potential to be X it might well be highly inappropriate to treat them as if they were already X. It is never inappropriate to treat someone with an ability as if they had that ability (although it may be inopportune). If you are a doctor of medicine it is not inappropriate for me to ask your medical advice (although it may be inopportune if you happen to be asleep or unconscious at the time) but if you are only a potential doctor, the 2-year-old object of a proud parental 'my son the doctor', it is quite another matter.

How permanent is permanent?

If I had the capacity to run a four-minute mile and then lost one of my legs it would be fair to say of me that I had permanently lost the capacity to run a mile in under four minutes. If I am permanently unconscious, where 'permanently' means that there is zero probability of my ever regaining consciousness, it seems fair to say that I have ceased to be a person, for there can be no self-consciousness and so no ability to value my existence if I am permanently unaware of my existence.

A difficulty might arise in the case of people who are about to die of a disease to which there is at present no cure, and are then frozen in the hope that a cure might be found in the future, at which point they might be thawed. If it cannot be said that a cure will never be found have they ceased to be persons? Indeed are they dead? It is sometimes thought that the spare embryos that are produced in *in vitro* fertilisation programmes should be frozen because since this does not amount to killing them it is morally preferable to simply throwing them away.[28] I'm not sure if there is any simple answer to such a conundrum and so I'll postpone consideration of this issue until the last.[29]

VI Conclusion

We have, I think, arrived at a workable and useful conception of the person and one we will be relying on increasingly in subsequent chapters. It is a concept which enables us to distinguish between persons and non-persons and which, as we shall see as the discussion develops, will help us to solve some of the most intractable problems of medical ethics. Many will regard this concept of the person as highly suspect if not positively wrongheaded. But if the concept of the person outlined in this chapter is rejected we will none the less require some such concept that will perform the same range of very important functions. These are:

1 To enable us morally to distinguish between persons and animals, fish, plants and so on.
2 To have an account of the point at which and the reasons why the embryo or any live human tissue becomes valuable.
3 To recognise when and why human beings cease to be valuable or become less valuable than others.
4 To provide a framework that would in principle enable us to answer the question 'are there other people in the universe?'
5 To give us an account of what it is that's so great about ourselves.

Until a better account emerges, I will continue to use this one, and we must begin to see how it helps us with the moral dilemmas that face health care professionals.

2 Above all do no harm

It is widely accepted that doctors and other health care professionals should 'above all do no harm' to their patients or clients.
In order for someone to follow even this apparently unexceptionable directive, it is important to have a lively sense of the ways in
which his or her conduct may affect others. Although in many
circumstances the scope of our individual or collective impact on
the world is entirely unproblematic, there is an important dimension of conduct where this is not so. The problem is precisely
whether or not we have two equally effective 'ways of determining
the state of any world in which we are able to intervene. One is
to intervene and to change the state of that world, the other is to
refrain from intervention and leave everything as it is.'[1] This is
the problem that is at the centre of the recent debate about killing
and letting die, about acts and omissions.

Are we responsible for the consequences of our omissions? Indeed, do omissions have consequences? If so, to what extent are
we responsible for them? Is letting-die as bad, morally speaking,
as killing? These questions are particularly important in medical
contexts and the problem is at its most acute when we consider
whether there is a moral difference between active and passive
euthanasia. But the same issues arise whenever decisions are taken
about whether or not to treat an individual or about where to
allocate resources.

This problem is one of the most frequently and fervently debated issues in contemporary moral philosophy and requires, and
has more than once received, a book-length study.[2] In much less
space I shall try to do two things. The first is to show how far
our conduct affects the world, and so how far we are responsible
for how the world stands at any particular moment; and of course
and in particular how far we are responsible for what happens in

medical care and research. The second is to say something about how far we are morally accountable for our part in the way of the world and so also about whether or not there is a moral difference between active and passive, positive or negative ways of influencing events.

Positive and negative

The distinction between positive and negative ways of influencing the world can be drawn in many ways, and in each case the apparent force of the distinction and the meaning of the terms may be slightly different. We can act or we can fail or omit or decline to act. We can do things, or we can forbear or neglect to do things, or we can refrain from doing them. We can sometimes make things happen, and sometimes we allow or permit or let them occur. We can set trains of events in motion, or we can fail to stop them or derail them. To emphasise just one example of the differences of meaning here, a simple *omission* to act may bear a different construction than an emphatic *neglect* of an action. To make things more complicated it is always possible (albeit with some labour and loss of elegance) to re-formulate any action description or any omission description so that each becomes the other. I can for example shoot you or fail to omit to shoot you.

For our purposes I think the best way of drawing the distinction is in terms of positive and negative responsibility, and I'll try to make clear exactly what is meant by these terms and the importance of drawing the distinction in this way. Quite simply, *where something happens, or a state of affairs obtains because someone did something, I will say that the agent is positively responsible for its occurrence;* and *where a particular state of affairs obtains or something happens because an agent did not do something I will say that the agent is negatively responsible for its occurrence.* For example, a piece of apparatus—a respirator—may be off and the patient connected to it dead because someone switched it off (positive responsibility) or because someone did not switch it on (negative responsibility). Of course for someone to be negatively responsible for the machine's being off it must have been *possible* for her to switch it on—she could not possibly be responsible for the occurrence of something the prevention of which would have been impossible.

So, someone will be responsible for an event or state of affairs when that event or state of affairs obtains and the agents could have so conducted themselves that the event or state of affairs did not obtain. When their conduct is positive the responsibility is positive, and when the conduct is negative the responsibility is negative.

I must make two further features of this account of the difference between positive and negative responsibility clear now, although these features will become more obvious when we turn in a moment to some examples. The first is that we can be negatively responsible for something even though it is not the case that we ought to have prevented its occurrence, or where we had no duty or contractual obligation to prevent it. I will be negatively responsible for the occurrence of something I could have prevented simply because I could have prevented it, not because I should have prevented it. The second, related qualification is that this will be the case, even where I did not know that I could have prevented the event. So where I am negatively responsible for something that I genuinely didn't realise I could prevent, I may well not be to *blame* for its occurrence, but I am still *responsible* for it.[3]

The point of drawing the distinction in this way is to reveal what I take to be a truth about our ability to affect the world and it is simply this: that where we are able to intervene decisively, whether or not we ought to intervene, whether or not we have a duty to intervene, and even whether or not we know we can intervene, our conduct is crucial. It makes the whole difference between an event's occurring or a state of affairs obtaining, and their not so doing. To put this point in the language of probability, where someone's conduct can make the entire difference between probability $= 0$ and probability $= 1$ for the obtaining of some state of affairs, then that person is responsible for that state of affairs. And again, where the conduct is positive the responsibility will be positive and where negative the responsibility will be negative. Of course where the agent's conduct does not make the whole difference between the occurrence or non-occurrence of an event and where the probabilities consequently are less, the responsibility will be lessened in direct proportion.

By now it will be clear that I believe that we can be equally responsible for what happens because of our actions and what happens because of our inaction or non-action. I also accept that if the occurrence of a particular event or state of affairs would be a disaster it makes no moral difference whether our responsibility for that disaster is positive or negative. In the rest of this chapter I will try to show why this is so.

Some people deny absolutely that we can ever be negatively responsible for anything. Others take a marginally milder view and deny only that positive and negative responsibility are either equally strong or equally morally serious.

No negative responsibility

Those who deny absolutely that there is any such thing as negative responsibility must take a very odd view of the world.[4] Suppose I can save your life by telling a lie, say where I could be your alibi for a capital crime. Then, saving your life is something I have done and can be responsible for. Conversely, if I tell the truth and as a result you die I have straightforwardly caused your death and can be similarly responsible. But now, if only my silence can save you and knowing this I keep quiet, then those who deny the existence of negative responsibility must believe that I have not in these circumstances saved you at all. Similarly, if I could save your life by speaking out but remain silent they cannot hold me morally responsible for your death. And of course I may have no duty to save you—you may be guilty or I may know that you will commit some much worse crime if you are released.

An even more unsatisfactory consequence of denying the possibility of negative responsibility is that where either keeping silent or telling a lie will save your life, then, if I wish to save you I must not remain silent rather than tell a lie, for remaining silent cannot be a way of making a difference to what happens in the world. Those who deny negative responsibility would have to recommend lying to those who wish to save others in such circumstances; and needlessly, since keeping silent and telling a lie *are* here both equally effective ways of saving life!

Decisions can be decisive

Both those who deny absolutely the possibility of negative responsibility and those who think less severely that it is somehow less effective or less morally significant than positive responsibility will have difficulty making sense of quite commonplace things like how to decide what to do. For example, the decisions of health care professionals do make a difference to what happens to their patients, and I take it that decisions not to do things, to take no action or make no interventions, are as important and crucial, and as consequential, as various sorts of treatment and interventions. The day-to-day care of most patients will involve innumerable decisions to do and not to do various things, and each will have its effect on the course of the patient's illness and on his chances of recovery. More dramatically, consider the case of the known diabetic admitted to the casualty department of a hospital in a hypoglycaemic coma. If the casualty officer, suspecting this condition, failed to take the blood sugar level of the patient, and so also failed to give glucose in an appropriate form and the patient died, there would be surely no difficulty in recognising that the patient died as a consequence of that decision not to treat. Or, if a patient was admitted to hospital having obviously lost vast quantities of blood and a decision was taken not to replace this with an appropriate saline or other solution pending transfusion of blood, and the patient died, there would again be no problem in recognising that the patient died because of the decision not to take appropriate measures to make good the loss. In either case the first question any investigation into the causes of the patients' deaths would want answered is: why were they left untreated?

In these examples, of course, the patients have been admitted to hospital, and so in a sense the hospital has taken responsibility for them, and so has either accepted that there is an obligation to treat them or has, by accepting the patients, created the obligation to treat them. Is it not therefore the breach of this obligation that makes it the case that if the patients die, their deaths will be the result of the decision not to treat them? This objection is not well founded, for we can clearly see the connexion between failure to treat and death quite independently of the existence of any obligation to treat.

Suppose that as a result of our deliberations in the next chapter, we conclude that doctors and other health care professionals have in fact no moral or other obligation to treat patients. Our reaching this conclusion would not prevent us from seeing that the diabetic and haemorrhaging patients died because they were not given appropriate treatment. We would understand very well that this was the reason for their deaths but accept, presumably, that it is morally permissible to be responsible for their deaths in circumstances like these. How plausible a judgment this might be is of course a consideration to which we will return.

A set of cases which even more clearly illustrate this point are those where decisions are taken not to resuscitate elderly terminal patients, or where severely handicapped infants are put on a regime (like selective treatment) which is well known to lead almost inevitably to death.[5] In either case, when the patients die, our understanding of the connexion between the decision not to resuscitate or the decisions not to give antibiotics for infections or food or remedial surgery and so on (which are part of selective treatment as we shall see in a moment) is not dependent on either course of treatment involving any breach of duty or obligation. For those taking such decisions understand full well that the patients will die as a result, but none the less judge that these decisions are fully consistent with their duty to treat their patients caringly, properly and professionally.

We must now turn more singlemindedly to the case of the selective treatment of severely handicapped children, because this practice raises most clearly almost all the important issues surrounding the differences between active and passive euthanasia or positive versus negative responsibility for death. The difference between selective treatment and active euthanasia illustrates both the tenacity of the belief that negative responsibility is somehow a weaker sort of responsibility than is positive responsibility, and also the view that passive euthanasia is somehow morally preferable to its active counterpart. Selective treatment is thus well worth an extended examination in the hope that we may be able to resolve these vexed and controversial issues.

Selective treatment

Selective treatment of severely handicapped children is calculated to result in their deaths. I am thinking particularly of the management of children with severe spina bifida.[6] Such a policy has been justified on the hypothesis that it is reasonable to conclude that the child would be better off dead. This paradoxical sounding conclusion means simply that it is judged to be in the child's best interests to die. I am assuming that the children in question are too young, or too severely handicapped, to be themselves consulted. I assume also that this sort of judgment, while difficult to make, is unproblematic in that we can all imagine many cases in which life is so intolerable, so painful, so miserable, so difficult and so utterly without reward, that we would not wish to live such a life and that it is reasonable to suppose that no one would. I assume also that severe spina bifida is such a case.

What is, however, highly problematic is the judgment that it is

morally preferable to withhold treatment from such children so
that they die slowly, rather than to kill them quickly and painlessly. Since 'selective treatment' in this context usually means
not treating and often not feeding either, I will use the term
'selective non-treatment' to refer to this procedure.

Many in the medical profession and many relatives of patients
do not regard this as problematic and accept that selective non-
treatment of severely handicapped children is morally preferable
to killing and it is worth looking at the reasons that one eminent
practitioner in this field has advanced for this view.

In a paper entitled 'Ethical Problems in the Management of
Myelomeningocele and Hydrocephalus', John Lorber[7] makes out
his case for selective non-treatment. Lorber sees clearly that it is
in his severe spina bifida patients' interests to die, and his programme of selective non-treatment is calculated to bring about
the speedy deaths of the patients. 'It is essential', Lorber em-
phasises, 'that nothing should be done which might prolong the
infant's survival'[8] and that the temptation to operate should be
resisted because 'progressive hydrocephalus is an important cause
of early death'.[9] An early death is of course desirable both to
shorten the suffering of those marked for death and so that ex-
pensive and scarce resources should not be wastefully employed.

It may seem tendentious to talk of patients 'marked for death',
but non-treatment is a death-dealing device. If all patients what-
soever were treated as Lorber treats his selected spina bifida
children (fed only on demand, given no tube feeding, no oxygen
or resuscitation and no antibiotics for infections)[10] and they died,
their deaths would be treated at 'best' as resulting from criminal
negligence and at worst as culpable homicide. Indeed non-treatment is so effective a killer that Lorber is able to report that 'of
the first 41 untreated infants in Sheffield none survived beyond
eight months and 60 per cent were dead before they reached one
month of age'.[11]

The tragedy is, of course, that these children or their families
should suffer unnecessarily for even one month. Lorber sees this
and records that 'It is painful to see such infants gradually fading
away over a number of weeks or months when everybody hopes
for a speedy end.'[12] Lorber's motives are of the highest, he wants
to save children and their families as much suffering as in conscience he can, and he has been courageous in pioneering selective
non-treatment which is more economical of suffering and of resources than is the active treatment of severe spina bifida. It is

therefore particularly poignant that he believes it right to stop short of killing and particularly worthwhile examining his arguments for so doing.

Although Lorber's paper is ostensibly about the ethical problems of selective non-treatment, he in fact relegates discussion of these to the final page and a half of his paper. After noting 'a major inconsistency and perhaps hypocrisy'[13] in his opposition to active euthanasia, Lorber sets out the arguments which he must believe to be strong enough to outweigh charges of hypocrisy and inconsistency and to justify those painful weeks and months which, in this case, represent the moral difference between killing and letting die. His arguments must be such as to pull the moral difference back in favour of selective non-treatment. We will take the arguments in order.

The argument from brutalisation

This argument has two parts which are stated in two sentences, 'active euthanasia may brutalise the persons who carry it out.... It would be wrong for a doctor to order his junior or his nurses to carry out such a task if he cannot bring himself to do it.'[14] To 'brutalise' in this context is I suppose to render individuals more insensitive to the pain and suffering of others and more careless of or callous about the value of their lives. Evidence of brutalisation would be very hard to find and Lorber cites none. But what we have to balance here surely is a remote and imponderable danger of sensitive medical staff becoming 'brutalised' to an unknown (but perhaps insignificant) degree, against real and present pain, suffering and distress to the patients, their loving ones, *and* the medical staff who have to preside over their slow demise. We must also take into account the equally probable brutalising effect of taking responsibility for a slow and distressing rather than a quick and painless end. In the absence of any evidence, it is plausible to suppose that the responsibility of bringing about a slow and distressing death would be more rather than less brutalising than would a quick and merciful killing.

Certainly we can agree that doctors should not order others to do what they themselves cannot in conscience bring themselves to do, and others should not take such 'orders'. But again we are discussing what people ought to do in these cases, and what they feel they can in conscience do will, one hopes, be determined by what, after considering carefully evidence and argument, they think they ought to do.

The argument from lack of consent

'I strongly disagree with active euthanasia', Lorber states, 'especially for babies and children, who cannot possibly ask for it or give their considered consent.'[15] Consent is worrying, but it is no more worrying for active euthanasia in the cases under consideration, than it is for selective non-treatment. As we have seen, selective non-treatment is intended to result in death and it does, and those who die cannot possibly ask for it or give their considered consent.

The slippery slope argument

> It would be impossible to formulate legislation, however humane are the intentions, that could not be abused by the unscrupulous. There have been plenty of examples in the past, especially in Hitler's Germany. Few just or compassionate persons would wish to give such a dangerous legal power to any individual or group of people.[16]

There are two points that need to be made here. The first is again that Lorber and others already have this power, they decide to act so as to bring about the speedy deaths of their patients and they are very successful. Whatever the dangers of legislation are, it must surely be possible to make them less than those that already exist *without* specific legislation. The power is awesome but it is already exercised. The second point is about the spectre of Hitler and Nazism. By raising it, Lorber invites us to see the difference between active and passive euthanasia as the difference between humane medical practice in a civilised society and the first step on the road to the holocaust. But the Nazi euthanasia programme was nothing like the possibilities we are considering. Under the Nazis euthanasia was simply one way of exterminating those racially or politically beyond moral consideration. And the Nazis were not short of other ways to achieve the same ends. It is precisely because we care about spina bifida children, precisely because we are in no doubt that they must not suffer, that we are concerned about what it is in their best interests to do. The spectre of Nazism offers no analogy at all and so only fogs the issues.

We must again remind ourselves that doctors already take decisions which result in death with no legal or publicly debated safeguards. If we do not cry 'Nazism' it is simply because we know there is no analogy and we know that all concerned are concerned only about the welfare of their patients. But if we fear even the slimmest chance of abuse, we should take care that all decisions in these areas are taken in the open with the widest possible public debate and scrutiny.[17]

The last door argument

The argument here is that active euthanasia closes the last door on an individual's life whereas 'No treatment with normal nursing care is a safeguard against wrong diagnosis ... If an infant's condition is not as grave as was thought, he will live and he can then be given optimal care....'[18] But this is just not true on Lorber's own account of the treatment. If a child selected for non-treatment contracts an infection and dies because it is not given antibiotics or, if it requires resuscitation which is not given and it dies, there will be no opportunity to discover whether the diagnosis was wrong or not. So this 'safeguard' is hit and miss at best. If the child *per* almost *impossible* lives, we may find reason to say the diagnosis was wrong, but if the child dies we cannot say the diagnosis was right unless the non-treatment played *no role at all* in the death, for otherwise the diagnosis is self-fulfilling. Whether closing a particular door on life chances is closing the last door will be a question of fact in each case. If the child dies of an untreated infection, then the withholding of the antibiotic drugs was in fact the closing of the last door, just as the administering of a lethal injection would be.

There can surely be no doubt that active and passive procedures which are both consciously designed to result in death and which do equally result in death are both forms of euthanasia. The crucial question must surely be: are there any reasons against the advocacy of active euthanasia in these cases which are of sufficient moral weight to tip the scales in favour of an alternative which involves weeks and possibly months of the very suffering that the alternative was embarked upon to minimise?

The argument from self-deception

One argument that is sometimes advanced is the suggestion that parents and relatives of severely handicapped children would not accept or consent to anything resembling killing, and so if doctors are to be able to recommend what they see as the most humane couse, such a recommendation or, if that is too strong a term, such a possible course of treatment would be useless if it were always rejected by those whose consent is judged necessary.[19] But this, even if true, should not prevent us from seeing clearly what the most humane course of action is and advocating its acceptance. Unless we do so those concerned will continue to deceive themselves as to the reality of what they are doing, or consenting to have done, and will continue to choose a programme which involves weeks and months of avoidable suffering. And we should be clear that it is self-deception unless it can be unequivocally demonstrated that one procedure is of different moral quality to the other. The only palpable differences demonstrated by Lorber are that non-treatment takes longer to bring about death than would active euthanasia and is minimally less certain to result in death. And both these features seem to count against rather than in favour of selective non-treatment, given the reasons which justify its being undertaken at all.

Indeed self-deception is sometimes advanced as *itself* constituting the moral difference between active and passive euthanasia. The argument here is that it is only because the medical staff and the relatives of the children are able to protect themselves from full awareness of what they are doing that they are able to bring themselves to do what they judge to be morally required by the circumstances. Here the idea that they are only 'letting nature take its course' allows them to distance themselves from the death of the child and fit their part in events more comfortably into their conception of the medical role.[20]

There is a terrible irony here in that the whole practice of medicine might be described as a comprehensive attempt to frustrate the course of nature, of which disease is after all a part, and to prevent 'nature' from killing people in its usual extravagant fashion. There is undoubtedly a widespread, but equally undoubtedly an irrational, respect for what is natural or part of the course of nature.[21] Famines, floods, droughts, storms are all natural and all disastrous. We only, and rightly, want the natural when it's good for us. What is natural is morally inert and progress-dependent. It was only natural for people to die of infected wounds before antibiotics were available and it is only natural for spina bifida children to die if their condition is inoperable, but it is not natural if they are selected for non-treatment, when with full treatment they would live.

It is also perhaps worth emphasising that if we are ever to feel confident that the right thing is for the child to die in these circumstances then we should face the decision under its most stark and 'non-distanced' description. One might say that there is a moral requirement that in matters of such importance where the lives of others are at stake, we should be absolutely sure that we have faced squarely the full import of what we are doing. Whereas if we disguise the facts from ourselves and others by various distancing strategies, we may permanently shield ourselves both from full awareness of what we are about and from the possibility of thinking through all the implications of such consequential decisions.

Ordinary and extraordinary treatment

An argument that has appealed particularly to Catholic theology involves putting moral weight on the distinction between ordinary and extraordinary treatment.[22] Extraordinary treatment is not obligatory and its extraordinariness consists in its involving great costs, pain or inconvenience, or in being a great burden to the patient or others, without a reasonable hope that the treatment will be successful. Almost all the terms of this distinction cry out for analysis, but where resources are not scarce and not competed for by needier or worthier patients, it seems that the crucial issue is whether just staying alive is a 'success'. So long as it is reasonable to suppose that it is, and to suppose this I think we must judge it to be in the patient's interests to live, then it seems difficult to justify the withholding of even extraordinary treatment. For to come to the conclusion that it is in the patient's interests to live we must believe that the costs, pain, inconvenience and burden of the treatment to the patient are compensated for by being alive. And if it is not in the patient's interests to live it would require a pretty strong accumulation of pain, distress, costs or whatever to *others* or to society to justify the patient's being sacrificed to secure their own or society's freedom from such burdens.[23]

Law, logic and journalism

The law, to be sure, forbids active euthanasia, but passive euthanasia is outlawed only where there exists a positive duty to save life. I should stress that I am not here urging people to break the law, but examining what might constitute good reasons to change the law governing these matters. Thus while the current state of the law is a good reason for not *implementing* a policy of active euthanasia, it is not a good reason for not *advocating* such a policy. Perhaps because of the legal position it is 'abundantly clear', as one commentator reminds us,[24] 'that doctors are not in

favour of [active euthanasia] principally because they regard
themselves as being under an obligation not to take any active
steps to end the lives of their patients.' The law may explain this
but it does not justify it. The question for anyone interested in
doing what's right must be: can there be a moral obligation not
to take active steps to end the lives of patients, and at the same
time no moral obligation not to take passive steps to this end? Or,
to put the point in the way that it presents itself in the cases we
are considering, can it be right to take passive steps to end the
lives of patients (as in selective non-treatment) but wrong to take
active steps to the same end?

The *Guardian* newspaper in its first leader commenting on the
case of Dr Leonard Arthur (who was prosecuted for murder following the death of a child suffering from Down's syndrome for
whom he was caring by selective non-treatment) conceded, referring to the arguments above, that 'it would be hard to gainsay
such arguments' but then proceeded to reject argument entirely!

> Casuistic it may be but doctors feel the distinction passionately; to
> adopt the narrow rules of logic would turn them, in their own
> estimation, into killers. They say their patients would come to see
> them as executioners, and that active euthanasia would be even
> more traumatic for parents and professional staff. Who is to say
> that the weight of this professional opinion, rooted in practical
> experience, is any less valid than the relentless logic of Dr Harris?[25]

When logic and reasoned argument are abandoned in favour of
casuistry and passion, further discussion seems pointless. But one
of the tasks for medical ethics, and the *Guardian* leader shows
that it is by no means an easy one, is to try to understand the
value of the obligations we intuitively feel and the distinctions we
feel passionately. What, for example, is the good of feeling that
positive steps to end life are forbidden but negative or passive
ones permitted? What is the point of feeling such an obligation?
What values do such feelings express or subserve?

If this passionate feeling is the product of a reverence for
human life, then if both active and passive steps lead inexorably
to death can a distinction between active and passive euthanasia
be part of such an attitude of reverence? If, on the other hand,
the distinction is not so much part of what it is to have reverence
for life, but is rather expressive of our care for the interests and
welfare of others; then if it is seen to be in their interests to die,
we might come to feel that the obligation as expressed is self-

defeating in that it leads us to sacrifice rather than promote the interests of others.

Feeling guilty

Guilt feelings, like the sense of obligation discussed above, can be similarly misplaced or irrational. So that when John Lorber notes that 'the aftermath of thought and guilt complexes in the parents and persons involved (in active euthanasia) is likely to be much worse than caring for the baby in a humane way until it dies',[26] we must ask whether such guilt is appropriate, whether there is anything to feel guilty about? Indeed, as we have seen, it might be more appropriate to feel guilt were the children to be allowed to die slowly rather than assist them to a speedy end. The mere fact that guilt is sincerely felt does not of course indicate that there is anything to feel guilty about.[27] We are all prone to feel irrational guilt, particularly when we are forced by circumstances to choose between evils. We should not allow the feeling of guilt to prevent us from choosing the lesser evil.

Active euthanasia is not the best solution?

It may be that it is better all things considered for children in these circumstances to fade away slowly rather than to die quickly from a lethal injection. There are a number of reasons why this might be so. The first is that parents and relatives may need time to get used to the idea that their child is going to die, have time to be with the child and prepare themselves for losing a loved one, make their farewells and so on.

It may also be better for the parents if they are able to be with their child at the end, nurse him until the last, see him quietly fade away and so know that he is gone. If this is so and if it can be accomplished without added distress to the child, then it may well be preferable both morally and emotionally.

Whether this sort of end for the child will be achieved by a policy of selective treatment is more doubtful. This may after all involve a rather prolonged waiting and hoping for the child to contract an infection, or to become so weak that it cannot further survive. Parents may not be able to be present during this protracted period, and may become distressed at the unnecessarily long and drawn-out process.

If it is accepted that in principle in cases like this there is no moral difference between active and passive euthanasia, and it is clear that the best course is that the child should not survive, then it will be open to health care professsionals and families to arrange matters in the best interests of the child, whatever that turns out to be.

Selective treatment or active euthanasia?

It comes down to this: if, for whatever reason, we feel justified in concluding that it is in this particular individual's own best interests to die or, if there are any other reasons why he should die,[28] then it cannot be better or more morally sound to be negatively rather than positively responsible for his death. If, on the other hand, this individual should not die then we cannot be justified in being either positively or negatively responsible for his death. Indeed, as we have seen, so far from being morally preferable to active euthanasia, selective non-treatment may actually be morally worse in that it may well involve more of the very pain and distress, both to victims and to their loving ones, which made the individual's death desirable in the first place. Worse also because it may involve both self-deception and a, perhaps unwitting, deception of others which prevents a clear view of, and so clear judgments about, what is happening.

The case of selective non-treatment has enabled us to examine in the context of a real and not uncommon dilemma, many of the important differences between positive and negative responsibility, and to see that such differences as exist are not such as to permit our approving of one type of responsibility for the consequences of our decisions, and disapproving of the other. There are, however, a number of supposed differences that do not emerge from a discussion of selective non-treatment and these we must now examine.

A difficulty with omissions

It is sometimes said that an important difference between positive acts and omissions is that 'Blame for a positive act seldom depends on how difficult not acting would have been. Blame for an omission must take account of the difficulty, inconvenience, etc. of the omitted act.'[29] It is difficult to meet such a suggestion with the many counter-examples that spring to mind, since it is always open to those who accept such a view to say that while it is *seldom* the case, this particular example just happens to be one of the exceptions. However, and for the record, duress and provocation are two very standard cases where blame is often mitigated because of how difficult not acting would have been. But instead of rehearsing further counter-examples, it is perhaps more instructive to remind ourselves of the basis of the distinction between positive and negative responsibility. If I am responsible for some evil, and if it would have been difficult for me to behave in a way that would have avoided the evil, it is bizarre to suppose that this fact does nothing to diminish the degree to which I am blameworthy in the case where my responsibility is positive, but *can* do so where my responsibility is negative. Without any argument as to why this should be so (and I have never seen any), we can reject this suggestion as totally implausible.

Side-effects and double-effects

The principle of double-effect, which appears in Catholic theology, is often cited as explaining an important difference between positive and negative responsibility. It is not clear that it operates on this distinction at all but we will examine it because it is often believed that it does. I will take as an authoritative statement of the principle the explanation of it given in a recent Linacre Centre publication:[30]

> the term 'double effect' relates to 'side-effects'.... The principle of the side-effect merely states a possibility: where you may not aim at someone's death, causing it does not necessarily incur guilt—it can be that there are necessities which in the circumstances are great enough or there are legitimate purposes in hand of such a kind to provide a valid excuse for risking or accepting that you cause death. Without such excuse foreseeable killing is either murder or manslaughter.[31]

We should be clear also that you may not aim at someone's death either as an end or a means. There is an immense, and I think insoluble, problem about deciding when a death (or any other consequence) is aimed at as an end or a means and when it is merely a side-effect. It all depends on how the action is described, and crucially on how to set limits to the re-description of any action. This can clearly be seen if we examine the Linacre Centre's own example in illustration of the distinction.

> Imagine a pot-holer stuck with people behind him and water rising to drown them. And suppose two cases: in one he can be blown up; in the other a rock can be moved to open another escape route, but it will crush him to death . . .
> There might be people among them who, seeing the consequence, would move the rock, though they would not blow up the

man because that would be choosing his death as the means of
escape. This is a far from meaningless stance, for they thus show
themselves as people who will absolutely reject any policy making
the death of innocent people a means or end.[32]

It is difficult to see how anyone could read this and not be im-
pressed by it as an example of the most comprehensive sophistry.
If this example has any plausibility, it depends on our accepting
that blowing up the potholer can only be described as killing him
whereas moving the rock is a complete action description, of
which crushing the man is a mere side-effect. It is a feature of
any action that its description is almost infinitely expandable or
contractable. My crooking my finger, is my pulling the trigger, is
my shooting at Samson, is my hitting Delilah, is my killing the
President, is my orphaning her children, etc., etc. The problem
is to set a limit to the legitimacy of characterising the action in
one way rather than another. The above description of what went
on in the cave could seem plausible only because the whole distinction between direct means and ends on the one hand, and
side-effects on the other, has already been rigged by a particular
choice of action descriptions. This can easily be seen if we change
the phraseology slightly:

> ... suppose two cases: in one he is crushed leaving room to escape;
> in the other a hole can be blown in the rock at its weakest point
> but this will dismember the potholer ...

These descriptions are equally plausible but the impression of
which course of action involves direct killing, and which involves
death as a side-effect of what is done, is different. The crucial
point for anyone who wishes to have a realistic appreciation of
what is involved in one choice rather than another is surely not:
'which description makes the most undesirable consequence a
side-effect?' but 'am I justified in behaving in a way that has these
consequences?'

Anyone who thinks that, in the Linacre Centre example, those
who choose to save themselves by crushing the potholer rather
than by blowing him up are those who 'show themselves as people
who will absolutely reject any policy making the death of innocent
people a means or end' is simply and comprehensively deceiving
himself.

The distinction between effects and side-effects, and between
effects and double-effects, drawn in this way is entirely without
moral significance. What matters, as I have tried to show in this

chapter, is how our decisions and actions affect the world, not whether that effect is direct or indirect.

The reason that the principle of double-effect has often been thought relevant to the distinction between positive and negative ways of influencing events is simply because positive actions have seemed to be more obviously 'direct' and negative actions more obviously 'indirect'. While this may sometimes (perhaps even more often) be true, it is by no means necessarily true. I can deliberately set out to ensure your demise by withholding life-saving measures that it is within my power to provide, and where I do so my moral responsibility for your death will not be one jot reduced by the fact that the responsibility was negative. Most recent Catholic thinking on responsibility, including the Linacre Centre report, accepts this; but the belief that the doctrine of double-effect is somehow relevant to the difference between acts and omissions or between positive and negative responsibility is tenacious, and it is as well to clear it away at this early stage of our investigation.

Side-effects revisited

I should emphasise that there is a perfectly respectable everyday use of the term 'side-effects' and I am not denying that for some purposes it may be useful to distinguish between the direct effects and the side-effects of a drug or a course of treatment. But it is important to be clear that this distinction is entirely without moral significance and cannot be used to limit our responsibility for bringing about those side-effects.

A usual way of drawing the distinction in medical practice is to characterise the hoped-for result of the treatment as its direct effect, and any unwanted or redundant effects as side-effects. So, for example, the degree to which it diminishes pain is the direct effect of an analgesic, and any consequent drowsiness or toxicity a side-effect. However, those who administer[33] the analgesic remain responsible for the drowsiness and the toxicity, and will be justified in producing these effects along with the reduction in pain only if, all things considered, the reduction is worth having at the cost of the side-effects.

Terminal care

The importance of this point is revealed when we look at one of the most sensitive areas, the care of the terminally ill. In the care of patients who are both terminally ill and in great pain, it is often only possible to control the pain effectively if analgesics are given in quantities, where the toxicity of the drugs inevitably further curtails the lives of the patients. Thus the patients die sooner than they would have if the pain were not controlled. Now, of course, doctors do not want the drugs to kill their patients. They would like to be able to control the pain without any increased morbidity. They do not then aim at their patients' deaths, either as a means or as an end; it is a side-effect of the treatment but it is still an effect. If it is justified, it is justified not because the death is a side-effect rather than a direct effect, but rather because, in these circumstances, hastening death is a price worth paying for the relief of pain. It's not the fact that the side-effect is unwanted that makes it permissible, but rather that the total package of consequences including unwanted side-effects is morally preferable to the alternative.

This can be seen very clearly if we imagine an alternative case in which premature death is a consequence of effective pain control. Suppose a patient were suffering from a condition (if there is one) that subjected him to terrible pain for two years, but thereafter, if appropriate treatment had been given during the two years, he could be expected to make a complete recovery. The pain is as bad or worse than in the case of the terminal patients. The only way to control the pain is to give drugs that would have as a side-effect the effect of killing him shortly after the two years had elapsed. Here I think we can see that although the morbidity of the drug is still a side-effect, if doctors were to administer it in such circumstances, they could not plausibly evade responsibility for the patient's premature death.

Of course, if the pain were very great, they might well be justified in controlling it at such a cost if the patient so wished; that is a different question. What we can see, however, is that the fact that morbidity is a side-effect of treatment does not diminish responsibility.

Unmasking the difference
In his discussion of a doctor's duties to terminal patients, Ian Kennedy, in his stimulating *The Unmasking of Medicine*[34] displays uncharacteristic nervousness in dealing with the distinction between positive and negative responsibility. He believes that the 'question which fascinates so many, that of when it is proper to turn off a respirator, can be shown to be one of the more simple

questions to answer'.[35] There are two strands to his solution. One is to show, quite rightly, that the crucial issue is the effect the respirator's being on has on the patient, and to argue that if that effect is deleterious the respirator should not be on. However, the nervousness emerges in his discussion of just how the respirator comes to be off. Kennedy seems to think that the moral dilemma is somehow solved if circumstances can be so arranged that the machine is off when the crucial decision is taken, rather than on. The trick is to take the patient off the respirator for some independent reason, like testing his breathing, and then to decide not to put him back on again:

> If the patient's condition is so irreversibly hopeless, the doctor is entitled to desist from returning him to the respirator.... The ethical question thus becomes not one of turning off the respirator but rather of turning it back on again.[36]

After showing us three separate sorts of circumstances in which this trick can be accomplished, Kennedy concludes:

> From this brief outline it can be seen that the ethically relevant decision is not whether to turn off the respirator. Rather, it is the decision whether to put the patient on the respirator, or to turn it back on again having turned it off in the light of the prognosis.[37]

I hope it is now clear that this cannot be the ethically relevant decision. Nothing of moral significance can hinge on whether the patient dies as a consequence of the respirator's not being turned on, rather than as a consequence of its being turned off. The ethically relevant decision is quite different. It is contained in the other strand of Kennedy's account, and it is simply 'in all the circumstances of the case is it better for this patient to be connected to the respirator or not?' If the answer is 'yes' then the respirator should not be switched off or should be switched on, whichever is required to keep the patient on the machine. And if the answer is 'no' then the machine must not be switched on if it happens to be off and must be switched off if it happens to be on. Nothing can hang on the issue of whether the relevant decision is to switch off the machine or not to switch it on.

It is this conclusion that is of fundamental importance in medical care: that what matters is how our actions and decisions affect the world and other people, not whether our responsibility for the effect is positive or negative.

3 Must doctors help their patients?

There is a question here which needs discussion: whether, when and why a doctor has an obligation to do anything for someone? I mean: to do anything in the way of medical treatment. Has he such an obligation simply because of (say) the existence of a National Health Service, and because he belongs to it? Can't a doctor sometimes say: 'I do not want to treat this patient, I actually don't want him as a patient of mine?' Can he sometimes, or can he never say the following?: 'I do not want to prolong this person's life by taking medical measures to do so. I am not saying it is *better* not to; I would say nothing against another practitioner who might want to. But I don't want to. And I don't have to.'

This question of G.E.M. Anscombe's[1] she rightly identifies as 'a deep and important question of medical ethics', and it is this question, or rather these questions, that I wish to attempt to answer in this chapter.

These questions are deceptively straightforward, and deceptively narrow, despite their obvious profundity and difficulty. A proper answer to them may well prove to be an answer to the very general and much larger question: what is our obligation to care for one another? Or, scarcely narrower, what is society's obligation to care for and protect its citizens? With these possibilities in mind we will try to maintain a sharp focus and talk for the most part of doctors, nurses and other health professionals.[2] Here Professor Anscombe identifies two questions: the first is the question of whether or not there is any obligation to do *something* in the way of medical treatment for others, and second asks whether there can be any obligation to do *something 'medical'* to *prolong the life* of another person?

What is 'medical treatment'?

Before looking at these questions however we must ask what is implied by the use of the term 'medical' to qualify what is or is not done for other people.

Much of the 'treatment' offered by doctors and other health care professionals is in the form of advice or counselling. This may be as to diet, rest, exercise, cleanliness and so on, or it may be very general advice about the probable effects of a particular lifestyle or habit. This advice may well help to prolong life or it may not. Where more palpable treatment is offered, say in the form of drugs, the question of what is specifically 'medical' about the treatment may remain problematic. The drugs may be proven therapies appropriately prescribed; they may or may not help. They may be placebos, given to the sick in the absence of anything proved to be more efficacious, or they may be given to hypochondriacs; either group may consequently recover or they may not. The necessity to test drugs complicates the issue still further. People involved in a test as a control group might be given nothing at all, but they are still in a sense the subjects of medical treatment. Treatment then may range from major surgery or chemotherapy through 'nursing care only', to simple observation.

Because of the wide variety of activities or absences of activity that may be described as 'treatment', and because of the wide variation in probable, expected or hoped for, actual or imagined success, indeed because of the great difficulty in defining 'success', we should be wary of thinking of medical treatment exclusively in terms of any of these. I shall in consequence take a very broad view of what constitutes medical treatment or care and take these terms to refer *to anything done by health care professionals or at their direction (or done by amateurs working for or in place of professionals) which affects people for whose care they are responsible.*

Postponing death

So, having been called on for help, does a doctor's obligation (whatever that obligation turns out to be) differ when her judgment is that such help as can be given (say comfort, or relief of pain or setting a broken limb, or advice, or simply diagnosis) will not (probably) prolong life, and those cases where it (probably) will? Clearly, life-saving, or more accurately death-postponing, actions are of the highest moral importance. And they are so for precisely the same reasons that death-dealing or murderous ones

are, generally, the most serious of crimes. This is not of course
to say that many of the things that we do for one another which
are not death-postponing are not, morally speaking, very important indeed. But while the prolongation of life is not necessarily
or always more important than that of giving the other sorts of
help that may be required, it is always of the first importance,
and except in very rare cases, the saving of life, or the attempt so
to do, is the first and most urgent requirement. So that while we
may want to rank order the multifarious varieties of care and
other treatment that doctors may perform, there is no need to
grade the importance of saving life.

There may then be a fairly systematic difference in our judgments about the importance of medical treatment which does not
save or prolong life and that which does; and this may well influence our judgments about the force of whatever obligation there
may be to give treatment, or even our judgment as to whether or
not there is any such obligation at all. To avoid this further
complication of our investigation we will concentrate on those
cases which are always of the first importance and so on to Professor Anscombe's second question: is there an obligation to prolong life by taking medical measures so to do?

Refusing patients and refusing treatment

Can a doctor say of a dying patient, 'I do not want to treat this
patient, I actually don't want him as a patient of mine?' There
are two possibilities here: in one a doctor refuses to accept someone as her patient and in the other she refuses to treat one of her
patients. How different are these and do they indicate different
possible obligations on the part of the doctor?

Superficially the difference between these two possibilities is
that in the first a doctor refuses to take responsibility for someone,
refuses to ascertain whether or not they need her help and
whether or not she can or cannot do anything for them. In the
second she takes, or somehow has, responsibility for the patient,
and refuses to discharge that responsibility. In a society which
has many doctors (even if that 'many' are in fact a scarcity) refusal
to accept someone as a patient may just mean that some other
doctor will (will have to?) accept them. Similarly, refusal to treat
will just mean that some other doctor will (will have to?) treat
them. There may of course be a long line of such doctors but we
must concentrate on the doctor at the end of the line, or on the
doctor who for a particular patient (because that patient will not

survive being moved along to the next practitioner) is the doctor at the end of the line. We must concentrate on this doctor just because it is here that the buck stops. The doctors up the line have passed on the responsibility for the patient, but they have also passed on whatever force there is in the obligation of doctors to treat the sick. This force can be fully felt only at the point where a person's fate hangs upon whether or not he gets the treatment he needs here and now from this doctor. For it is difficult to see a particular doctor's obligation as especially strong when the sick person who, so to speak, attempts to force the obligation to treat him upon that doctor, can *and will* be equally well treated by the doctor next door. But when this doctor is the last doctor, then we can clearly see the urgency of the question of whether this doctor is entitled to say 'I don't want to and I don't have to.'

Now if you are that doctor the consequences for the patient of your saying 'I do not want to treat this patient' are the same as saying 'I ... don't want him as a patient of mine'. Of course you, the doctor, may not know that they are the same, indeed, if you refuse to take on the patient you may effectively shield yourself from any knowledge of his condition let alone of his fate. This may or may not affect moral assessments of your character and we will return to this point, but for now it is important to stress that this makes no difference to the patient. In both cases the patient will die and he will die because you refused to treat him.

We saw in the previous chapter that this conclusion is inescapable. The question that remains, is, however, whether the doctor is morally obliged to avoid all such consequences, whether, in short, the doctor is obliged never to refuse to treat a patient whom she can help, or whose life she can save. We are here interested just in the question of what moral obligations there are which derive purely from the fact that one party is a doctor and that the other needs her help. Many doctors would have all sorts of contractual obligations in such circumstances and, irrespective of the legal status of these, there will also perhaps be a moral obligation to honour contracts freely entered into. But our interest is concentrated entirely on the question of what moral obligation there is on a doctor to treat those who need her help.

What is a doctor's business?
It is sometimes said that saving life is always a doctor's business, that is what she is trained for, it is her vocation. This, while

perhaps uncontroversial, is too weak a consideration upon which
to found moral obligation. For playing cricket is (if anything is)
always a cricketer's business, it is what he is trained for, it is his
vocation. But that does not mean that he is obliged to play in
every match, or every time someone turns up wishing to see him
play. Perhaps this analogy misses an important point, that medicine is special, and its specialness just consists in its role in saving
life and in healing or caring for health and in the special priority
we give to all these things.

First, and of course, we do attach special importance to prolonging life and to recovering from illness and injury, and to relief
of pain. We attach the same importance to the avoidance of subjection to involuntary and substantial risks to life and health, and
to the risk of being subjected to pain. However, it would be odd
to think that there was some special category of person whose
unique and first responsibility it is to refrain from killing or injuring us or from subjecting us to substantial risk of death or
injury or pain. No one at all should subject us to these or the risk
of them. Similarly, and for the same reasons, anyone who can
should save or help save our lives and preserve our health.

But surely, it might be argued, a doctor would be specially
blameworthy if, knowing how incompetent a physician she was,
she allowed a patient to die rather than risk the disgrace of muff-
ing a simple life-saving procedure. She would, moreover, be more
blameworthy than would a lay bystander who happened to know
the appropriate procedure, but was unwilling to risk employing
it. The same difference would lead us to judge a lifeguard more
blameworthy for failing to rescue a drowning man than we would
another competent swimmer who also witnessed the drowning,
but did nothing to help.

Wicked men and evil deeds

It is important here not to confuse the moral assessment of
character with the moral assessment of actions. This important
distinction can be illustrated by the case of a completely innocent
ordinary man. Of course no one at all should murder him, and
everyone's obligation to refrain from so doing is equally strong.
All have an obligation, rated at 100 per cent, to refrain from
killing the innocent, and no one's obligation is less or more than
100 per cent. However, if the man's son were to murder him we
might think the son more wicked than we would a murderous
stranger. It does not follow from this that his son was somehow

under a *stronger* obligation not to murder him than was the stranger, nor that his murder was somehow a greater calamity in the one case than in the other, or somehow more to be deplored. In each case the murder was equally bad and the obligation to refrain from it equally strong—only our moral assessment of the character of the murderer differs. We regard someone who could bring himself to murder his father as more wicked than someone who could bring himself to murder a stranger. Similarly, we may think that the doctor and the lifeguard are more to blame for their cowardice than were the others, but not that their obligation was stronger, nor that the victim was more wronged by one of them than by any other.

Two faces of the obligation to treat

There are then two sorts of moral obligation here, or rather as I think, two ways of thinking about one and the same obligation. I won't enquire where this obligation comes from because in one or other of its forms it is almost universally recognised. For our present purposes we will have gone a long way to make clear the nature of the moral obligations of health care professionals if we can show that they fall under one or other aspect of this more general and widely recognised duty.

The first way of thinking about this duty sees it as part of our duty to refrain from killing or injuring others. Because, as we have seen, where we decide not to treat someone knowing that they will die or suffer as a consequence, or decide not to rescue someone knowing that they will die or suffer as a consequence, then their death or suffering is, in either case, a consequence of our decision.[3] If we believe, as most of us do, that we should not behave in ways that cause death, injury, or suffering to others, then our obligation is clear.[4]

The second way of thinking of this obligation is to see it as part of what it is to value human life. An irreplaceable part of what it is to value life must be a belief that it is better that people live rather than die, and die later rather than earlier and also that their lives be as unimpaired by ill-health, injury, suffering and so on as it is possible to make them. Moreover that it remains better that death should be postponed and life chances made as good as they can be for so long as the individual's life remains valuable to that individual. These remarks are not of course intended to provide anything like an exhaustive account of what it is to value life.[5] They are none the less an irreplaceable part of any such account, in that no one could plausibly claim to value life, unless she were also committed to postponing the deaths of those individuals whose lives were valuable as long as possible, or as long as the individuals themselves wanted their deaths postponed. Similarly it would be part of what is involved in valuing life to attempt to ameliorate its quality so long as the individual concerned wanted this.

Rescue is everyone's business

On either account of our obligations to others, in addition to refraining from murder and other forms of bodily harm, we should also rescue others so that they do not lose or otherwise involuntarily impair their valuable lives. We believe for example that we should rescue trapped miners and other victims of accidents, or those shipwrecked, or the victims of hijackers or other hostage-takers; and, not least, those who can be rescued only by medical care. Some of these rescues can be performed by anyone who is on hand; others require all sorts of expertise from that of potholers, sailors, miners, engineers, firemen and so on, to specialised military personnel and those with medical skills. Very often, those of us who lack these skills can best help, and thus discharge our obligation to those at risk, by keeping well out of the way. All of this is perhaps obvious enough but it helps us to see two important features of the obligation of health care professionals. The first is that *there is nothing special about their obligation in particular.* Just as there is no special category of person whose unique and first obligation it is to refrain from inflicting death, injury or suffering on the rest of us, so there is no one who is specially required, morally speaking, to undertake rescues. We can see this more clearly if we consider the obverse side of the same coin.

Contract killers
Suppose someone to have a contractual obligation to take innocent life rather than to save it, a contract killer or professional 'hit-man' for example. What extra moral obligation does such a person have which derives from the existence of his contract? If someone were to have any extra moral obligation to kill the innocent, deriving from the existence of a contract, this would amount to their having *that much less* of a moral obligation to refrain from killing those innocent people they had contracted to

kill! Contractual obligations must be irrelevant to the moral obligation to save life, precisely because they must be irrelevant to the obligation to refrain from taking life. In so far as the possession of a contract to kill is not a plausible plea in mitigation of the killer's moral responsibility for the demise of the person whose life he has wrongly ended, so the contract rescuer's or health care professional's contract does not place upon her any extra moral responsibility to save the life of someone she ought in any event to save.

Although I have said that there is nothing special about health care professionals, this was perhaps hasty. What's special about them is simply that they possess skills which enable them to rescue others from a particularly pervasive and heterogeneous group of dangers. But we should be clear that the reasons why they should do so are the same as the reasons why any of us should rescue any others of us if we can, or the reasons why we should refrain from decisions which we know will result in harm to others. Of course it may well be that health care professionals have acquired what skills they have expressly for the purpose of effecting rescues and have thus in a way 'undertaken' to carry out the job. But we are here interested in the question of what general moral grounds there are for thinking them obliged to continue to do that job when perhaps they have withdrawn their undertaking, or feel like withdrawing or cancelling their undertaking, or perhaps dispute its precise terms or even its existence. Where any of these things are true and this doctor is say the last doctor, the only one who can help or who can help in time to be of use, then if contract were the source of obligation, there would be no moral duty to save lives. Here the doctor who repudiated her contract, or had yet to enter into it, would apparently have less of a duty than the rest of us.

The contractual obligation

As far as life-saving or other crucial forms of rescue go,[6] a doctor or any health care professional has the same moral obligation to undertake these as anyone else who is in a position to help and is able to do so. The doctor's contract, whatever its fine print, cannot vary this obligation, for it falls equally on us all. And in so far as contracts impose this very duty the fact that they are also contractual as well as moral obligations imposes no additional duty, for the duty is already as strong as it can be.[7]

What the professional's contract might well do, however, that is not part of the general moral obligation that we have to one another, is impose on doctors and other professionals the obligation to put themselves *in a position* to render aid at particular times and places. For example to be present in a hospital or clinic, or to be 'on call'. It might well also put them under a contractual obligation to *maintain their ability* to render aid. This may involve an obligation to 'keep up with developments', perhaps by study or 'refresher' courses, or by practice. These obligations may fall on health care professionals in virtue of their being, or claiming to be, *professionals*, whatever the fine print of their actual contracts provides. These obligations will be part of the actual or implied contract between professional and client which do not form part of our general moral obligations to one another. It may be that obligations such as these cannot be varied so long as the professional still continues to offer professional services.

Yet other conditions may be part of specific and actual contracts that professionals have with their employers or their clients or both. These may well be varied without loss of professional standing, and might concern anything from the specific hours of employment, to appropriate dress or remuneration. They are of no concern to us for we are interested in the moral obligations of health care professionals.

Saving life is a moral issue

The second important feature of the obligations of health care professionals made clearer by seeing those obligations as the same as those which fall on the rest of us is that professionals have *no special prerogatives in the interpretation of that obligation.* In deciding, for example, who should and who should not be the beneficiary of their power to save life or prevent suffering,[8] doctors have no special status because such a decision is a moral and not a medical or clinical decision. Of course, medical opinion may be part of the *data* required in order to come to a moral decision, just as the opinion of a mine engineer may well be an important part of the data upon which to base a decision as to whether or not to attempt a rescue of trapped miners. But the decision will be a moral and not an engineering decision. The point is worth labouring because doctors are very apt to claim that only they can decide these matters, firstly because the decisions are supposedly 'medical', and secondly because it is they, the doctors, who will have to carry through whatever decision is taken. We have seen that such decisions are by no means medical, in the sense that doctors have any special competence or right to exclusivity in making them. The second point is even less well taken. It would be like a hangman claiming that it is he who must decide the guilt or innocence of the accused because it is he who will have to carry out the sentence.

Given what is at stake, when might anyone at all say 'I don't want to and I don't have to' save the life of another person? Clearly there would have to be something which could plausibly be claimed to be of comparable moral importance at stake or some other equally forceful moral consideration that would show why one shouldn't save (or one should end) this life in these circumstances. The answer would thus seem to be not unless either:

(a) It is probable that I would suffer significant injury (or death) or undergo great hardship in the attempt or as a result of it.

(b) There is something of comparable (or greater) moral importance I must do and I cannot do both.

(c) It would be better for that person if I did not attempt to save them or some other good will be achieved by their death or by my refraining from saving them for which end I would be justified in sacrificing their life.

(d) They don't want to be saved.

(e) They would be better off dead.

Conditions (c), (d) and (e) are all exceptions because morality requires, or it is claimed that morality requires, that the person whose life is in the balance be not saved. Or perhaps at its weakest, that there are moral reasons for not saving the victim and we can appreciate that reasonable and humane people would find these reasons compelling. Conditions (a) and (b), on the other hand, both involve cases in which the potential victim's life should undoubtedly be saved but the potential rescuer believes that there are moral reasons why they should not be, or need not be, the rescuer. In these two cases there need be no judgment that it would be better for anyone if the victim were not saved, only that particular people are not required, in these circumstances, to do the saving.

We will take the last three conditions first and look at them just long enough to see the sorts of cases to which they would apply. We will then turn in more detail to the first two conditions because it is these to which doctors must appeal if they are ever to decline to treat the generality of patients.

In what circumstances would condition (c) apply? I suppose it would be better for someone if I didn't attempt to save them if either, they would be better off dead (see (e) below) or the process of saving them would either be so painful and protracted for them that death would be preferable to experiencing it, or their rescue would involve the sacrifice of some other value that *they* believed to be more important than their own life, as perhaps is the case when Jehovah's Witnesses require, but refuse, blood transfusions. Where some other good will allegedly be achieved by the death of the person I could save, it must be the sort of scale of good for which I would be justified in sacrificing his life. Some will hold that this could never be the case, but I suppose most of us would accept that saving one or more other lives who can be saved only if this person is left to die would be an example. Another might be using the resources required to rescue certain individuals to prevent the certain occurrence of a greater number of deaths from another danger.

How we respond to the request of those under condition (d) that they be not saved will depend very much upon whether we judge 'the value of life' to be primarily a value to the person whose life it is or of some independent importance; or perhaps, upon whether we accept that an individual must be free to determine his or her own fate even at the cost of their own life. Broadly, those who think suicides should be left alone will accede to such requests and those who think they should be prevented and/or revived will not. We can, however, understand someone's finding the fact that a person has sincerely and soberly asked not to be saved a morally compelling reason for allowing them to die.

Condition (e) is both important and problematic. It is important for this discussion because, where doctors have judged that it is in their patient's best interests to die, they have felt supported in their decision to let a patient die by the belief that they are in any event under no compelling obligation to provide treatment.[9] It is problematic because of the difficulty in being satisfied that it is in a patient's best interests to die, particularly when, either through disability or infancy, the patients cannot themselves be consulted. Some will claim that we can never come to such a conclusion, others will be able to imagine cases in which they feel that it would be better for someone not to survive any longer. We cannot resolve this very difficult question here, but it will be examined in detail in the next chapter. For now we must simply note that for some people (e) will be an empty category and for others not. Either way, given that one form or other of the very general moral requirement is accepted, that we either refrain from decisions the consequence of which is death and other disasters for others or we act consistently with our belief in the value of life; then unless as in conditions (c), (d) and (e), the particular individual whose life is at risk should die, we must save them if we can. Or, we must do so unless conditions (a) or (b) hold.

What is worth a life?

Condition (a) reflects our acceptance of the futility of requiring that people lay down their lives for one another. Equally we recognise that it is unrealistic to expect that anyone will willingly run substantial risk of significant injury or undergo great hardship to rescue others although we may regard them as saints or heroes if they do. While it may be hard to specify with any confidence or exactness what is to count as 'significant' or as 'substantial' for these purposes, we do, I think, retain a general idea of the sorts of thing that might be proportionate here and this is all we need. For while many would doubt that anyone ought to sacrifice say, a finger to save the life of another, most people would accept that working longer hours or taking a (small?) cut in salary would be a price that anyone ought to be prepared to pay to save a life.

Condition (b) is similar, and reminds us that life and our commitment to it is so important that we cannot lightly sacrifice the one or turn our backs on the other. What is in fact of moral importance comparable to saving a life may be difficult to specify for all sorts of reasons. There will be those who place an infinite value on life and so deny that there is anything to compare with it in importance. Others claim that certain values are incommensurable and cannot simply be traded off, one against the other. Further difficulties will have to do with the estimation of the probability of various outcomes and other uncertainties, others still will turn on weighing the moral importance of various projects and activities.

Those who place an infinite value on human life will have many problems to resolve.[10] They would have to believe that they must go on saving lives even if the consequences of so doing were ruinous for many other important aspects of life. And of course, if such things as housing, sanitation, and other areas of social welfare are to be neglected so that resources may be directed to more immediate life-saving measures, there will be a delayed feedback effect and the lack of these services will begin to cost lives.

Incommensurability of values

While the difficulty of weighing up the comparative moral importance of different values may be extreme, those who hold that there can be no way of trading off the importance of one value, or one sort of value, against another face a different difficulty. Since deciding what to do is inescapable, in a way that deciding what to value or what to value most is not, those who hold that values are incommensurable will have to choose to do one thing rather than another while maintaining that this does not commit them to any judgment about the greater value or moral importance of what they have chosen, as compared with rejected alternatives. Such people will face acute moral dilemmas in which they have to choose between respecting one sort of value or another, while believing that there is no reason to regard one alternative as more morally important than the other. Unless such choices are always and deliberately made at random, a pattern of preference is likely to emerge. It would be difficult not to think of such preferences as moral preferences. But even if the choices were made consistently randomly, those making them would have to be confident that there was literally nothing to choose between them or the justification of a random choice would be impossible. In other words, to know that two values were incommensurable, one would have to have a sense of just how valuable each was, of what made it so important, of what made it a *value*, and moreover one of such a kind that it could not simply be traded off against another value.

And this is perhaps enough, for it is not necessary that we have a comprehensive or even a well-worked-out system of priorities that we can rank order with confidence; nor do we need a foolproof method of calculating probabilities or resolving uncertainties, though all or any of these would be useful. However, if anyone is to decline to save the life of another person because there is something else they must do instead, then if they are to retain any moral credit at all, they must be able to give a plausible (though not necessarily a decisive) account of how the moral importance of their alternative project compares with that of saving a life. Or, given the probability of saving a particular life, that there is a better way to use time or resources. If they maintain that values are incommensurable then they must still justify their choosing *to do* one thing rather than another.

Sharing the burden

If we return now to the problem of how these conditions apply to the obligations of health care professionals a number of apparently special problems apply. The sorts of cases conjured up by thinking of the obligation as a perfectly general one, to save life where we can, tempt us to imagine rather exceptional circumstances in which we find ourselves with the opportunity to save life and readily recognise the lameness of saying 'I can't save that child from drowning, I've not finished my tea.' Those in health care are presented with life-saving opportunities rather more often than most of us imagine that we are. These apparently special problems are all to do with how burdensome a business life-saving is, or might be, for particular individuals. I say they are apparently special because, as we saw in the previous chapter, we all of us have more of such opportunities, and therefore more of a burden, than we imagine; but I will concentrate just on the case of doctors and on how the burden which falls on them is to be shared between them and the members of the society of which they are a part.

Let's suppose that the last doctor happens to be the only doctor, because say, she is first on the scene of a huge disaster and no help can be expected for a long while, then so long as her skills are essential to life it is clearly her moral obligation to provide them. She cannot insist on normal office hours, or that she is in vacation time or that she has decided as of now to give up medicine for a career in television. But this seems reasonable only in an emergency. The burden of such unremitting life-saving might be too great to bear on a long-term basis, at least if all the burden fell on one individual.

Suppose a particular doctor always found herself as the last doctor because her colleagues played elaborate games of 'pass the patient', and consistently cheated so that when the music stopped she was always left holding the baby. We would think it unjust that *this* doctor must devote twenty-four hours a day to caring for the sick, when her colleagues merely shared the burden of minding the gramophone. But here our judgment would not be that there was *no* obligation, rather that the obligation should be fairly distributed. So that although, with exceptions already noted, the last doctor is obliged to treat her patients rather than let them

die, there is also an obligation on the rest of us to see to it that
the burden (even if it isn't a burden?) of being the last doctor is
shared equally or at least fairly.

Scarcity of doctors

More common than being the only available doctor will be the
situation of doctors in a society which has insufficient doctors.
We would say I think that a society is short of doctors when, if
the burden of treating those who need care were to be spread
fairly through the population of practising doctors, a doctor could
not then discharge her obligation to the sick or dying without
either working significantly harder than people in that society
normally work or without hardship to herself. A society will thus
be short of doctors in this sense even where perhaps some doctors
are unemployed or otherwise present but unable to practise. Well,
where doctors are in short supply they will clearly have a hard
time of it if they are to rescue all those who need to be and could
be saved. But unless this hard time is so hard as to bring it under
condition (a) then their obligation to save life remains. But we
must remember that this obligation falls equally on anyone and
everyone who could help, and while it may be that only medically
qualified people can help those in immediate danger there is
something that the rest of us can do to help as well. We can
provide the resources that will remove the scarcity of doctors.[11]
Unless we are willing to work at least as hard as the doctors to
remove the shortage, then we can hardly complain if they are
unwilling to fulfil their obligations to the dying. Of course, if we
work harder then the doctors will have to work harder as well,
until rough equilibrium is reached.

Comparative judgments

It is important here to keep clear the distinction between judging
people and judging actions or between assigning blame and assigning responsibility. Because doctors are *no more* obliged to
rescue the dying than any other members of society, their complaint (or anyone's) against a society that allows there to be a
shortage of doctors is at least as great as the complaint of any
member of that society against the doctors for failing to do more
than others are doing to save the dying. So that while the obligation of doctors to rescue those they can rescue is not lessened
by the burden of the task (unless that burden amounts to grave
hardship) it would be wrong to think that doctors are morally

worse for not working much harder as a matter of course than other members of the society.

And of course, where doctors are not in short supply they seem clearly obliged to help the dying unless conditions (a) to (e) apply, even if this involves occasional emergencies where much harder work than normal is required.

We have concentrated on saving life as the clearest and most important obligation to our fellows. Whether the same arguments can be applied to the general question of the obligation to provide all the various things that count as medical care is less clear. It may well be that we could make rough but workable judgments as to the importance of each sort of treatment and *pro rata* judgments about the importance of alternative projects that those who could provide the care might wish to undertake. Many injuries, illnesses and conditions which are not lethal may, to those who suffer from them, be a fate almost as bad as death (and perhaps sometimes worse). Here the obligation to cure or heal if possible and to relieve terrible pain may be clearly as important as life-saving or death-postponing. In other cases day-to-day medical care may be a fairly low personal and social priority, and the obligation to provide it weak or even non-existent. Of course it may sometimes (or always?) be necessary to see patients to decide which is which, and the obligation to assess may be much more comprehensive than the general obligation to treat. How all these problems are to be resolved will require much more detailed study than can be given here.

We should note finally that special difficulties will arise when a particular society, community or state cannot afford all the doctors (let alone all the other medical resources) it needs however hard the people work. Such a society will effectively be a permanent disaster area and what morality requires of doctors, or anyone else, in such circumstances may be a problem of a different order. We should note, however, that the same general moral principles that require us to save the lives of our fellows if we can are not parochial and do require us to work to save lives in that society as well as in our own. I do not know whether adequate principles for distributing the burden of life-saving and other health care would reveal the whole world to be a disaster area or not. But the obligation to share this burden fairly does not wait upon our knowing how great a burden it is.

4 Killing: a caring thing to do?

Perhaps there were times when the idea of a fate worse than death was familiar and unsurprising. In these days, the phrase usually occurs, if it occurs at all, as a joke or a grim irony, so much has life become in a sense the ultimate value, the value against which all other values are measured. The idea that there are fates worse than death has, however, remained with us, but in a self-defeatingly isolated and attenuated form.

Most sensitive people would probably regard death, when it comes to the very old and infirm, or to individuals who are suffering from a painful and terminal illness, as a 'blessed release' or a 'merciful and welcome end'. But many of these same people would regard death as acceptable only if it comes, so to speak, unbidden, of its own accord. If death is commanded or encouraged to appear, then however welcome or merciful its appearance, those who have issued the commands or provided the inducements are thought guilty of a moral wrong and perhaps also of a criminal offence. But, if death is a benefit, how can those who confer it fail to be benefactors? And if they are benefactors, and no third parties suffer from, or lose by, the benefaction, how can it be morally wrong?

In this chapter we will consider the ways in which killing might be a caring thing for one person to do for another and in so doing try to arrive at a general account of the circumstances in which it is wrong for us to kill others and those in which it is not. In order to accomplish this our discussion will range far from the immediate concerns of health care professionals. This is unavoidable for, as we saw in Chapter 2, our responsibility for what happens to others, and in particular for their premature demise, is wider than has been generally accepted; and it is of some importance to be clear about the circumstances in which we might justifiably be responsible for the death of another person.

In the euphoria following the murder of Julius Caesar, Shakespeare's conspirators convince themselves that they have done Caesar a great service by killing him; for as Casca says:

> Why he that cuts off twenty years of life
> Cuts off so many years of fearing death.
> *Brutus.* Grant that, and then is death a benefit:
> So are we Caesar's friends, that have abridg'd
> His time of fearing death.[1]

The cynical absurdity of this reasoning is accentuated by Caesar's own attitude to the prospect of his death:

> Cowards die many times before their deaths;
> The valiant never taste of death but once.
> Of all the wonders that I yet have heard,
> It seems to me most strange that men should fear;
> Seeing that death, a necessary end,
> Will come when it will come.[2]

While the fear that people might falsely or implausibly decide that others might be better off dead and act on that decision is a real one, and is one that clearly animates much of the opposition to euthanasia, it is not an objection in principle but rather a demand for safeguards. We shall return to the issue of safeguards, but for the moment it is the question of what objections there are in principle to such killing that must be answered. However implausibly the conspirators argued the case for Caesar's murder being a benefit to Caesar their main argument was that it was a benefit to *others* and indeed to Rome itself. By so arguing the conspirators attempted to show that there were moral reasons for the assassination of Caesar. There seem to be four principal types of cases in which there are moral reasons for killing and it is worthwhile reviewing them to get our bearings in this very difficult terrain. Firstly, and of course, to say there are moral reasons for killing is not to say that there are *decisive* moral reasons for killing. The cases we shall review are those in which one can appreciate the moral concern which underpins the reasons for killing and in which it makes sense to ask whether these reasons are adequate.

Speaking from the point of view of the potential 'victim', one might say that persons become *vulnerable* to another's moral reasons for killing them in four sorts of circumstance: where they are a threat, where they themselves want to die, where they would

be better off dead and where their death would secure a value
sufficient to outweigh the moral cost of securing it.³ We will examine each of these sorts of case in turn. The first, where death
removes a threat, will engage us the longest and will prove the
most difficult. Its examination will take us furthest from the normal concerns of health care professionals but its interest and importance is such that this is unavoidable.

I Death removes a threat

Self-defence is often taken to be a paradigm of justified killing.
But the acceptability of this defence depends in large part on the
assumption that the attack was 'lethal', in the sense that it was
the sort of attack that would put its victim in danger of death,
and that killing the assailant was the only available method of
stopping or disarming her. It must be literally 'her or me'! While
such killing in self-defence might seem entirely unproblematic, a
difficult question that immediately arises is: does the justifiability
of eliminating lethal threats extend to so-called 'innocent threats'
and to 'innocent shields of threats'?⁴ 'An *innocent threat* is someone
who innocently is a causal agent in a process such that he would
be an aggressor had he chosen to become such an agent.'⁵ The
unknowing carrier of a deadly infectious disease who is attempting to clamber aboard my lifeboat would be an example. If I
know that I will die if he succeeds in getting aboard, and he is
unaware of the danger that he presents, then I can only defend
myself by keeping him off or by pushing him off if he succeeds
in getting aboard (either of which would in the circumstances be
fatal). If he knows that the disease he is carrying will be lethal to
me (but not to him) and he tries to get aboard, he is not exactly
an 'innocent' threat although he is not straightforwardly an aggressor either. For both of us self-defence consists in bringing
about the death of the other.

'Innocent shields of threats' are persons 'who themselves are
non-threats but who are so situated that they will be damaged by
the only means available for stopping the threat.'⁶ Hostages are a
classic example here. If the hostage-takers plan to kill hostages
sequentially until their demands are met then, to would-be res-
cuers who might have to kill some hostages to effect the rescue
each hostage is an innocent shield of a threat to the other hostages
and to anyone threatened by the demands made by the hostage-

takers. An example nearer our present interests is the familiar *vaccination dilemma.* If we don't vaccinate babies, against whooping cough for example, many will die and there may be an epidemic. If we do vaccinate, a few will suffer brain damage and one or two will die. These victims of a policy of vaccination are in a sense innocent shields of threats; we can only attack whooping cough and the threat it poses to all children by doing so 'over the dead bodies' so to speak of those few who will be injured by the vaccine.

Does the principle of justified self-defence extend to innocent threats and innocent shields of threats? One way of trying to answer this question is to ask what precisely makes killing in self-defence a case of justified killing?

Understanding and justification
First we must distinguish between an action's being psychologically understandable, perhaps even psychologically inescapable, and its being morally justified. We can recognise that people will defend themselves against lethal attacks if they can, and that it is unreasonable to expect them not to. This is not, however, the same as accepting that they are morally justified in resisting such attacks. If someone had attempted to assassinate Hitler in 1940, we might well *understand* that Hitler would defend himself if he could, without being in any way committed to the view that he was morally justified in so doing or to its corollary, that the would-be assassin was morally unjustified. Of course Hitler might have had moral reasons for killing his assailant but these would have to have been unconnected with the morality of self-defence. Self-defence is not a moral reason but a psychological appeal, it says in effect, 'she was trying to *kill* me! What did you expect me to do?' And of course we may not have *expected* anything else (and neither would the assailant), but the fact that our expectations have been fulfilled is no evidence at all of the moral respectability of the actions which fulfil them.

It seems strange to demand the moral justification of self-defence. This is largely because the disposition of most creatures is to defend their lives if they can, and we have come to regard this as a sort of brute and immovable fact with which all societies and all moralities have had to cope. This they tend to do by accepting the inevitable, and treating self-defence as a right. However, the moral force behind the psychological appeal of self-defence can be important, particularly where, either as individuals or as

society, we have to decide whether to aid someone in their defence
of self. This is not only of jurisprudential interest, for people may
reasonably wish to defend themselves against disease or infection,
and it may only be possible for them to do this by defensive
assaults on people who carry infection, or whose continued life or
health is incompatible with the survival of the person who wishes
to enlist our aid.

   This, as we have seen, is just what happens in cases like that of
the 'vaccination dilemma', where babies are quite literally as-
saulted by third parties on each others' behalf; if some die as a
result, they are the victims of an assault in the defence of those
who survive. The same is true, less dramatically, in cases of quar-
antine, where people may be subjected to non-lethal assaults (imprisonment) if they are a danger to others because they carry a
harmful contagion or infection. Another case which may be of
increasing importance in medical ethics (as we shall see in Chapter 6) is where some can only defend their lives by receiving
transplants from other living beings. The following extract from
a newspaper report highlights this issue:

> A young man, gravely ill with advanced leukaemia, is engaged in
> a remarkable legal battle with the University of Iowa for the name
> of a woman who could offer him the hope of life. All she has to do
> is donate some bone marrow.[7]

Here again, the woman, who virtually alone has the right type of
marrow to save this man's life, is the innocent shield of a deadly
threat to him. It is because of cases like these that the vexed
problem of the justification of self-defence becomes of crucial
importance to medical ethics.

The justification of self-defence

We saw in Chapter 1 that there were good reasons for thinking
it wrong to take any life that was valued by the individual whose
life it is, and that the best reason for thinking life valuable was
that the individual concerned is capable of valuing it. We saw also
that because each life is valuable, two lives are more valuable than
one, and we thus have a reason always to save as many lives as
we can. This of course might involve sacrificing a particular life
so that others may be saved; as where a crashing aeroplane is
directed away from a crowded school and on to an isolated farm-
house. Or, more remotely but as surely, in the cases like that of

the 'vaccination dilemma' we have just reviewed. So that while usually no one can be justified in taking the life of an innocent person against her will, a justification is available to those who take life while sincerely, plausibly and fairly attempting to save the lives of others.

Guilty threats

Where someone attempts to kill me in circumstances other than those which would involve a saving of life,[8] my attacker is giving the world a reason to value his life less than that of others. This is because his attack will itself represent an attack on the very value that must support any defence of the value of his own life.

The argument which underpins what is called the right of self-defence appeals to a moral view about the value of life and claims that an aggressor, by himself wishing to deny that value, has forfeited his claim to have his own life valued equally with that of his victim. This is because he has in a sense undermined or made hollow his claim to have his own life valued equally with that of his intended victim. For to preserve his own life in such circumstances, he must appeal to the very value he is attempting to subvert. An aggressor could not then consistently claim that his own life should be respected while attempting to kill his victim. Of course, if the aggressor does not wish to live, or doesn't care if he is killed, then neither his victim nor any third parties have any reasons not to defend themselves against his attack by killing him if they can.

A useful test, and one which we will apply at a number of points, is to ask what a third party who is capable of decisive interference should do? For us, third parties to the assault, to respect the aggressor's claim to live rather than that of his chosen victim would be inconsistent with our belief that we should value life and try to preserve as many lives as we can. Inconsistent, because it is only the aggressor's decision to kill another that has put either of the lives in question at risk, and only his actions which prevent the possibility of preserving both lives rather than merely that either of the aggressor or of his victim. So whether we are victims of murderous assaults or bystanders, it is our belief in the value of life that justifies our defending either ourselves or others against an assault that attacks the value of life, by seeking to kill in circumstances in which a net loss of life will result. We will shortly be examining cases in which lethal assaults may be justified where they will actually save life and in which some acts of self-defence may consequently not be justified.

Before considering such cases we should be clear that there is no suggestion that an aggressor's life has somehow *lost* its value, or that the obligation on others to respect its value has been extinguished. For once the aggressor no longer poses a threat, his life ceases to be 'at risk', and his wish to live must then be respected as much as that of anyone else. This account of the principles underlying self-defence offers no support to retributivist theories of any kind. People who have ceased to constitute threats, whether or not their threats were actually carried through, are equally strong candidates for rescue with any other members of society.[9]

Innocent threats and shields

Suppose two people are drowning and only one can be saved. If we know nothing about either of them, it is a matter of moral indifference which we save. All that matters morally is that we save as many as we can—in this case one of them, but we have no moral reason to *prefer* one to the other. But, if one of them is trying to kill the other without justification, then we have a reason to save the victim rather than the aggressor. The victim of course has *the same moral reasons* to save himself as we have to save him, but with rather more personal and psychological investment in their success. So 'self-defence' is shorthand for an argument which shows who ought to be saved where lives are in the balance one against another and not all can be saved. Where it's either you or me it shows why if I survive I was justified whereas if you, the aggressor, survive you were not; and equally it shows third parties on whose side they should intervene and who they may kill to bring hostilities to an end and rescue the innocent.

With these points in mind we can begin to see an answer to the problem of innocent threats and innocent shields of threats. Consider Robert Nozick's[10] example of the collision between an innocent 'victim' and an innocent threat: 'If someone picks up a third party and throws him at you down at the bottom of a deep well.... Even though the falling person would survive his fall onto you, may you use your ray gun to disintegrate the falling body before it crushes and kills you?' What is the answer to Nozick's question? Both parties are involuntarily forced into a situation where they cannot both survive, both are innocent.

What for example should a third party do? Which one should she rescue by using her ray-gun to 'zap' the other? The third party is in the same position as a bystander who can rescue one but not both men drowning in different parts of the lake. She must rescue one and it doesn't matter which so long as she chooses between them in a way which does not display a vicious preference for one over the other, a preference that effectively treats one as of less value than the other.

The principle of non-vicious choice

If one of the drowning men were white and the other black, then the bystander should not allow any prejudice she might have against either blacks or whites to influence her choice of whom to save, for to do so would involve vicious[11] discrimination. It would be vicious not because the black man who was left to drown was entitled to be rescued *rather than* the white man, but because he was entitled not to be the victim of vicious discrimination. He was, in short, entitled to have his life valued equally with that of the other man. In cases such as the one we are considering a bystander who thinks she might be prejudiced should perhaps spin a coin to determine which man to save.

But now suppose that one of the drowning individuals is the bystander's child and the other a complete stranger. What should she do, may she save her child rather than a complete stranger or must she toss a coin? It would not be vicious discrimination for her to save her child for if everyone were to act on this principle no systematic (and deadly) disadvantage would accrue to any identifiable group, no one could say they died because of the prejudice of rescuers, nor would any group of people be able to claim that the lives of members of that group were valued less than others. One doctor who has to cope with hundreds of victims of a disaster cannot treat them all. She must not for example separate the whites from the blacks and treat one group first, but she may treat her children first if they are victims and equally in need of immediate treatment to save their lives.

The doctor's choosing to save her own children first is not then a case of what I have called 'vicious choice'. She has to start somewhere and her preference for her own children is benign in a way that preference for, say, her own race is not; benign for two reasons. Firstly because as we have seen this preference generalised would not lead to any group being systematically and unfairly disadvantaged. Benign also because we can see that the disposition to love one's family (and one's friends) is a disposition that generally speaking makes life better all round, better for everyone. We want all people to love their families and friends, we want to live in a world where people are like that. The disposition to prefer one's fellow racists, as one might term it, or one's co-religionists, on the other hand, is one we want everyone not to have. It makes the world a worse place.

But now suppose that the doctor's decision to save her children first means that in total fewer lives are saved. She can either save the lives of both her children and ten other people on the one hand or save twenty strangers on the other (perhaps her children's injuries are complex and require a disproportionate amount of attention).

We can see that in this special case the doctor ought to save as many lives as she can, even at the expense of her children, but we can also see that she should not be blamed if she saves her children. This would be a case of what Derek Parfit[12] has called 'blameless wrongdoing'. The doctor might defend herself as follows:

> I had no reason to believe that my love for my child[ren] would have this very bad effect. It was subjectively right for me to allow myself to love my child[ren]. And causing myself to lose this love would have been blameworthy or subjectively wrong. When I save my child[ren] rather than strangers I am acting on a set of motives that it would have been wrong for me to cause myself to lose. This is enough to justify my claim that, when I act in this way, this is a case of blameless wrongdoing.[13]

We will see these principles at work in some of the following examples.

If we return to Nozick's well, a bystander has no reason to intervene on behalf of either party; if the person at the bottom of the well has a ray gun he will survive, if not, not. If the bystander were to choose to 'zap' the falling individual and make good the absence of a ray gun at the bottom of the well, she would not achieve a more just outcome. Likewise if she were to kill the ray-gun-holding man at the bottom of the well, thereby securing happy landings for the innocent fall-guy, again, no gain for justice would be recorded. If she were to spin a coin to see whom to save she would simply be subjecting the outcome to chance twice over and for no gain in lives saved since chance has already either provided one with a ray gun or the other with a soft landing.

If we shift the perspective from that of the third party to that of two innocent mutual threats, may either kill the other? If a third party has no moral reason to choose to save one rather than the other, then neither do either of the innocent mutual threats have such a reason, at least so long as one life is balanced against another. But suppose five innocent and immune carriers of a deadly disease attempt to climb aboard a lifeboat inhabited by one vulnerable individual, may he ward off these five innocent threats, thereby killing them? (We will assume that the five will soon cease to be carriers and so will not pose threats to those who eventually rescue them.) Here a third party would have a moral reason to prevent the lifeboatman saving himself from the five innocent threats and would be justified in doing so at the cost of the lifeboatman's life. Here, too, the lifeboatman might see that he was not justified in saving himself at the cost of so many other innocent lives. We might well understand his none the less trying to save himself, and we might not wish to punish him for so doing (these are separate questions) but we and he should see that he is not justified in so doing.

Equally, where the man threatened cannot defend himself from the innocent threat but can merely 'take him with me', then again we would rightly regard such gratuitous killing as unjustified because instead of an optimum (in the circumstances) outcome with one survivor out of two at risk, there would then be no survivors. And here again, a third party would be right to prevent such an outcome.[14]

The same is also true of innocent shields of threats. Where it is simply a case of one life balanced against another (where perhaps a terrorist holds one hostage while he attempts to kill a policeman) then if the policeman can only save his own life by killing the innocent shield, then it is difficult to think that he would not be justified in doing this. But where the innocent shields are many and those threatened are few, it clearly cannot be justified to kill those innocent people. And again, if we ask which group of people an omnipotent bystander should protect if she cannot protect both, we will have some sort of check on our intuition. Of course, as in the vaccination dilemma, where the innocent shields are few and those threatened are many, then again it seems clear that both our intuition and our principles pull the same way, that we should act so that as many innocent lives be preserved as is possible.

Innocent threats and scarce resources

We should note finally that innocent threats and innocent shields of threats occur in any circumstances where scarce resources mean that some will suffer or die for want of resources allocated to or possessed by others. If you and I need a blood transfusion, or a vital drug, and there is only enough of either for one of us, then the allocation of that resource to me makes me an innocent threat to you. Are you entitled to kill me either directly so that you can take the resource or indirectly *by* taking it? (and, of course, there is no moral significance in the directness or indirectness of the killing). Again we can ask what the omnipotent bystander should do here? Such a bystander is in the position of the person who allocated the drug to me in the first instance. As long as that choice was exercised non-viciously then there is no gain either for justice or in lives saved if circumstances are reversed so that you and not I are saved. So that while *ex hypothesi* there was no reason to save me rather than you, there is, once a decision has been made, no reason to reverse it. Of course *you* have such a reason and since again *ex hypothesi*, neither of us is more entitled to the resource than the other, it cannot be simply morally wrong for you to defend yourself by killing me. The reasons against your doing so or being permitted to do so by bystanders have all to do with what may be called the *side-effects* of such actions. In most circumstances it would be disfunctional in terms of the numbers of lives that could be saved and in terms of social order to permit or encourage those who lose out in a fair distribution of a vital resource from attempting any re-distribution.

Where the drug or the blood were not allocated to me but were somehow already owned by me then again, so long as that acquisition was just, bystanders have no reason to re-distribute the resource. It will now be obvious that the problem of innocent threats and scarce resources cannot be adequately solved without a theory of just distribution, and just acquisition of resources that would apply not only between individuals but across societies and national boundaries. Such a theory, if one could be found, is quite beyond the bounds of this essay. Although, in the absence of such a theory we may, indeed we must, use the moral principles that would be part of such a theory to try to decide hard cases that arise in the everyday world. In such a world the state of the law of particular societies will in circumstances short of complete catastrophe be very influential in determining lawful acquisition of resources but we will still need our moral principles to determine how far we should respect the law.[15]

Non-lethal threats

A problem arises as to how to meet non-lethal threats. To know how to meet non-lethal threats is to reveal more about the value of life because it is to have a view about how to weigh other values against the value of life. 'Suppose Thomson tries to rape Jacobson, Jacobson kills in self-defence because there was no other way of preventing the rape, though not only was there in reality no threat to her life, but Jacobson did not believe that there was one.'[16] Where it was either kill or be raped, Robert Young has offered an account of what makes killing morally wrong which he believes would not permit Jacobson killing Thomson in these circumstances. Young holds that 'what makes killing another human being wrong on occasions is its character as an irrevocable, maximally unjust prevention of the realization either of the victim's life purposes or of such life purposes as the victim may reasonably have been expected to resume or to come to have.'[17] 'Maximally unjust' here means 'that there are not present any overwhelmingly significant redeeming consequences', as for example in the cases we have just been considering where one unjust killing is morally required to save other innocent individuals who would otherwise unjustly die.

Young concludes that if Jacobson kills Thomson in such circumstances it is a wrong act because 'Thomson's attempted rape may not have been a grave attack on Jacobson's ability to achieve her life purposes.'[18] Locating the wrongness of killing in its prevention of the realisation of life purposes seems over-restrictive. Rape would not usually prevent the realisation of these, nor would the loss of a limb (unless one was an athlete) nor perhaps would disfigurement (unless one's face was one's fortune) nor would very intense but temporary pain—so the same account would rule out killing to prevent oneself from being tortured. This difficulty for Young's account (although he does not see it as a difficulty) could be overcome by defining a 'life purpose' as including remaining un-raped and un-tortured, etc., but Young rightly perceives the oddity and artificiality of such a move and in any event remaining un-raped would be only one among a

large set of life plans. These problems do, however, highlight this
rather restrictive nature of Young's account of the wrongness of
killing, and hence by implication of his account of the value of
life as consisting principally in the realisation of life purposes.

Clearly a very important and indispensable part of the value of
life for most people is the wants and wishes they have for themselves and for others. These would not usually amount to anything as grand or well-worked-out as a 'life purpose' but would
certainly include the wish to remain healthy (or become healthy)
and the wish never to experience great pain, or be tortured or
raped. Being tortured or raped may not significantly affect someone's ability to achieve their projects or formulate and pursue
new ones, but it might also be true that someone would be willing
to forgo or abandon many of their life purposes to avoid rape or
to cut short torture. And, of course, the purpose of torture is very
often to make them do just this.

But there are other difficulties with Young's account which
reveal the necessity for and indicate the structure of a different
account of the wrongness of killing.

A terminal but otherwise 'fit' patient with, say, only three or
four weeks left to live, would have already suffered Young's 'grave
attack on (her) ability to achieve her life purposes'. But if she
fervently wishes to live out what little time remains to her in her
own way then it would still seem to be a terrible wrong to kill
her against her will.[19]

But suppose this lady wishes to take her own life now rather
than wait for her illness to overcome her. Again, if her clear wish
is to kill herself in her own way and in her own time then it
would still surely be wrong to kill her in our own way and in our
own time (even if our and her way (method) and time would have
coincided). Wrong *inter alia*, because it would rob her of the
opportunity to determine her own fate (albeit for the last time).
This sort of case shows I think that the wish to live and the
wrongness of frustrating that wish and the wish to die in one's
own way if one can and the wrongness of frustrating that wish
are a very important part of any account of what is wrong with
killing someone on a particular occasion.

There is another difficulty which is highlighted by the problem
of non-lethal threats, and that is the need to distinguish between
guilty and non-guilty non-lethal threats (and of course shields of
such threats).

Guilt and innocence

If Young is right and Jacobson may not kill Thomson to protect herself from rape then would-be rapists would do well to
make sure that potential victims can only resist by killing them.
Shakespeare's Duke of Gloucester is a master of such techniques
and no doubt they could be further refined. Gloucester combines
the 'you'll have to kill me to stop me' technique with the threat
of suicide and the combination is too much for his victim. In a
burst of cynically splendid bravado he reminds the Lady Anne that
he has already killed her father and her brother as he hands her
his sword and invites her either to kill him or marry him. When
she drops the sword Gloucester neatly forecloses all the options:

> Take up the sword again, or take up me.
> *Anne.* Arise dissembler: though I wish thy death,
> I will not be thy executioner.
> *Gloucester.* Then bid me kill myself and I will do it.[20]

Torture and rape and maiming and disfigurement are terrible
and fearful injuries and even where, as is perhaps usual, they do
not amount to a fate worse than death, it is incumbent upon us
all, whether we are victims or bystanders, to try to prevent the
infliction of such injuries if we can. And if those who would do
such things are killed in the attempt they 'have only themselves
to blame'. It is this feeling that those wicked enough to attempt
to inflict such damage on others have, as the English Common
Law maxim *volenti non fit injuria*[21] so well states, in a sense 'vol-
unteered' for any injury that preventing them may involve, that
makes us distinguish such guilty attackers from innocent third
parties in such circumstances.

So, if on the other hand I can only protect myself from being
tortured by killing an innocent person then I may well not be
justified in resisting at such a cost (although you may understand
and perhaps forgive me if I do) but neither justice, nor any other
moral principle, requires me to protect, at the cost of terrible
injury to myself, those who would inflict such injuries upon me.

II Death is a benefit

We have seen that where killing removes a threat the death is a
benefit to those threatened and that in many circumstances this

may count as an adequate justification for the killing. But what of those cases where death is supposedly a benefit to the person who is to die? Initially there seems to be a strong logical objection to this way of speaking since death cannot be a benefit when manifestly there is no beneficiary! But this is a quibble. What is meant is simply that for a particular person the prospect of continuing to live under certain conditions is a worse prospect than immediate death.

Although there are people who would hold that there is no such thing as a fate worse than death in this sense, there seem to be numerous cases where it would be difficult to fail to conclude that particular people are facing or experiencing such terror and pain and misery that immediate death is a benefit. We are all familiar with the cliché of American Westerns in which the hero's friend is being tortured to death by savages (red or white) and the hero is left no choice but to kill his friend rather than let him go on suffering a moment longer. Real life, however, provides at least as many clichés and many more disasters than does fiction. There was a famous American case in which a driver trapped in the flaming wreck of his truck following an accident asked a policeman to shoot him dead rather than let him be burned alive when it became obvious that he could not be rescued nor the fire put out in time. A final horrifying prospect is that held out in a recent statement on health care planning following nuclear war.[22] It is certain that following such a war there would be 'large numbers of people so severely injured by blast or heat that their death within hours or days is wholly unavoidable'.[23] Because of the shortage of surviving medical staff and the necessity for such trained medical personnel as do survive to tend those who have a chance of recovery, it would be impossible to either tend, nurse or administer analgesics to such 'inevitably moribund individuals'.[24] One could well understand that such individuals might prefer a quick death to the lingering pain-ridden alternative.

There can surely be no doubt that killing such people who want to die, for whom death is the best prospect, and who cannot kill themselves, is not only the right moral choice but also a caring and humane thing to do.

Much more difficult is the case of those who are living in circumstances to which death is preferable or who face a future in which this will be true, but who are unable to express a preference for death. They may be too ill, too feeble-minded, or too young to say so, but it is as clear as these things can be that life is or will become so bad that the prospect of its continuing is horrifying and the prospect of its ending as quickly as possible is by far the lesser evil. Where this is so, what should we do? If the case is such that no humane person could stand by and let such suffering continue or commence and the only prospect of its cessation is through the death of the sufferer then again it is not only a caring but surely a moral thing to do.

Would we, for example, applaud the actions of a wandering cowboy who, coming upon our hero about to shoot his friend to save him from being lingeringly tortured to death by the exemplary savages, promptly shot our hero to save his friend from a premature violent end?

III Wanting to live and wanting to die

The last two sorts of case that we need to consider are best taken together. The first is where someone faces life prospects that are so dreadful as to make death the more attractive prospect but who none the less wishes to go on living and the second is the obverse case where someone seems to have a reasonable or at any rate not dreadful life or life prospect but who none the less wants to die.

In the first case the person in question may agree that their life is not worth living but none the less wishes to continue to live for any number of reasons. They may wish to punish themselves for real or imagined wrongs committed, they may believe that suicide or voluntary euthanasia violates God's law or they may be worried about vitiating an insurance policy.[25] They may, on the other hand, not accept that their life is not worth living or that living it is worse than an immediate death. Is it possible for someone to be wrong about whether or not staying alive is a worse prospect than death? Surely they are the best judges? Who is to say if not the person most concerned that their life is too terrible to continue it another moment. Surely the person in question is not merely the best judge of just how bad things are for her, she is in a sense the only person in a position to judge of such matters? Interestingly, our reluctance to contradict people who think (in our view erroneously) that their lives are worth living is not echoed by an equal reluctance to contradict those who think (in our view wrongly) that their lives are not worth living. Many people are only too ready to say to would-be suicides that 'things are not so bad' as they imagine, whereas few are ready to tell the non-suicidal that things are really much worse than they think.

Certainly we can know both that things are not so bad for others as they imagine them to be and that things are much worse than they imagine them to be. But how far we feel entitled to act on that judgment contrary to the wishes of the person most concerned depends crucially on the importance we attach to autonomy. To deny people the direction of their own lives, even of lives we know to be terrible or that we know to have little time left to run, is to do them a great wrong. To deny people the power of choice over their own destiny is to treat them as incompetent to run their lives and is thus to make their lives subordinate to *our* purposes for their lives rather than to treat their lives as *their own*. It is therefore to offer them the most profound of insults. Autonomy has a very special and central role in the value of life. People have been and continue to be prepared to sacrifice their lives in order to win for themselves or others autonomy over relatively minor sorts of decisions. Many things that we would find delightful if we had chosen them for ourselves lose all charm when they are seen to have been chosen for us or imposed on us by others. A life that seems thoroughly rich and worthwhile may be so only because we choose freely to live it. If we are *condemned* to live it, it may be worthless to us. And if life is far from rich and worthwhile, how much more terrible to be condemned to live it against our will?

The contrary case is also persuasive. If my life is so terrible that no one would wish to live as I do, then since it is *my life* its value to me consists precisely in doing with it what I choose, regardless of whether what I choose is to live on in great suffering or to end it in my own way rather than in your own way.

Third parties must decide whether they do someone a greater wrong by allowing them to suffer when their sufferings could be ended by death or by denying them autonomy by killing them against their will. But since, as I have suggested, the value of someone's life is primarily a value *to them* we should perhaps take that value as far as is possible at their own estimation of it.

The final sort of case is thus comparatively easy to resolve. Where someone has a life which holds out for them a worse prospect than immediate death and we and they agree about this and they wish to die then everything speaks for their being allowed to die and for our helping them by killing them at their request.[26]

IV Death promotes other values

We have reviewed cases in which killing is justified because it removes a serious threat, and where it may be said to benefit those whose death is in question. Killing may also be a caring thing to do to people who want to die, particularly if they cannot bring about their own deaths. But are there any values which are so important that one could be justified in killing completely innocent people to protect or promote them?

Many people claim that they are willing to die for various causes and, although the cynical may feel that this claim is made more often by people willing to kill for causes than to die for them, there are cases in which this latter claim is genuine. The willingness to die for a cause is, however, no evidence that the cause is worth the sacrifice of even one life any more than someone's willingness to commit suicide is evidence that their life is worthless. We have seen in our discussion of threats that there may be causes for which the guilty may be sacrificed where the guilty are those who seek wrongfully to impose their will damagingly upon others but we also saw the dubious nature of the claim that the innocent could be sacrificed to preserve such values.

If there are any causes which justify the sacrifice of unwilling innocent people and for which the justification does not at some point turn on the other lives that may now or later be thereby saved I do not know what they are. They would have to be very weighty causes, indeed their weight would almost certainly have to consist in avoidable human suffering both widespread and severe. So that whatever the title or ostensible purpose of the cause, if it were to hope to justify the sacrifice of innocent lives in its name it would have to appeal either to the value of life by showing that only by adhering to this cause will lives be saved. Or, it would have to show that the level of suffering in the world would be greatly diminished by adhering to such a cause at such a cost.

V Safeguards

But if we accept that killing is permissible because it is a caring thing to do, because it saves lives, because it reduces suffering ... in short, because it is right, how can we be sure that it will only be done when it is right and when it does achieve all these things? Once accepted, might not such killing become more and more common and the horror of ending the lives of others less and less real, until something approaching a Nazi callousness became pervasive? The answer of course is that we cannot be sure.

One good reason for not looking at the problem of the justification of killing solely through health care spectacles, but right across the spectrum of cases where we judge killing to be justifiable, is to put our judgments into some sort of perspective. All killing, whether in self-defence, or in defence of one's country, or of innocent third parties, might have the sorts of fearful effects we have imagined. What we have always to decide is how real such possibilities are likely to be, and to set against this the real disaster that would be consequent upon our not defending ourselves, our country or other people against an unjustified lethal attack. We must also bear in mind the brutalising effect that just standing by and allowing lethal attacks free rein would have on those who acquiesced in such atrocities.

There is no such thing as playing safe. To make a choice is to entertain the possibility of making a wrong choice. But a wrong choice is no less likely when the decision is not to entertain the idea of euthanasia, but rather to countenance the suffering of the individual who can only be released from suffering by death.

The only way to increase the probability of being morally right is to increase one's practice in thinking through difficult dilemmas and in making difficult decisions.

VI The justification of euthanasia

Now that we have reviewed in general the problem of how and when it might be justifiable to kill another person, the problem of the justification of euthanasia is relatively straightforward.

Euthanasia is simply the implementation of a decision that the life of a particular individual will come to an end before it need do so—a decision that a life will end when it could continue.

Voluntary Euthanasia occurs when that decision coincides with the individual's own wishes and he or she consciously approves of it, and of all aspects of its implementation.

Involuntary Euthanasia occurs whenever such a decision is implemented against the express wishes of the individual and

Non-voluntary Euthanasia occurs whenever such a decision is made without the consent of the individual concerned, whatever the reason for the absence of such consent.[27]

We have seen that the wrongness of prematurely ending the life of another person consists in depriving that person of something they value, and usually of something they value above all else, namely life itself. So that involuntary euthanasia will always be wrong, although it may be *justifiable* for any of the reasons considered earlier.

Non-voluntary euthanasia, on the other hand, will be wrong unless it seems certain that the individual concerned would prefer to die rather than go on living under the circumstances which confront her *and* it is impossible to find out whether the individual concerned shares this view. These will be extreme and rare cases, and we have already considered two sorts of circumstances in which it might be reasonable to judge that an individual would prefer death to the only alternative existence. One is that of very severely handicapped babies which face a painful and short life and whose handicap is irremediable.[28] The second sort of case might be that of someone who is perhaps being tortured to death and whom we can neither consult nor rescue—all that can be done is to put an end to his sufferings.

Voluntary euthanasia on the other hand, like suicide, will never be wrong morally, although like any other human choice it might be ill-advised. But so long as someone has genuinely ceased to value life, and prefers death to continued existence, then they are not morally wrong to take their own life and neither is anyone who assists them or who acts for them where they cannot act on their own behalf. We will look more closely at the problem of gauging the genuineness of consent in Chapter 10.

The real problem of euthanasia

Whenever the so-called problem of euthanasia is debated, or wherever it appears as an issue in morality generally or more particularly in medical ethics, the issue is almost always seen in terms of whether or not voluntary euthanasia is or is not justifiable, and so whether or not it should be permitted. This is a small and relatively straightforward issue compared with the problem that the widespread and disastrous use of non-voluntary euthanasia poses for many societies. Its continued and unrestricted use is seldom reviewed or criticised, and in most of its applications it is perfectly legal. So that the moral issue concerning euthanasia that most urgently requires consideration is not that of voluntary euthanasia, which concerns relatively small numbers of people and is so clearly something that society should permit. Rather the problem is the massive level of non-voluntary, and in some cases involuntary, euthanasia that society already permits and practises and which equally clearly should be outlawed or in its relatively few benign forms more closely regulated and supervised.

Euthanasia within health care

There are two sorts of cases which require most urgent consideration. The first concerns a number of practices falling broadly within the area of health care provision, where decisions are taken to curtail lives that could continue or be prolonged, and where the individuals concerned are not informed or consulted. They are not usually referred to (or perhaps even thought of) as cases of euthanasia; human beings have a habit of bringing their actions under the most agreeable description available. But if they are examined they share all the central features of euthanasia. Three examples must suffice.

We have already examined at length the widespread practice of 'selective treatment' where severely handicapped children are neither given food nor are infections treated in order that they do not survive. It may or may not be morally justified—only the circumstances of each individual case will reveal that; but it is euthanasia just the same.

The practice of declining to offer or to give resuscitation to a wide variety of patients in hospitals who suffer cardiac arrest, or some other crisis, is known and acknowledged to be widespread. Wherever patients are not consulted as to whether or not they wish to be resuscitated in case of crisis, and they are not resuscitated where it is possible to do so, or to attempt to do so, then their deaths are a consequence of that failure and are part of the hospital's euthanasia programme. Again, such a programme may or may not be justified; what is disturbing is that it is not acknowledged to exist, and the decisions are seldom scrutinised.

In the care of terminally ill patients, particularly those suffering from cancer or other painful conditions, there may come a point where the administration of pain-killing drugs hastens death. We have seen[29] how successful pain management may only be achieved at the cost of a foreshortened life. Where the patient is not told that this will be the consequence of pain control he is again the subject of non-voluntary euthanasia.

By far the most massive administration of non-voluntary and involuntary euthanasia is or is a result of government policy or action. And this forms the second group of cases requiring the attention of all those concerned about euthanasia.

The government's euthanasia programme

This is quite extraordinarily comprehensive, and has been much discussed in the press, although not always under this heading. I'll confine myself here to three illustrations from respectable and authoritative medical experts, although there are numerous other examples available.[30] The *Guardian* newspaper quoting a letter sent to the *Lancet* by Professor John Cameron, head of renal medicine at Guy's Hospital London, Dr Chisholm Ogg, director of Guy's dialysis and transplant unit, and Dr Daniel Glyn Williams, a consultant also at Guy's, said that an instruction from Birmingham Health Authority to turn away patients dying of kidney failure because the authority had run out of money was, 'effectively an order to allow patients to die within weeks or within months at the most'.[31] 'Doctors could not allow patients to die because the state ordered cut-backs', the letter had said.[32]

It has been clear for a decade at least that 'some 2000 or more patients (have died) each year because sufficient treatment is not available for them all', and this in the area of kidney disease alone.[33] If we add to this all the other areas of health care where lack of resources has caused avoidable deaths, the number would be many times greater. One such area is the treatment of heart disease. 'Heart patients at Wythenshawe Hospital Manchester, who could have been saved by open heart surgery, are dying because of a shortage of nurses and beds, caused by the crisis over hospital funding.... Six patients waiting for surgery died within four weeks just before Christmas.'[34]

All these people, and thousands more, have died as a direct and avoidable consequence of decisions taken by government about which they are not consulted, and to which they certainly do not consent. This is the real problem of euthanasia, and it is a sad irony that those concerned about euthanasia have concentrated on the tip of the iceberg represented by voluntary euthanasia, and have neglected the much larger, more significant and more sinister covert euthanasia, widely practised in the area of health care, and particularly by the government itself.

It has never, I believe, been suggested that this killing is in any sense a caring thing to do, and a traditional but inexcusable myopia as to negative responsibility has allowed this area of euthanasia to flourish while the government and other agencies continue to show moral disapproval for the only morally respectable form of euthanasia.

5 The value of life

Suppose that only one place is available on a renal dialysis programme or that only one bed is vacant in a vital transplantation
unit or that resuscitation could be given in the time and with the
resources available to only one patient. Suppose further that of
the two patients requiring any of these resources, one is a 70-
year-old widower, friendless and living alone, and the other a
40-year-old mother of three young children with a husband and
a career.

Or suppose that following a major disaster medical resources
were available to save the lives of only half those for whom
medical care was vital for life. Or, less dramatically, suppose that
in the next two years, only half of two hundred patients waiting
for surgery that will alleviate severe discomfort can be accommodated in the only available hospital. Suppose further and
finally that all candidates stand an equal chance of maximum
benefit from any of the available treatments. Whom should we
treat and what justifies our decision?

Many will think that in the first case preference should be given
to the young mother rather than the old friendless widower, that
this is obviously the right chôice. There might be a number of
grounds for such a decision. Two of these grounds have to do
with age. One indicates a preference for the young on the grounds
that they have a greater expectation of life if they are restored to
health. The other favours the young simply because their life is
likely to be fuller and hence more valuable than that of the older
person. Another consideration to which many will want to give
some weight is that of the number of people dependent on or
even caring about a potential victim. It is sometimes also considered relevant to give weight to the patient's probable usefulness to the community or even their moral character before a final

decision is made. And of course these considerations may be taken together in various combinations.

In the case of a major disaster related problems arise. If say a policy of triage[1] has identified the only group of victims to be treated, those for whom medical intervention will make the difference between life and death, but there are still not enough resources to help all such persons, then, again, many will hold that the right thing to do is help the young or those with dependants and so on first.

Those who believe that they ought to select the patient or patients to be saved on any of the above criteria, will believe that they must show preference for some types or conditions of person over others. Another available strategy is of course to decline to choose between people in any way that involves preferring one patient, or one sort of person, to another. Perhaps the easiest way of declining to show such a preference is to toss a coin or draw lots to decide who shall be helped. I want to consider what might count as a good reason for preferring to help some patients rather than others where all cannot be helped and also whether our intuitive preference for saving the younger and more useful members of society can be sustained.

I The moral significance of age

Many, perhaps most, people feel that, in cases like the one with which we began, there is some moral reason to save the 40-year-old mother rather than the 70-year-old widower. A smaller, but perhaps growing, group of people would see this as a sort of 'ageist' prejudice which, in a number of important areas of resource allocation and care, involves giving the old a much worse deal than the younger members of society. This is an exceptionally difficult issue to resolve. A number of the ways of thinking about the issue of the moral relevance of age yield opposed conclusions or seem to tug in opposite directions.

I want first to look at an argument which denies that we should prefer the young mother in our opening example. It is an anti-ageist argument so that is what I will call it, but it is not perhaps the usual sort of argument used to defend the rights of the old.

The anti-ageist argument

All of us who wish to go on living have something that each of us values equally although for each it is different in character, for some a much richer prize than for others, and we none of us know its true extent. This thing is of course 'the rest of our lives'. So long as we do not know the date of our deaths then for each of us the 'rest of our lives' is of indefinite duration. Whether we are 17 or 70, in perfect health or suffering from a terminal disease we each have the rest of our lives to lead. So long as we each fervently wish to live out the rest of our lives, however long that turns out to be, then if we do not deserve to die, we each suffer the same injustice if our wishes are deliberately frustrated and we are cut off prematurely. Indeed there may well be a double injustice in deciding that those whose life expectation is short should not benefit from rescue or resuscitation. Suppose I am told today that I have terminal cancer with only approximately six months or so to live, but I want to live until I die, or at least until I decide that life is no longer worth living. Suppose I then am involved in an accident and because my condition is known to my potential res-cuers and there are not enough resources to treat all who could immediately be saved I am marked among those who will not be helped. I am then the victim of a double tragedy and a double injustice. I am stricken first by cancer and the knowledge that I have only a short time to live and I'm then stricken again when I'm told that because of my first tragedy a second and more immediate one is to be visited upon me. Because I have once been unlucky I'm now no longer worth saving.

The point is a simple but powerful one. However short or long my life will be, so long as I want to go on living it then I suffer a terrible injustice when that life is prematurely cut short. Imagine a group of people all of an age, say a class of students all in their mid-20s. If fire trapped all in the lecture theatre and only twenty could be rescued in time should the rescuers shout 'youngest first!'? Suppose they had time to debate the question or had been debating it 'academically' before the fire? It would surely seem invidious to deny some what all value so dearly merely because of an accident of birth? It might be argued that age here provides no criterion precisely because although the lifespans of such a group might be expected to vary widely, there would be no way of knowing who was most likely to live longest. But suppose a reliable astrologer could make very realistic estimates or, what amounts to the same thing, suppose the age range of the students to be much greater, say 17 to 55. Does not the invidiousness of selecting by birth-date remain? Should a 17-year-old be saved before a 29-year-old or she before the 45-year-old and should the 55-year-old clearly be the last to be saved or the first to be sacrificed?

Our normal intuitions would share this sense of the invidiousness of choosing between our imaginary students by reason of their respective ages, but would start to want to make age relevant at some extremes, say if there were a 2-day-old baby and a 90-year-old grandmother. We will be returning to discuss a possible basis for this intuition in a moment. However, it is important to be clear that the anti-ageist argument denies the relevance of age or life expectancy as a criterion absolutely. It argues that even if I know for certain that I have only a little space to live, that space, however short, may be very precious to me. Precious, precisely because it is all the time I have left, and just as precious to me on that account as all the time you have left is precious to you, however much those two timespans differ in length. So that where we both want, equally strongly, to go on living, then we each suffer the same injustice[2] when our lives are cut short or are cut further short.[3]

It might seem that someone who would insist on living out the last few months of his life when by 'going quietly' someone else might have the chance to live for a much longer time would be a very selfish person. But this would be true only if the anti-ageist argument is false. It will be true only if it is not plausible to claim that living out the rest of one's life could be equally valuable to the individual whose life it is irrespective of the amount of unelapsed time that is left. And this is of course precisely the usual situation when individuals do not normally have anything but the haziest of ideas as to how long it is that they might have left.

I think the anti-ageist argument has much plausibility. It locates the wrongness of ending an individual's life in the evil of thwarting that person's desire to go on living and argues that it is profoundly unjust to frustrate that desire merely because some of those who have exactly the same desire, held no more strongly, also have a longer life expectancy than the others. However, there are a number of arguments that pull in the opposite direction and these we must now consider.

The fair innings argument

One problem with the anti-ageist argument is our feeling that there is something unfair about a person who has lived a long and happy life hanging on grimly at the end, while someone who has not been so fortunate suffers a related double misfortune, of losing out in a lottery in which his life happened to be in the balance with that of the grim octogenarian. It might be argued that we could accept the part of the anti-ageist argument which focusses on the equal value of unelapsed time, if this could be tempered in some way. How can it be just that someone who has already had more than her fair share of life and its delights should be preferred or even given an equal chance of continued survival with the young person who has not been so favoured? One strategy that seems to take account of our feeling that there is something wrong with taking steps to prolong the lives of the very old at the expense of those much younger is the fair innings argument.

The fair innings argument takes the view that there is some span of years that we consider a reasonable life, a fair innings. Let's say that a fair share of life is the traditional three score and ten, seventy years. Anyone who does not reach 70 suffers, on this view, the injustice of being cut off in their prime. They have missed out on a reasonable share of life; they have been short-changed. Those, however, who do make 70 suffer no such injustice, they have not lost out but rather must consider any additional years a sort of bonus beyond that which could reasonably be hoped for. The fair innings argument requires that everyone be given an equal chance to have a fair innings, to reach the appropriate threshold but, having reached it, they have received their entitlement. The rest of their life is the sort of bonus which may be cancelled when this is necessary to help others reach the threshold.

The attraction of the fair innings argument is that it preserves and incorporates many of the features that made the anti-ageist argument plausible, but allows us to preserve our feeling that the old who have had a good run for their money should not be endlessly propped up at the expense of those who have not had the same chance. We can preserve the conclusion of the anti-ageist argument, that so long as life is equally valued by the person whose life it is, it should be given an equal chance of preservation, and we can go on taking this view until the people in question have reached a fair innings.

There is, however, an important difficulty with the fair innings argument. It is that the very arguments which support the setting of the threshold at an age which might plausibly be considered to be a reasonable lifespan, equally support the setting of the threshold at any age at all, so long as an argument from fairness can be used to support so doing. Suppose that there is only one place available on the dialysis programme and two patients are in competition for it. One is 30, and the other 40 years of age. The fair innings argument requires that neither be preferred on the grounds of age since both are below the threshold and are entitled to an equal chance of reaching it. If there is no other reason to choose between them we should do something like toss a coin. However, the 30-year-old can argue that the considerations which support the fair innings argument require that she be given the place. After all, what's fair about the fair innings argument is precisely that each individual should have an equal chance of enjoying the benefits of a reasonable lifespan. The younger patient can argue that from where she's standing, the age of 40 looks much more reasonable a span than that of 30, and that she should be given the chance to benefit from those ten extra years.

This argument generalised becomes a reason for always preferring to save younger rather than older people, whatever the age difference, and makes the original anti-ageist argument begin to look again the more attractive line to take. For the younger person can always argue that the older has had a fairer innings, and should now give way. It is difficult to stop whatever span is taken to be a fair innings collapsing towards zero under pressure from those younger candidates who see their innings as less fair than that of those with a larger share.

But perhaps this objection to the fair innings argument is mistaken? If seventy years is a fair innings it does not follow that the nearer a span of life approaches seventy years, the fairer an innings it is. This may be revealed by considering a different sort of threshold. Suppose that most people can run a mile in seven minutes, and that two people are given the opportunity to show that they can run a mile in that time. They both expect to be given seven minutes. However, if one is in fact given only three minutes and the other only four, it's not true that the latter is given a fairer running time: for people with average abilities four minutes is no more realistic a time in which to run a mile than is three. Four minutes is neither a fair threshold in itself, nor a fairer one than three minutes would be.

Nor does the argument that establishes seven minutes as an appropriate threshold lend itself to variation downwards. For that argument just is that seven is the number of minutes that an average adult takes to run a mile. Why then is it different for lifespans? If three score and ten is the number of years available to most people for getting what life has to offer, and is also the number of years people can reasonably expect to have, then it is a misfortune to be allowed anything less however much less one is allowed, if nothing less than the full span normally suffices for getting what can be got out of life. It's true that the 40-year-old gets more time than the 30-year-old, but the frame of reference is not time only, but time normally required for a full life.[4]

This objection has some force, but its failure to be a good analogy reveals that two sorts of considerations go to make an innings fair. For while living a full or complete life, just in the sense of experiencing all the ages of man,[5] is one mark of a fair innings, there is also value in living through as many ages as possible. Just as completing the mile is one value, it is not the only one. Runners in the race of life also value ground covered, and generally judge success in terms of distance run.

What the fair innings argument needs to do is to capture and express in a workable form the truth that while it is always a *misfortune* to die when one wants to go on living, it is not a *tragedy* to die in old age; but it is on the other hand, both a tragedy and a misfortune to be cut off prematurely. Of course ideas like 'old age' and 'premature death' are inescapably vague, and may vary from society to society, and over time as techniques for postponing death improve. We must also remember that while it may be invidious to choose between a 30- and a 40-year-old on the grounds that one has had a fairer innings than the other, it may not be invidious to choose between the 30- and the 65-year-old on those grounds.

If we remember, too, that it will remain wrong to end the life of someone who wants to live or to fail to save them, and that the fair innings argument will only operate as a principle of selection where we are forced to choose between lives, then something workable might well be salvaged.

While 'old age' is irredeemably vague, we can tell the old from the young, and even the old from the middle-aged. So that without attempting precise formulation, a reasonable form of the fair innings argument might hold; and might hold that people who had achieved old age or who were closely approaching it would not have their lives further prolonged when this could only be achieved at the cost of the lives of those who were not nearing old age. These categories could be left vague, the idea being that it would be morally defensible to prefer to save the lives of those who 'still had their lives before them' rather than those who had 'already lived full lives'. The criterion to be employed in each case would simply be what reasonable people would say about whether someone had had a fair innings. Where reasonable people would be in no doubt that a particular individual was nearing old age *and* that that person's life could only be further prolonged at the expense of the life of someone that no reasonable person would classify as nearing old age, then the fair innings argument would apply, and it would be justifiable to save the younger candidate.

In cases where reasonable people differed or it seemed likely that they would differ as to whether people fell into one category or the other, then the anti-ageist argument would apply and the inescapable choice would have to be made arbitrarily.

But again it must be emphasised that the fair innings argument would only operate as a counsel of despair, when it was clearly impossible to postpone the deaths of all those who wanted to go on living. In all other circumstances the anti-ageist argument would apply.

So far so good. There are, however, further problems in the path of the anti-ageist argument and some of them are also problems for the fair innings argument.

Numbers of lives and numbers of years

One immediate problem is that although living as long as possible, however long that turns out to be, will normally be very important to each individual, it seems a bad basis for planning health care or justifying the distribution of resources.

Suppose a particular disease, cancer, kills 120,000 people a year. Suppose further that a drug is developed which would prolong the lives of all cancer victims by one month but no more. Would it be worth putting such a drug into production? What if, for the same cost, a different drug would give ten years' complete remission, but would only operate on a form of cancer that affects 1,000 people? If we cannot afford both, which should we invest in? Or, what if there is only one place on a renal dialysis programme and two patients who could benefit, but one will die immediately without dialysis but in six months in any event. The other will also die immediately without dialysis but with such help will survive for ten years. Although each wants the extra span of life equally badly, many would think that we ought to save the one with the longer life expectancy, that she is the 'better bet'.

All of these cases are an embarrassment for the anti-ageist argument, for our reaction to them implies that we do value extra years more. But how much more?

Extra life-time versus extra lives

> If we choose to save one person for a predicted span of sixty years, rather than saving five people each for a predicted span of ten years, we have gained ten extra life years at the cost of overriding the desires of four extra people.[6]

So far we have looked at the issue of whether we should count length of life or desire to live as the most important factor when deciding which of two people should be saved. If all things are equal, there can be no reason to prefer one to the other and so we should choose in a way that does not display preference, by lot, for example. The question that seems so difficult is what, if any, difference should length of life make to such choices?

The anti-ageist argument says that it should make no difference, but the cases we have just been examining seem to pull the other way. And if we are persuaded by such cases this seems to imply that we do think length of life or life expectancy give additional value to lives and so constitute a factor which must be given some weight. One consequence of this is that we should think it more important to save one 10-year-old rather than five 60-year-olds (if we take 70 as an arbitrary maximum).[7] Equally, it would be better to save one 20-year-old rather than two 50-year-old people, for we would again save ten life years by so doing. Or one 15-year-old rather than two 45-year-olds (a saving of five life years) and so on.

It is just at this point that the anti-ageist argument seems to require resuscitation, for there is surely something invidious about sacrificing two 45-year-olds to one 15-year-old. To take the 'life years' view seems to discount entirely the desires and hopes and life plans of people in middle age, whenever an importunate youngster can place herself in the balance against them. But we

do not normally think it better to save a 15-year-old rather than
a 45-year-old when we cannot save both, so why should we think
it better to save a 15-year-old rather than *two* 45-year olds?

For those who do favour saving one 15-year-old rather than
two 45-year-olds, there is another difficulty. The life-time view
seems to commit us to favouring total life-time saved rather than
total number of people saved, with bizarre consequences. Suppose I could prolong the lives of 121,000 people for one month?
This would yield a saving of 121,000 life months. Alternatively
I could develop a drug which would give ten more years of life
to 1,000 people. This would yield a saving of 120,000 life months.
Thus, on the timespan view, we should choose to extend the lives
of 121,000 people by one month rather than 1,000 people by ten
years each. So, what started out by looking as though it consti-
tuted an objection to the anti-ageist argument actually supports
it in some circumstances. For, while we should favour length of
life, where numbers of lives balanced against one another are
equal, we should favour numbers of lives where, summed together, they yield a greater contribution to the total amount of
life-time saved.

Unfortunately the force of the comparison between extending
the lives of 120,000 people for one month or 1,000 for ten years
was to encourage us to think that life-time saved was more important than numbers of lives saved. Its support for this conclusion now seems less decisive. What it seems to indicate is a very
complicated calculus in which allocation of resources would be
dependent on the amount of life-time such allocation could save.
It would also lead to some bizarre orderings of priority, and not
necessarily to those envisaged by enthusiasts of such a scheme.

One such enthusiast, Dr Donald Gould, produced the following scenario:

> Calculations are based on the assumption that all who survive their
> first perilous year ought then to live on to the age of 70 ... In
> Denmark for example, there are 50,000 deaths a year, but only
> 20,000 among citizens in the 1–70 bracket. These are the ones that
> count. The annual number of life years lost in this group totals
> 264,000. Of these 80,000 are lost because of accidents and suicides,
> 40,000 because of coronary heart disease, and 20,000 are due to
> lung disease. On the basis of these figures, a large proportion of
> the 'health' budget ought to be spent on preventing accidents and
> suicides and a lesser ... amount on attempting to prevent and cure
> heart and lung disease. Much less would be spent on cancer which

is predominantly a disease of the latter half of life, and which therefore contributes relatively little to the total sum of life years lost ... No money at all would be available for trying to prolong the life of a sick old man of 82.[8]

The first thing to note about Gould's scenario is, that while deaths before the age of seventy may be the only life years *considered to have been lost*,[9] it does not follow that there is no reason to attempt to *gain* life years by prolonging the lives of the over-70s if that seems feasible. For example if a reasonable prognosis is that the life of the 70-year-old could be prolonged for five years by some intervention, then that is still a gain of five life years. This can have important consequences for it means that it would be quite wrong to write-off all care for the over-70s. Suppose a simple procedure would add one year to the lives of all septuagenarians. This would yield a huge gain in life years spread over a whole population. Suppose, as is perhaps likely, the number of septuagenarians in Denmark was over 260,000, then the number of life years saved by adding a further year to their lives would exceed the total to be gained by all the measures to prevent accidents, suicides, heart disease and so on. This would then become the chief priority for health care spending.

Gould starts his calculations after 'the first perilous year' but this cut-off point would require justification. We might well conclude, persuaded by his general line of argument, that neo-natal and postnatal care would have the first priority for resources.

The life-time position then can support a wide variety of practices and may lead to a policy of achieving small gains in lifespan for large numbers of people rather than to the sorts of substantial gains for those individuals with most to lose that its supporters seem to have principally in mind.

Threshold of discrimination

It is tempting to think that we might be able to get over some of the problems of the life-time position by arguing that we can discount small gains in time as below the level of discrimination, in the sense that the benefit to the individual which accrued from living for a comparatively short period of extra time was nugatory. This might solve a few of the problems for the life-time position which arise from the necessity it imposes of favouring one group of people over another, wherever and whenever they are sufficiently numerous that the total life-time saved by rescuing them, even for a negligibly short period, exceeds that which might be saved by rescuing another smaller group who would live longer individually, but shorter collectively. However, the problem will remain wherever the amount of life-time to be saved is just enough to be worth having (or is thought so to be by those whose time it is) but seems a poor return on the investment required to procure it or in terms of other savings, including savings of longer individual life-time, that might be made instead.

People versus policies

We are strongly inclined to believe that where, for example, we can prolong the lives of 120,000 people by one month or 1,000 people by ten years that we should do the latter and that it is better to use a scarce resource to save the life of someone who is likely to live on for at least ten years rather than that of someone who will die in six months in any event. This inclination makes it look as though what we must in fact value is length of life-time rather than simply saving lives. But valuing life-time can be as dangerous to our moral intuitions as is the anti-ageist argument. Again, it might be tempting to believe that a policy of devoting resources to saving individual lives for as long as possible was better than simply maximising life-time saved. There might be a number of different grounds for such a belief. One such ground would be the expectation that procedures which could prolong individual lives by a substantial period would lead to a greater saving of life-time in the long term than would procedures which merely postponed death for a month or so. But in the absence of any strong evidence for such a conclusion this expectation would be at best an act of faith and at worse a pious hope. Is there any way out?

The fallacy of life-time views

Suppose various medical research teams to be in competition for all research funds available and that one team could demonstrate that it was capable of producing an elixir of life that would make anyone taking it immortal. Suppose further that the entire world medical research budget, if applied to this end would produce just enough elixir for one dose, and that nothing less than a full dose would have any effect at all. The life-time view suggests that all the money should go to making one person immortal rather than say to an alternative project by which another team could make everyone on earth live to a flourishing 80![10]

But there is an obvious fallacy in this argument which reveals a defect in the whole life-time approach. Making one person immortal will produce a saving of no more life years than would the alternative of making everyone on earth live to a flourishing 80. So long as the world itself and its population lasts as long as the immortal (and how—and where—could he last longer?) there would be no net increase in life years lived. Indeed so long as there is either a stable or an increasing world population, from the life years point of view, it matters not at all who lives and who dies, nor does it matter how many years anyone survives. For, so long as those who die are replaced on a one-for-one, or better than a one-for-one basis, there will be no loss of life years. Nor will there be any gain in life years when particular individuals live for longer. For if the overall world population is stable, then prolonging the life of particular individuals does not increase the total number of life years the world contains. And if the world population is increasing then it is highly unlikely that prolonging the lives of particular people will fuel that increase. Indeed the reverse is more likely to be the case with the survival of people beyond child-bearing age having a retarding effect on the rate of increase.

In the context of a stable or of an increasing world population, any idea that any policy which did not have the effect of increasing the population in fact made any contribution to the amount of life-time saved would be an illusion.

We do not then have always to calculate the probable net saving in life-time of any particular policy or therapy, before knowing what to do, and can revert to the more customary consideration of the numbers of lives that might be saved or lost. This, however, highlights once again the problems of whether lives that can only be saved for relatively short periods of time (that can only be prolonged by a few months say) are as worth saving as those for whom the prognosis in terms of life expectancy is much longer. A manœuvre that seems to capture our intuitions here involves modifying the life-time view into a worthwhile life-time view.

Worthwhile life-time

While to many just staying alive may be the most important consideration, and while they may even wish to continue to live even at appalling cost in terms of pain, disability and so on even, as we have seen,[11] where their lives are hardly worth living, they of course prefer to live worthwhile lives. So that while any life might be better than no life, people generally expect medical care of concern itself not simply with preventing death but with restoring worthwhile existence.

Many sorts of thing will go to diminish the worth of life just as many and various considerations go to make life valuable and these will differ from individual to individual. For the moment we are just concerned with the question of how life expectancy operates as one of these.

If someone were sentenced to death and told that the execution would take place at dawn the next day, they would not, I imagine, be excessively overjoyed if they were then informed that the execution had been postponed for one month. Similarly if the prognosis for a particular disease were very accurate indeed, to be told that one had only seven months to live would not be dramatically less terrible than to be told one had six months to live. There are two related reasons for this. The first is simply that the prospect of imminent death colours, or rather discolours, existence and leaves it joyless. The second is that an almost necessary condition for valuing life is its open-endedness. The fact that we do not normally know how long we have to live liberates the present and leaves us apparently free to plan the future without having to be constantly aware of the futility of so doing.[12] If life had a short and finite (rather than indefinite) future, most things would not seem to be worth doing and the whole sense of the worth of life as an enterprise would evaporate.[13]

In the light of these considerations many people would not much value such short periods of remission, and support for policies which could at best produce such small gains might well be slight. However, some might well value highly the chance of even a small share of extra time. So far from emptying their life of meaning, it might enable them to 'round it off' or complete some important task or settle or better arrange their affairs. It might, so far from being of no value, be just what they needed to sort their life out and make some sort of final sense of it.

We have frequently noted the extreme difficulty involved in discounting the value of someone's life where we and they disagree about whether or not it is worth living, and we have also noted the injustice of preferring our assessment to theirs when so much is at stake for them. In view of all this it would be hard to prefer our judgment to theirs here.

Perhaps the problem would in reality be a small one. These dilemmas only arise where we cannot both help some people to live for relatively short periods *and* at the same time help others to live for much longer ones. Where there is no such conflict there is no question that we should go on helping people to stay alive for just so long as they want us to. However, the fact that hard cases are rare does not mean that we can turn our backs on them.

Fair innings or no ageism?

We have then two principles which can in hard cases pull in opposite directions. What should we do in the sorts of hard cases we have been considering? First, we should be clear that while the very old and those with terminal conditions are alike, in that they both have a short life expectancy, they may well differ with respect to whether or not they have had a fair innings. I do not believe that this issue is at all clear cut but I am inclined to believe that where two individuals both equally wish to go on living for as long as possible our duty to respect this wish is paramount. It is, as I have suggested, the most important part of what is involved in valuing the lives of others. Each person's desire to stay alive should be regarded as of the same importance and as deserving the same respect as that of anyone else, irrespective of the quality of their life or its expected duration.

This would hold good in all cases in which we have to choose between lives, except one. And that is where one individual has had a fair innings and the other not. In this case, while both equally wish to have their lives further prolonged one, but not the other, has had a fair innings. In this case, although there is nothing to choose between the two candidates from the point of view of their respective will to live and both would suffer the injustice of having their life cut short when it might continue, only one would suffer the further injustice of being deprived of a fair innings—a benefit that the other has received.

It is sometimes said that it is a misfortune to grow old, but it is not nearly so great a misfortune as not to grow old. Growing old when you don't want to is not half the misfortune that is not growing old when you do want to. It is this truth that the fair innings argument captures. So that while it remains true, as the anti-ageist argument asserts, that the value of the unelapsed possible lifespan of each person who wants to go on living is equally valuable however long that span may be, the question of which person's premature death involves the greater injustice can be important. The fair innings argument points to the fact that the injustice done to someone who has not had a fair innings when they lose out to someone who has is significantly greater than in the reverse circumstances. It is for this reason that in the hopefully rare cases where we have to choose between candidates who differ only in this respect that we should choose to give as many people as possible the chance of a fair innings.

Before considering what moral advantage the wishes of third parties, friends, relatives and dependants might give to an individual, we must consider a further argument against the principle just reaffirmed.

II Worthwhile lives

The more usual way in which 'quality of life' appears as a way of deciding who to save is where the competition for rescue is between someone thought to have a very poor quality of life, and the familiar family figure, with an apparently full life. In discussing this particular dilemma Jonathan Glover sees the problem thus:

> If we accept that some people have lives so terrible as to be not worth living, it seems hard to deny the existence of a neighbouring grey area where a life may be worth living but is less worth living than normal. It would clearly be absurd to give priority in life saving to someone whose life is not worth living. Yet it is hard, without making an artificially sharp cut-off point, to accept this while refusing to be influenced in selection by the fact that someone is in a state only a little less bad.[14]

I argued in Chapter 1 that there were good reasons for taking an individual's estimation of the desirability of continuing their own life as the crucial factor, and similar considerations give much of the force to the anti-ageist argument. So there is no absurdity in giving priority in life-saving to someone who wants to live, even though we do not think that they ought to want to live. In the sorts of cases we examined earlier, where we cannot consult the individual, but where humanity seems to require us to end their acute and irremediable suffering by death, then of course we should do so, and the absurdity of saving them is evident. On the other hand, if we conclude that they would not be better off dead, however difficult that decision is, or whether they want to live, then in either case the fact that someone else's life is in the balance against them, should make no difference. If we cannot conclude that they ought to die, then we should not do so merely because there is now someone else balanced against them, who is marginally a clearer case of a person who should not die.

Suppose someone is badly injured and in agony after a cliff fall. We know that if rescued she will be permanently paralysed from the neck down but, although her quality of life will be poor, we cannot conclude that she would be better off dead. We cannot justify killing her nor yet leaving her to die. However, the rescue will be difficult and will involve risking the life of the healthy vigorous and happy rescuer. His life now becomes in a sense balanced against hers. Do we conclude because of this that she is not worth rescuing? Is it right to risk the life of the happy rescuer to save a less badly injured victim but not to save her? Should the less badly injured victim be saved rather than her?

While these are difficult decisions I assume that the badly injured girl does not suddenly become not worth rescuing because of the risk any more than would anyone else. Nor is she less worth saving than someone less badly injured, unless she is less likely to survive at all, which we assume is not the case. The invidiousness of choosing between people on these grounds is worse, if anything, than using life-expectancy as the measure of individual value. For even people with severely impaired lives can see their lives as enterprises they wish to control, bringing delights and events they wish to experience, and the loss of all of which would be as much of a tragedy as the loss of life ever is.

III The moral advantage of dependants and friends

If there are two people whose lives are in question and we have to choose to save only one, the number of people dependent on them should be regarded as very important. If other things are equal, but one has no family and the other is the mother of several young children, the case against deciding between them randomly is a strong one ... Refusal to depart from random choice when knowledge about their dependants is available is to place no value on avoiding the additional misery caused to the children if the mother is not the one saved ...

In a case like this it seems perverse to allow the drawbacks of
interventionism to outweigh the great loss to the children, particularly since one of the main drawbacks seems less serious here. A
large part of the case against interventionism is the undesirability
of creating a two-tier community, saying that we value some people
more than others. This seems obviously objectionable if our preference is based on the belief that one of the people is nicer, more
intelligent or morally superior to the other person. But the objection loses a lot of its force when the preference is justified by citing
the interests of dependants rather than the merits of the person
selected.[15]

I've quoted this passage of Jonathan Glover's at some length
because it elegantly and concisely summarises both the case for
preferring to save those with dependants and also deals with one
of the chief objections to a policy of intervening purposively
rather than randomly and positively preferring some people to
others. I've also introduced it because it seems to offer danger-
ously inadequate reasons for saving one person's life at the expense of another's and it is important to explain why this is so.
I do not imagine that any knock-down arguments are available in
territory as complex as this but there do seem to me to be weighty
objections to a preference for those with dependants.

A first difficulty is that of justifying saving the life of one person
and condemning another to death by citing the interests of third
parties (albeit related and dependent third parties) in the continued existence of a particular individual. If the interests and desires of third parties are to be sufficient grounds for granting a
stay of execution, why are they not considered sufficient grounds
for justifying an execution? Suppose Jane's friends and children
announced that so far from being the occasion of their misery,
Jane's death would rather be the only event that could alleviate
it? Should we regard this fact as sufficient (or indeed as any)
reason to save the other candidate? If the desires of someone's
dependants are not to count against them, why should they be
allowed to count for them at the expense of a third party? If the
fact that Jane has children who want her to live, and are dependent on her, is a good reason for saving her rather than me, why
shouldn't the fact that she has children who want her dead be a
good reason for saving me rather than her? If we do not like the
idea of the preferences of third parties counting as justifications
for the condemning of one person rather than another, we should
remember that this is just what would happen if we allow the

interests of third parties to count in favour of someone. For if Jane's children want her to live, they want the other candidate for rescue to die, or at least to die rather than Jane. It seems safer in such cases to stick to the Benthamite maxim that everyone is to count for one and none for more than one.

Another problem is that the feeling that it is somehow more important to rescue those with dependants, when elevated to the level of policy, amounts to a systematic preference of those with families over those without. How can it be the case that such a practice would avoid 'the offensive division of people into grades that we have seen to be one of the most serious disadvantages of interventionism'.[16] At first glance and particularly to those without dependent children, this looks very much like a covert grading of people into the 'haves' and the 'have-nots'—those who have dependants and those who don't. It might even be seen as a clandestine introduction of some reinforcement of a moral preference for the nuclear family and as an attack both on the childless, and on those with less family-oriented ideas about child-rearing. This attitude to family preference may seem paranoid[17] and extreme, but unless the arguments in favour of 'systematic family preference' as I shall call it, are substantial and compelling it will be difficult to stop such a policy appearing in this light to those who are its victims.

Two sorts of considerations are adduced by Glover to justify systematic family preference. The first is the idea of dependence, and the second is the weight to be accorded to the avoidance of the misery and loss to the bereaved. Many are called 'dependants' who are in no way dependent. Indeed, I believe that the dependence of children upon adults let alone on parents is usually grossly exaggerated and likewise the independence of adults, but that is another argument.[18] However, even if we grant the dependence of children this is not necessarily dependence on their parents or relations. So long as children are provided with someone to depend on in the requisite sense, they will survive. Of course it would be better for them (and for their parents) if their parents survive. But is this a good so clear and powerful that the lives of others may be automatically sacrificed to it, or the lives of parents automatically preserved at the expense of others, to protect it? No doubt the death of a parent usually causes great misery and sense of loss to her child, but whether on this account children have a right to be, or ought to be, protected against such misery and loss, at the expense of the lives of others who also would be miserable and suffer great loss if they were to die prematurely, is another matter.

It is not, of course, only children who grieve, but also friends, and I know of no evidence to show that the grief of children is necessarily greater or more deserving of prevention than any other sort. Short of a 'leaping-into-graves' competition there is no generally accepted and reliable method of measuring grief or the extent of personal loss at the death of another. And since there is no reliable way of discounting the grief of friends in favour of that of children we would have no reason to confine the class of grieving saviours of the unfortunate, to dependants. This being the case the way would be open to the undignified spectacle of legions of weeping (and perhaps paid) 'friends' coming forward to plead on behalf of one candidate or the other. The possibility of such a charade should be sufficient to dissuade us from allowing the misery of third parties to dictate who should live and who should die.

Dependence then is not simply dependence on parents, and grief and misery are not confined to family relationships. But even if they were, it is unclear that they would constitute adequate reasons for preferring to save one person rather than another. We should not forget that while the bereaved deserve sympathy, by far the greatest loss is to the deceased, and the misfortune of her friends and relations pales into insignificance besides the tragedy to the individual who must die. It seems as obviously offensive systematically to inflict this loss on the childless, and perhaps the friendless, as it would be to grade people in any other way. It seems less than convincing to argue that concentration of attention on 'the interests of dependants' rather than on the merits of individuals, rescues such a policy from the opprobrium of an arbitrary division of society into grades of people, with priority always and automatically accorded to those with families.

Finally, if systematic family preference became overt public policy, it might begin to seem that a relatively cheap form of insurance against a low-priority rating in the rescue stakes would be the acquisition of a family. Of course one would have to make sure that the children were spaced so as always to have at least one or two dependants on hand to plead one's case. And this would not only require that children be spaced prudently, but that they stayed one's own dependants, and did not for example become the dependants of an estranged spouse. This might lead to more durable marriages or even to more bitterly contested custody suits with perhaps the parent or guardian's very life at stake. Fostering and adoption might also become more popular, but whether, on balance, we would find such arrangements morally preferable to a situation in which children took pot luck on the survival of their parents and no one's life was discounted in favour of another merely because they could not produce the requisite quota of dependants, seems to me doubtful.

IV The moral advantage of usefulness

There are two sorts of usefulness, usefulness in saving lives and any other kind of usefulness. Usefulness in saving lives is in a class of its own simply because to fail to give extra value to the life of someone whose continued existence will save the lives of others is to discount entirely the value of those extra lives that will be lost if the life-saver dies. However the circumstances in which it is clear that others will die unless a particular individual is preserved will be very exceptional.

Heads of state, members of governments, chiefs of police and the like clearly believe that their usefulness is of this type since they arrange for themselves secure billets in fall-out shelters against the outbreak of nuclear war. Whether other citizens would take the value of these office-holders at their own estimation of it is more doubtful. It is sometimes said that 'leading surgeons' are a clear example of the sorts of people who have what might be called class-one usefulness,[19] although, again, this would not be an entirely uncontroversial classification. All that can safely be said is that all whose continued existence is clearly required so that others might live have a good claim to priority. Whether any other sort of usefulness is so important that those who possess it could claim to live on at the cost of the lives of others seems to me to be more doubtful.

A possible candidate, and one who appears from time to time in academic philosophical discussions, is the lady who has left half a million pounds to Oxfam or some other life-saving charity.[20] She has class-one usefulness but it consists, so the argument goes, not in her continuing to live, but in her rapid demise. The longer she lives, the more people will die whom her money would have saved. This seems to provide an argument for killing her now. Apart from the many independent objections to a policy of killing in such circumstances (the likelihood of a breakdown in law and

order and the negative feedback effect which would provide
everyone with a strong reason never to give others a beneficial
interest in their deaths) there is the obvious point that the lady
will die at some time and the same number of people (although
different individuals) will then be saved. We must of course be
sure that the lady's investments are inflation-proofed and that she
does not change her will.

There is another sort of person with what might be termed
class-one negative usefulness where we have a life-saving interest
in their demise and that is the case of people whose organs and
other tissue might be used in life-saving transplants. I have discussed the most extreme version of such a case elsewhere[21] and
further discussion of this rather specialised problem will be taken
up in the next chapter and in Chapter 7. I cannot think of any
other candidates for class-one usefulness, but if there are candidates, a very strong case indeed would have to be made out for
them. So strong indeed that it is clear either that their survival is
worth the sacrifice of another's life, or, that others should be
preserved at the cost of their life.

V Moral worth

Finally, we must look briefly at the question of whether the moral
character of an individual should weigh with those who have to
decide whether to save her life or that of someone else. Many
people believe that whether or not someone can be regarded as
moral depends at least in part on their sexual behaviour, so that
'immorality' is often thought to involve sexual immorality. We
shall see later, in Chapter 9, that this is not so, but for the moment
we are not concerned so much with what might lead us to conclude that someone was immoral, or less moral than another, but
rather with what follows from such a conclusion about their entitlement to treatment.

We all, of course, have a duty to encourage and promote morality, but to do so by choosing between candidates for treatment
on moral grounds is to arrogate to ourselves not simply the promotion of morality but the punishment of immorality. And to
choose to let one person rather than another die on the grounds
of some moral defect in their behaviour or character is to take
upon ourselves the right not simply to punish, but capitally to
punish, offenders against morality. Even in the, I hope unlikely,

event of our being satisfied that we were entitled or obliged to do this we would be attempting to discharge a quasi-judicial function without any of the safeguards or rigour of legal proceedings. What standards of proof would be required or discharged in such investigations, what right of reply or defence would be offered? Indeed, what would constitute moral crimes for these purposes? The morality of choosing between candidates for rescue on moral grounds would itself be much more likely to be profoundly immoral than anything any of the candidates is likely to be guilty of.

One fairly obvious exception, and one that we have already examined in Chapter 4, is that of the killer who can only be saved at the expense of either his intended victim or of some innocent third party. Either self-defence or the obligation to aid justified self-defence shows, as we have seen, why we should decline to help the would-be murderer at the expense of the innocent.

Should we, however, regard convicted murderers and other criminals as the lowest category or priority for rescue? Should we, for example, send the only available fire-engines and ambulances to a small hospital or a large prison, where both are on fire and only one or other can be reached in time?

Suppose I am standing on the bank of a river and can either rescue my own child from drowning or another stranger but not both. We saw in Chapter 2 that the principle of non-vicious choice does not require me to toss a coin rather than simply save my own child. My preference for my own child may be unjust to the stranger but it is not a vicious preference; whereas if the lives of two strangers were similarly at risk, but one was black and the other white, I am not entitled to exercise any racial preference I may have, for such a preference would be both unjust and vicious. Now, is the preference for non-criminals more like family preference or more like racial prejudice?

Well, clearly it is not simple prejudice for there are some good reasons for thinking murderers and criminals are somehow less worthy than others. Whether they are so much less worthy that it is reasonable to sacrifice their lives to save others is less clear. It would certainly be unjust, but would it be unjustifiable? Given that we do not think it appropriate to execute them for their crimes, I'm inclined to think so. It would amount to heaping an extra penalty on top of those already decided as appropriate for their crimes and doing so without any further judicial enquiry. It looks very much then as if we should not in any circumstances use the moral character of an individual as a reason for preferring to rescue her or of declining to rescue her and that there are no good reasons for permitting such criteria to be used in medical practice as an aid to selecting patients for treatment or the needy for rescue.

VI What should we do?

We have seen that the possession of dependants, friends, relatives, usefulness, moral worth, and even of a good quality of life, is not the stuff of which a greater entitlement to survival is made; and that for various reasons, considerations of this sort should not weigh with us when we are considering whom to rescue.

Neither should age normally be a criterion. I think the anti-ageist argument is powerful and, except where appropriately tempered by the fair innings argument, it should be respected.

So long as people want to live out the rest of their lives, however long this may be, or looks like being, then they should be given the best chance we can give them of doing so and we should not choose between such people on any other grounds, but treat each as an equal. The most moral and the most honourable way of dealing with the difficulties and anomalies that remain is to try to ensure that we have sufficient resources to devote to postponing death, wherever and whenever we can, whether for long or for short periods, so that we do not have to choose between people invidiously.

6 The beginnings of life

Human beings who appear to be attempting to play God attract the sort of hostility usually reserved for Gods who forget themselves so far as to aspire to do likewise. And just as 'acts of God' are synonymous with disaster, so acts of scientists can appear disastrously divine. The spectre of Dr Frankenstein, the representative 'mad scientist', is standardly invoked as a dire warning of what to expect when researchers tamper with the ultimate constituents of what matters. However grotesque, there is a certain appropriateness to its invocation in the context of the discussion and speculation surrounding recent work on so-called 'test-tube' babies.

The storm of interest and protest that this work has attracted and continues to attract[1] is, as is often the case, not on account of what is being done but for fear of what the work demonstrates can or might be done. The work in question,[2] initially undertaken to remedy infertility, involves the fertilisation of human eggs *'in vitro'* and the growing of the resulting embryos in the laboratory for subsequent transplantation into mothers who have experienced difficulties in conceiving by more economical means. However, two of the leading people in this field, Dr R.G. Edwards and Mr Patrick Steptoe whose work generated the first successful test-tube baby, have pointed the way clearly to new and controversial uses of their work[3] and others have been quick to follow. These controversial possibilities have led the British Medical Association first to condemn such work and to forbid their members to assist, then almost immediately to withdraw the ban and finally to set up an ethical sub-committee to report on the rights and wrongs of all such work. The moral concern of the government has also been stirred so far as to establish its own ethical committee, the Warnock Committee, to make a similar report.

For all its innocent beginnings (and maybe endings too) the work of Edwards and Steptoe and others has opened up possibilities and perhaps even more important, public discussion of possibilities[4] that have hitherto figured, if at all, only in the dreams and discussions of moral philosophers. I shall start in Section I by reviewing what is now being done by researchers in the field of *in vitro* fertilisation and indicate what such researchers believe will or may become possible in the relatively foreseeable future. Section II will examine the question of whether or not experiments on embryos raise different moral issues and require different justification from those involved in deciding whether embryos may be killed or aborted. In Section III we will consider whether the possibilities opened up by *in vitro* fertilisation constitute a slope so slippery that we dare not step on to it. Finally, in Section IV we consider the conclusions of the Warnock Committee.

I What's happening now

At the moment eggs can be removed from a woman and fertilised in a dish on the laboratory shelf. These embryos can then be implanted in a woman so that she can grow them and give birth to the resulting baby in the normal way. About fifty such children have been born to women treated by Edwards and Steptoe. If the embryos are not implanted, they can continue to grow *in vitro* (at the moment they have been so grown for up to nine days). They can then be 'flattened'[5] for examination, simply thrown away like most aborted embryos, used for experiments and/or for therapy (more of which anon), or they may be frozen for future use.[6]

The spare embryos
Most eggs obtained for fertilisation are provided by women who wish to have a child and the embryos are re-implanted in the donor mother. So called 'spare' embryos are produced when, usually as a result of fertility hormones being used, women produce multiple eggs which are all fertilised but of which only one (or perhaps two) are re-implanted because of the added risks attached to the prospect of multiple births. The remaining embryos are thus 'spare'. Of course other spare embryos could and have been produced deliberately and not as the bonus by-product of a fertility clinic. Indeed many such embryos were produced by Dr Edwards and other workers in order to test and develop fertilisation techniques.[7]

Permutations

We should note for the record a number of possibilities that arise. The eventual 'host' mother may not be the donor of the egg cell and the donor of the sperm may or may not be known to the donor of either the egg cell or to the eventual host mother. So the possibilities are that because of conceptual problems (though of course not necessarily so):

(1) A woman may donate her own oocyte or egg cell to be fertilised either by her husband or partner or by some other donor spermatozoa, for re-implantation into herself.

(2) A woman may donate an oocyte for fertilisation in any of the above ways for implantation in another woman either so that woman can have 'her own' child (perhaps fertilised by her husband or partner) or so that the original donor can (for whatever reasons)[8] avoid pregnancy but still have 'her own' baby.

Where a woman accepts a donor oocyte with the intention of giving birth to and bringing up the child as 'her own' we might call this 'prenatal adoption';[9] where the intention is that the resulting child be returned to the donor of the oocyte (or perhaps of the sperm) it is sometimes called 'uterine leasing' or 'postnatal parenthood'. And of course the baby might go to some 'stranger'.

Freezing

We have almost run ahead of ourselves, but not by very much. The question of whether or not it is dangerous to the embryo to freeze and thaw it is not yet finally resolved, and this is important if the above possibilities are to be realised, as we shall see. There have been decades of work on freezing and thawing mammalian embryos and other living tissue and very high success rates are now normal. Indeed, it is standard practice to freeze and 'bank' some strains of experimental mice. So that while the prognosis of success with human embryos is very good indeed the problem remains that, as Clifford Grobstein has said.

> Ninety per cent success rates ... may be acceptable for laboratory and domestic animals. In humans it is the ten per cent failure rate that is of concern—particularly if these are partial failures, not detectable until after birth or even later in life.[10]

But the prognosis for freezing is so good that in Australia, for example, it is regarded as morally acceptable to freeze spare embryos precisely because, since it may be possible to thaw them later and implant them, this does not amount to killing them.[11]

We should note also that one of the possibilities adumbrated above, that of donor embryos for 'host' mothers, could be achieved 'most effectively' with frozen-thawed embryos because these can be held until the uterus of the recipient is in the most receptive stage of the 'cycle',[12] although such donations are of course possible without resort to freezing.

Finally, freezing generates one further permutation, that of (3) *Post mortem* conception and birth, since frozen egg and sperm may be thawed and brought together after the death of either or both of the donors and frozen-thawed embryos may be implanted after the death of the donors.

Immediate and proximate possibilities

Firstly and of course the main use of *in vitro* fertilisation techniques is in the treatment of infertility. It is estimated that there are for example 2½ million infertile couples in the United States, 75 per cent of whom could be helped by the techniques now developed.[13] But although *in vitro* fertilisation techniques were developed primarily to treat infertility, many other uses immediately suggest themselves.

Suppose that a young woman were to have eggs removed from her ovaries and fertilised by her husband (or anyone), she could then freeze and store these for implantation whenever career permitted or fancy took and with a supply of embryos in the bank a couple or either one of them could be sterilised without losing the capacity to have children. These may seem frivolous uses to some but they have important effects. For example, since we know that the incidence of Down's syndrome increases sharply in the last decade of fecundity (between 35 and 45) a mother who wished to give birth during these years could *conceive* much earlier when the chances of avoiding Down's syndrome were much higher. But better still, the chances are that it will be possible to check whether the embryo had Down's or other genetic disorders before freezing and implantation and so virtually abolish this risk. Indeed as R. G. Edwards has noted:

> Identifying embryos with genetic abnormalities would offer an alternative to amniocentesis during the second trimester of pregnancy, and the 'abortion *in vitro*' of a defective preimplantation embryo, still free-living, minute and undifferentiated, would be infinitely preferable to abortion *in vivo* at twenty weeks of pregnancy or thereabouts as the results of amniocentesis are obtained.

It would also be less traumatic for parents and doctor to type several embryos and replace or store those that are normal rather than having the threat of a mid-term abortion looming over each successive pregnancy.[14]

Further, there are good prospects[15] of sexing embryos which will make it possible for parents to choose to implant 'boys' or 'girls' in order of preference. It will also be possible to implant only those embryos of the preferred sex. This may have more 'respectably medical' uses in that embryos can be screened for sex-linked disorders.

Cell and tissue banks

R.G. Edwards was able to report recently[16] that 'it is now possible to contemplate the use of "tailor-made" embryonic tissue grown *in vitro* for grafting into adults.' The special advantages of this possibility are that 'Grafts of embryonic tissue may offer a wider scope than those taken from neonates or adults, because tissue could be obtained from organs which do not regenerate in adults, and the risks of graft rejection can possibly be eliminated.'[17] Edwards goes on to list a number of specific possibilities that arise.

Foetal tissue can be used to replace bone marrow in patients that have for example been exposed to radiation, and foetal liver cells injected into the placenta can prevent the expression of inherited anaemia. It may be also that tissue grafted from neonates may be used to 'restore immune deficiencies in old people'[18] and a

> practical approach to controlling immunological ageing may involve a combination of dietary manipulation, chemical therapy and cell grafting ... Other recent reports have indicated that pancreatic cells may be used to repair diabetes and cultured skin cells grafted to repair lesions ... Human amniotic epithelial cells ... could be useful in repairing inherited enzyme defects in recipient children and adults.[19]

Further, Edwards reports that there are indications that foetal brain tissue might be capable of repairing neural defects in adults and 'There are reports that kidney cells may be transplanted into the human brain in order to cure illnesses such as Parkinson's disease.'[20] 'Myocardial tissue ... should be obtainable from embryos growing *in vitro* without great difficulty,'[21] and might be used by cardiologists for repair of the major vessels of the heart.

Finally, there are various indications that the ultimate and most intractable problems of tissue and cell grafting and of transplantation procedures may be solved by methods of *in vitro* embryology. Edwards notes a number of methods for completely avoiding rejection by 'tailoring embryos to suit a particular recipient'[22] and lists two strong advantages in using foetal tissue. The first is that 'foetal tissue ... might not be rejected by incompatible donors as strongly as adult tissue' and the second that 'Tissues compatible with an adult host might also be obtained through cloning' or by otherwise genetically tailoring matched or compatible tissue.[23]

We have for the moment looked sufficiently far into the future and we must now return to our starting point and ask what arguments there are against the continuation of such work and the realisation of these possibilities?

> There is only one argument for doing something; the rest are arguments for doing nothing.[24]

Cornford's jibe at academics in 1908 is particularly apposite in considering the case against *in vitro* fertilisation. The arguments for doing nothing or rather for doing nothing of the sort fall into two broad categories. There are the arguments which are all variants of the 'slippery slope' the upper reaches of which we have just been examining. The other arguments all turn either on the issue of whether it is morally permissible to kill the embryo or on whether it is morally permissible to use it or parts of it for our own purposes. We will examine both groups of arguments, attempting the slippery slope last.

Two reminders

Before moving on to a consideration of the morality of experimenting on human embryos, or of using them, or tissue from them, for therapeutic purposes, it would be as well to remind ourselves of two important considerations. The first is that in the United Kingdom alone we already perform some 150,000 abortions annually.[25] Many more embryos are lost through methods of contraception which prevent implantation of the fertilised egg. Those who accept such methods of contraception or the permissibility of abortions on anything like the present scale and for the current range of reasons must ask themselves whether there can be any moral reasons for preferring to grow hundreds of thousands of embryos *in vivo*, only to see them killed and their tissue go entirely to waste, rather than growing embryos *in vitro* and, instead of allowing them to die wastefully, using them to save and ameliorate the lives of existing people?

It is true that the embryos grown *in vitro* will add to the total lost, but it cannot be morally worse to grow embryos in glass and use them to save valuable lives or to cure debilitating disease, than it is to grow embryos in the body entirely wastefully. Nor can it be morally preferable to end the life of an embryo *in vivo* than it is to do so *in vitro*. Still less can it be worse to fertilise an egg *in vitro*, knowing that you will not allow it to be implanted or carried to term, than it would be to fertilise *in vivo* with the same attitude to implantation or the prospect of live birth.[26]

The second reminder concerns the moral status of the embryo (and I use the term 'embryo' to cover all stages of development from the zygote or blastocyst right through to the end of the third trimester of pregnancy). We saw in Chapter 1 that there were good reasons for thinking of the moral status of the human embryo in the same way that we think of that of any other creatures of comparable capacities. Such creatures are not persons and do not benefit from the same protections as those we accord to persons. The question we must now consider is that of whether there are any reasons why we should not use the embryo for experimental purposes, for observation or indeed for the provision of tissue and organs in any of the ways described above.

We should finally note that (even without accepting the arguments of Chapter 1) a society or individual that has concluded that IUDs and some forms of the contraceptive pill are permissible forms of birth control, or that abortion is permissible, either freely or where some disutilities can be shown to be involved in continuing a pregnancy, must conclude that *in vitro* fertilisation and the non-implantation of 'spare' embryos is also permissible on the same terms. That is either with the same freedom that is permitted to the use of IUDs and other methods of contraception that prevent implantation, or with the same freedom that abortions are standardly performed.

II Experiments on Embryos

Pain and suffering

Certainly it does not follow from our conclusion that there is nothing morally wrong with killing an embryo that there is nothing morally wrong with doing other things to or with it. For example, we may hold that it is wrong to inflict pain on creatures whom it is permissible to kill, and that if they are to be killed it must be done as painlessly as possible. This is, I suppose, the attitude of most people to the killing of animals for food and other human purposes. Where pain is inflicted on such creatures (and where it isn't for the creatures' own good as in most surgical operations) we demand, or we ought to demand, that the gains for humanity are of an importance to warrant the cruelty and suffering involved.

If, as seems likely, the embryo is not capable of feeling pain in the first few weeks of life (probably up to eighteen weeks) because it lacks a sufficiently established nervous system, then this reason for not interfering with it cannot apply, and it will not for similar reasons where adequate anaesthesia is used. We should also note and be concerned that many abortions are carried out after eighteen weeks and are performed in circumstances that are careless of the pain that might be inflicted on the embryo.

So, although the gratuitous infliction of pain gives us one reason to object to experiments on the embryo, it is an objection that can very easily be met.

Consent

To many people the idea of experiments on living human embryos is deeply disturbing as is the prospect of using tissue or organs from such beings to save the lives of human persons or to repair disabling defects. But the idea and the widespread practice of using tissue and organs from live adults seems to be far from disturbing. Skin grafts, cornea, kidney and bone-marrow transplants from children and adults to one another are not uncommon, nor of course is the use of cadaver organs and tissue. In each case, however, the crucial difference seems to be the ability to give and the actual giving of consent.

With live adults and children the wrongness of performing operations upon them and of taking away even 'spare' parts against their will is straightforwardly related to the wrongness of killing them against their will, and consent will remain effectively the *sine qua non* of such operations.[27] However, with cadaver transplants the situation is far from straightforwardly similar. The current practice is to require consent either from the potential donor while alive, perhaps in the form of a Will or kidney donor card or suchlike, or to obtain consent from the next-of-kin after death. And by and large people seem to want the obtaining of such consents to be mandatory. Now of course, all things being equal, it is always a good idea not to ignore people's wishes and sensibilities over such matters. However, all things are decidedly not equal.

The necessity of obtaining consent for cadaver transplants costs many hundreds of lives each year in this country alone. Where there is no kidney donor card, for example, the necessity to find next-of-kin and find them in any condition to entertain the question of transplants from their nearest and dearest means that many potential donor organs are lost. Other vagaries of consent can have more disastrous consequences. Following a BBC *Panorama* programme in 1981 on the subject of transplants, thousands of potential donors tore up their consent cards and the consequent shortfall of donors meant that many hundreds went without the transplants they desperately needed, either to stay alive or improve the quality of their lives.

Transplantation orders

The dead person cannot be wronged or harmed by the transplant of their organs 'against their will' for they have no will—they are not there to be harmed. Are the feelings or preferences of relatives of the dead a sufficiently important value to warrant protection at the cost of hundreds of lives annually?[28] The state has the power to order a *post mortem* examination regardless of the wishes of the deceased or his or her relatives and often does so when there is nothing so important as the saving of a life to be gained by so doing. (Little is so damaging to the dignity of the dead as a *post mortem*. The organs, liver, heart, lungs, kidneys, etc. are extracted, weighed, cut up, examined, tested and then dumped back in the chest cavity which is carelessly sewn together.) If the state can order such things to be done to the dead on the slightest of pretexts, where for example there is the slightest of suspicions as to the cause of death, how much more important and useful it would be to be able to order *post mortem* transplantation! If the ability to use cadaver organs for transplants were automatic there is no doubt that many hundreds, perhaps even many thousands, of lives could be saved annually at the same 'social cost' that we already (willingly?) pay for judicial certainty as to the cause of death.

If we return now to the issue of experiments with and transplants from the embryo we find related problems and issues. Unlike the articulate child or adult, the embryo cannot give or withhold consent, and this is not just a contingent difficulty about the development of speech, it reflects the fact that the embryo has no self-consciousness at all. If we are justified in killing or aborting the embryo, and do just this, its life will be lost and its death is a useless waste, not of life primarily, though living cells and tissue die, but of life-saving potential. If we can use it to save and ameliorate the lives of persons in being, would it not be both wasteful and morally wrong not to do so?

There are two sorts of problems here which turn on the question of whether the embryo can be said to be moribund or not and on the issue of whose consent is required.

Condemned to death?

> How about the fetus which is not growing satisfactorily or which is cleaving abnormally? Do we regard this embryo as having condemned itself to death ...? Is it not time that we started regarding these early embryos as collections of cells, and not as fetuses? Those that are not replaced in the mother are condemned to death, just as sperm that is spilt on the floor is condemned to death.[29]

These remarks of Patrick Steptoe strangely echo those of John Locke:

> Indeed having by his own fault forfeited his own life by some act that deserves death, he to whom he has forfeited it may, when he has him in his power delay to take it and make use of him for his own service; and he does him no injury by it. For whenever he finds the hardship of his slavery outweigh the value of his life it is in his power by resisting the will of his master, to draw on himself the death he desires.[30]

Although Locke was referring to slavery, the principle to which they are both appealing is the same. That death is wasteful and that when you are justified in ending a life you may also be justified in forbearing to take that life and making use of it instead. Of course, the issue of slavery is much more complex and for Locke the morality of the decision is in part determined by its being preferable to the slave given a justified alternative to death.

But Steptoe is surely right to suggest that if the embryo is moribund it is morally preferable to use it to save or benefit life than simply to waste both the embryo *and* the lives it might save or ameliorate? But is the spare embryo rightly to be thought of as 'condemned to death'?

Certainly if the embryo is not to be implanted either now or in the future then it is condemned never to become a person (if it is frozen indefinitely it may perhaps not be straightforwardly *moribund* either).[31] But might not a host mother be found or come forward to give the lie to the claim that the embryo is either moribund or condemned to refrigerated limbo? For if a woman were to say 'You may implant that embryo into me, I will carry it to term', then, although the embryo might have been 'condemned to death', an eleventh-hour reprieve seems possible.

Where such an eleventh-hour reprieve appears it will not of course be true that the embryo will inevitably die and if it will not die it cannot be claimed that its organs and experimental possibilities will go to waste. But of course if it is not morally wrong to kill the embryo, then it may be killed despite the appearance of such a reprieve; and if it is killed in these circumstances then, unless the organs and so on are utilised to benefit lives in being, they will be wasted.

Consent again

Who has the right to determine the fate of the embryo fertilised *in vitro*?

In the case of a normal pregnancy there is of course no question of aborting the foetus against the will of the mother. This is partly because such a course would involve a physical assault upon the mother. Now, if this mother has an abortion, who is to determine what happens to the aborted foetus? If for example medical researchers want the foetus for experiments, is the mother's consent required? We are inclined, I suppose, to think that the answer to this question is 'yes', who else if not the mother should decide such an issue? But suppose the foetus was aborted alive, late in pregnancy and could survive; should the mother be asked whether she wishes it kept alive or not? We cannot answer this question without knowing whether or not we are morally obliged to save the life of such a foetus. If we are obliged to save its life, if we are not entitled to kill it, then the mother cannot give the licence that morality will not grant.

If, as has been the argument of this chapter, we are *not* morally required to preserve the life of such a foetus, then again, why should we turn to the mother? Has she not already abdicated responsibility for the foetus by opting for abortion? We should turn to her only to see whether this is so. And of course if she hasn't thus abdicated responsibility for the foetus, perhaps because the abortion is being performed to preserve her own health and not because she doesn't want the baby, then the case is different. In this case, if the foetus can live it must be restored to the mother—this will be a case of premature birth.

Where the aborted foetus cannot live or is already dead, again why should we turn to the mother for a decision as to what should be done with the foetus? If experimenters ask her for, and are given, permission to experiment on the foetus this permission will not absolve them from the responsibility of deciding *for themselves* whether such a course of action is ethically sound. And if she withholds permission, we must ask what gives her the right to decide that others should not benefit from the research or from transplantation? This would be another case for transplantation orders.

Property rights
The only candidate for such a right vested in the mother is the claim that she has a property right in the foetus, deriving presumably from a view about the ownership of things growing either inside or on the surface of one's own body. This might well seem to be obviously the most basic and the most secure form of ownership possible. But there are obstacles to the idea that the foetus is owned by the mother simply in virtue of its growing inside her.

There seem to be powerful exceptions to the general theory that such things are simply owned by the 'owner' of the relevant body, at least in any absolute sense. For example, deadly and infectious viruses and so on may grow on or in someone's body but it is not clear that they are owned in any sense that would preclude society's right to kill or otherwise dispose of them against the will of the 'owner' where the social utility of their destruction is clear. It is also worth noting that any claim that the mother owned her foetus would seem to confirm that it cannot be considered a person because, since the abolition of slavery at least, it is generally agreed that persons cannot be owned.

We may conclude that even in the unlikely event of our being satisfied that the mother's relation to the embryo or foetus is one of ownership, we are not forced to accept that we may not vary such property rights where, as in the cases we are considering, there are clear gains in terms of lives to be saved and improvements to be made in the quality of lives in being.

To sum up this discussion of the fate of the embryo, the situation seems to be that where the foetus is aborted and can survive, then if the mother wants it to live it must be treated as a premature birth and restored to her. If she does not want it to live she has no right that it be killed wastefully rather than used for experiments or for transplants. The same is true of the embryo *in vitro*, except in this case there is no mother. No woman has a right that the egg she has donated be implanted. She has only a, perhaps contractual, right that it be implanted in *her* if she wants it.

Conclusion

It looks then strongly as though if the ends we purpose are themselves morally sound then we may pursue them by experimenting on or with the human embryo and by using tissue, cells and organs from embryos to benefit the lives of persons in being. Further, there is no moral virtue in killing or allowing embryos to die when they could rather be used to benefit us all and there is less virtue in allowing human cadavers to go to waste, when we could, with say transplantation orders or the like, save very many lives.

As we have seen, the objections to these conclusions must show either that the embryo is the sort of creature that is morally entitled to the same concern, respect and protections as are persons or that, failing this, there are other moral reasons why we should not experiment on or take tissue from such embryos. We have seen that neither of these objections holds and we must now turn to the remaining question, that of whether, despite the moral acceptability of these practices, to embark upon them somehow involves stepping on to a slippery slope of depravity.

III The slippery slope

In the first part of this chapter we reviewed a series of possibilities from the present to the reasonably foreseeable future and stopped short with Edwards' prognosis that *in vitro* embryology might well open the way to transplant procedures that would have surmounted the greatest risk, that of tissue rejection. We stopped, however, at a point which is artificially short, although, as we have seen, it is a point which is reached by morally justifiable paths. We must now explore the related questions of whether we are morally obliged to stick at that point and that of whether the gradient has become willy nilly so steep that if we go so far we will be unable to prevent ourselves from going further.

We should perhaps start by getting a clearer look at what lies in wait for us when we leave the nursery slopes.

Cloning

Cloning human beings would involve removing the nucleus of the fertilised egg cell (which contains the hereditary genetic material) and replacing it with the nucleus of a cell taken from the adult whom it is wished to clone. The resulting embryo would be the 'identical twin'[32] of the adult from whom the replacement cell nucleus was obtained. It would exactly replicate the genetic make-up of the adult and so its tissue and organs would be 'customised' to exactly match that of its adult 'progenitor'. It could then be grown to whatever stage was appropriate for development of the tissue or organs required for (or potentially required for) its adult twin.

The possibilities now become both mind and morality boggling, although it must be emphasised that these are not immediate possibilities and it is unclear how far off they are.

As we have seen, some tissue and some cells can be taken from the embryo *in vitro*. For the rest, the embryo would have to be grown, perhaps still *in vitro* if substitutes could be found for the mother's blood supply and other essential features of the womb, or perhaps in a surrogate mother. Here paths divide. Along one the foetus (and perhaps the neonate) would be grown until the organs or other tissue had reached a maturity sufficient for transplantation. Along the other, it might be possible to remove cells from the foetus as soon as they became distinct as potential organ tissue. It might then be possible to grow the organs themselves *in vitro* to the stage at which they could be used for transplantation. Both paths, of course, terminate in the death of the foetus or neonate.

There is one set of further possibilities we must consider and here the gradient, on what many will regard as a very slippery slope, becomes positively precipitous. The possibilities I have in mind, while extreme, are interesting both for the light they shed on the issues involved and for the sharp focus they give to the argument. Let us then examine the terrain at the bottom of the slippery slope, or at least as far down it as is presently visible.

Organ banks

One way in which adults could ensure for themselves a secure supply of appropriate organs for transplant when needed would be to clone themselves and grow the resulting clone, perhaps to adult size, for transplantation of organs as and when needed. The clone could be in all respects an identical adult and of course if it were it might well claim the right to be a recipient of the 'original's' organs rather than a donor of his or her own. To overcome this 'problem' originals might arrange for the brain of the clone to be destroyed as soon as it was differentiated in the embryo or enough of the brain to prevent the development of consciousness. The clone could be nourished and perhaps even exercised, and in the event of complete disaster to the original body his or her brain could be transplanted to the clone rather than the organs transplanted to the original, and life could continue. An endless supply of such clones at different stages of development could then keep the original going as long as its brain lasted. There might be a problem about the identity of the resultant beings or series of beings but they would (presumably) regard an identity crisis as less of a crisis than extinction.

The mad dictator problem

A fear that is perhaps worth recording is that recently expressed by Oliver Gillie[33] that these techniques might 'open the way for a self-infatuated millionaire or a mad dictator to produce hundreds of copies of himself'. Such self-infatuated individuals would have to be mad to suppose that anything of value to them could be thus gained. For one thing 'the best guess scientifically would be that the product of cloning would be less like the source than would be two identical twins'[34] because both physical characteristics and psychological and social characteristics also would be exposed to different time frames.

Genetic engineering

The techniques we have been considering also open the way to the possibility of influencing human evolution. But how and to what ends should this power be exercised? Clifford Grobstein puts the dilemma like this:

> ... many would be reassured to know that the intent of any intervention in human reproduction would be to benefit individuals and not to 'improve' the species as a whole. Though these two are linked, in contemporary thinking the first is generally understood and accepted, the second is burdened by suspicion and fraught with uncertainties as to how 'improvement' will be defined and by whom.

> It would also be reassuring to know that defects that *limit* self-realisation are the legitimate target; that conservation and fuller fruition of humanity as we know it is the goal, not the 'engineering' of new forms of human life.[35]

Worries about the engineering of new forms of life may be real enough, but the possibility of 'specialising' in existing forms may be equally disturbing.

Artificial parthogenesis

> Cloning may be possible with female as well as with male diploid nuclei, including a diploid nucleus from the egg donor. In the last case the product would be a female twin of the egg donor. By continued and exclusive application of the technique, an almost totally female and genetically homogeneous society could be created and perpetuated. The number of required males, as in the case of breeding bulls, would only have to be sufficient to provide sperm to activate the eggs
>
> Even that requirement could be eliminated if human eggs could be activated parthenogenetically. This occurs naturally in many animals but not regularly in any mammals. It can also be induced artificially in frogs and some mammals but with no normal offspring so far resulting in the latter case. If it could be accomplished externally, regularly and reliably on human eggs, it would open at lease a formal option for a totally female society.[36]

This prospect might be very attractive to a certain stamp of feminist and, disturbing as such a prospect would be to many, it is far from obvious that there are convincing moral arguments against the voluntary establishment of such a society. And if, for example, all the women in the world voluntarily decided that in future they would 'bring forth women children only' it is not clear that anyone, let alone any man, would have the right to force them to do otherwise.

The resolution of these dilemmas raised by the possibilities of genetic engineering is a large undertaking and one we must postpone until Chapter 8, but it is important to bear such possibilities in mind when considering what the policy of society should be towards *in vitro* fertilisation and the bio-technology it generates and utilises. For if we are on a slippery slope and it is towards such scenarios that we are sliding it is our attitude to them which will determine whether we set forth with skates or crampons.

It would perhaps be prudent to emphasise again that the possibilities we have just been considering are most certainly not yet even possible and perhaps may never be. But even fifty years is a long time in science, as the last fifty years have shown, and we should be clear as to what our policy should be in the face of such 'possibilities'. It will not be my purpose here to sift the cases one by one and review their general merits and defects. Some general conclusions however can safely be drawn.

Slippery slopes again

The first is the slopes are only slippery if they catch us unawares and we have strayed on to them inadequately equipped. It is up to us to decide not what we can countenance but what we ought to pursue. We would be both irrational and immoral if we cut ourselves off from options we clearly perceive to be the beneficial products of the procedures now being developed because we fear that we will be insufficiently resolute to resist the dangers. We do not outlaw effective contraception because we fear that to practise population control is to step on to a slope that leads inexorably to the extinction of the human race.

The principle of the dangerous precedent

In any event the idea that we can turn our backs on a slippery slope and thus avoid its dangers is an illusion. We are in fact only able to identify slippery slopes when we are already on them. What we can always do is decide in which direction to go and constantly review our decisions in the light of new information and revisions in our thinking. The feared slippery slope is just a variant of the well-known principle of the dangerous precedent so effectively lampooned by Cornford at the turn of the century:

> The Principle of the Dangerous Precedent is that you should not now do an admittedly right action for fear you, or your equally timid successors, should not have the courage to do right in some future case, which *ex hypothesi* is essentially different, but superficially resembles the present one. Every public action which is not customary, either is wrong, or, if it is right, is a dangerous precedent. It follows that nothing should ever be done for the first time.[37]

The artificiality of the dilemma of the so-called 'slippery slope' is precisely as identified by Cornford. It would be irrationally self-defeating if we decline to permit work which is in no way immoral and which can benefit us all, merely because we fear that at some future time we will not have the courage to object to work that *is* immoral. The arguments of this chapter indicate that it is not morally wrong to fertilise the human egg externally *in vitro* nor are there sound objections to our permitting researchers to end the lives of spare embryos nor to experiment upon, nor use cells, tissue or organs from them, so long as this does not involve pain or suffering to the embryo. If we can thereby learn much that is of benefit to us and eventually use such embryonic material to repair or prolong the lives of children or adults, the lives of persons, then we should clearly do so.

Whether we should permit, for example, the growing of clones to adult maturity as living organ banks in the way described earlier is a question we cannot address here. But we should note that we are in no way committed to a particular answer simply in virtue of our assenting to work on the embryo. It may be difficult to find convincing arguments against the realisation of such a possibility[38] but again, the fear that we might not be able to find such arguments is not relevant to our assessment of the morality of *in vitro* embryology.

What should we do?

As we saw at the start of this discussion, the advantages in terms of saving lives and curing or arresting disease, that are predicated upon the use of the human embryo, are substantial. If they are realistic as well, we would be more than foolish, we would be immoral to deny them to ourselves and others rather than experiment on or use tissue from embryos when we already abort 150,000 embryos a year (entirely wastefully in terms of lives we might save) and kill many more through widespread use of contraception. When we add to this the conclusions reached in Chapter 1 about the moral status of the embryo, the case for saving people's lives by using embryos becomes unanswerable.

A problem remains of how to define the embryo for these purposes. Most of the presently envisaged work can be done on the embryo before the end of the first month of development, but for the sake of avoiding foreclosing future options, I think we should define the embryo in the way that I have used the term in this chapter—to cover all stages of development from the moment of conception right through to the point where, were the embryo developing *in vivo*, it would be born. This period of nine months' development, like the event of birth, is an arbitrary point of no moral significance. It is, however, a point which, if it errs, does so comfortably on the safe side. Nine months' development leaves the human embryo far short of the emergence of anything that could be called a person, far short of an individual capable of valuing its own life or possessing any of the capacities that would be required for such valuing. I talk of 'nine months' development' rather than of birth, because birth lacks, or will soon lack, the clarity it once had as a point of clear transition from the womb to the world. Many babies in the future will never have been in the womb and so will never be 'born' (let alone 'untimely ripped').

Permitting work on the human embryo up until the end of the third trimester of development would allow most of the current and reasonably projected research to proceed, while leaving us time to review the moral and social implications of further developments. We should be clear, however, that the arguments we have been reviewing indicate that any moral objections to beneficial work on and use of even human non-persons who do not suffer in the process would be objections to the side-effects or extrinsic features of such work rather than objections to the work as such.

The cases that must be surveyed in order to adequately map *that* terrain, cases of the sort examined briefly at the beginning of this section, require a more detailed assessment than can be given here. It is not clear at first glance, however, whether such possibilities as living cell, tissue and organ banks, which involve development beyond the third trimester, cloning, genetic engineering to 'improve' human beings, artificial parthogenesis and the like, would involve a slide or an ascent on the slope or axis of morality.

IV The Warnock Report

The Committee of Inquiry into Human Fertilisation and Embryology set up by the British government under the Chairmanship of Dame Mary Warnock reported in July 1984.[39] As we noted at the beginning of this chapter, it was established to report on, among other things, the ethics of *in vitro* fertilisation and of experimentation on the human embryo. Some of its other concerns will be the subject of the next chapter, but to conclude our discussion of the ethical issues surrounding the beginnings of life, we should examine what the Warnock Report has to say about the conclusions that we have already reached. Before doing so, however, something should be said about the ethical presuppositions of 'Warnock' and about the methodology adopted by the report.

The ethical presuppositions

The Warnock Committee state clearly the ethical presuppositions of the report in their foreword. Briefly the Committee believe that:

> [M]oral questions ... are by definition, questions that involve not only calculation of consequences but also strong sentiments with regard to the nature of the proposed activities themselves.
>
> We were therefore bound to take very seriously the feelings expressed in the evidence. And ... it would be idle to pretend that there is not a wide diversity in moral feelings. ... What is common ... is that people generally want *some principles or other* to govern the development and use of the new techniques. There must be *some* barriers that are not to be crossed, *some* fixed limits, beyond which people must not be allowed to go. Nor is such a wish for containment a mere whim or fancy. The very existence of morality depends on it. A society which had no inhibiting limits, especially in the areas with which we have been concerned, questions of birth and death, of the setting up of families, and the valuing of human life, would be a society without moral scruples. *And this nobody wants.*[40]

The Committee conclude their foreword with some remarks about the way in which legislation, and particularly the legislation they recommend, relates to moral reasoning.

> In recommending legislation then, we are recommending a kind of society that we can, all of us, praise and admire, even if, in detail, we may individually wish that it were different. Within the broad limits of legislation there is room for different, and perhaps much more stringent, moral rules. What is legally permissible may be thought of as the minimum requirement for a tolerable society. ... The question must ultimately be what kind of society can we praise and admire? In what sort of society can we live with our conscience clear?[41]

There is much that is unexceptionable and even valuable in all this, but the crucial questions are fudged, or rather are never addressed. The Report says repeatedly that the Committee, and indeed anyone at all, is bound to take seriously people's feelings (and indeed the Committee is ready to express its own feelings from time to time).[42] However, not all feelings, however strongly held, are *moral* feelings—some feelings are immoral ones, that is they spring from immoral motives or are productive of morally bad consequences. Any moral agent must then be prepared and able to test her feelings about moral issues to see whether they are indeed morally defensible. But this the Warnock Committee does not itself do, nor does it recommend that others do so.

In this book I have suggested that moral motives are those directed towards making the world in some sense a better place and that good and bad consequences are simply those which make the world better or worse. Now of course this leaves open a wide range of possibilities, but at least it allows moral argument to get off the ground, because anyone claiming that what they propose will make the world a better place must be able and prepared to give some account of just how the world will be better for what they propose, and indeed of what a better world would look like and why. Moreover once a person's moral objectives are known, that is, once they have sketched at least some of the things that they believe will make the world a better place, it may become obvious that their present beliefs or proposals are not well calculated to achieve that better world.

Many of the things that make for a better world are almost universally agreed upon. Saving life or postponing death, reduction or elimination of pain, illness, misery, poverty and starvation are, for example, usually high on the list of most people, and are all things to which health care is directed. So that where people's feelings or instincts lead to policies, practices or states of affairs that in effect frustrate these ends and others that most people accept as making for a better world, we have good reason to regard them as immoral or at least as anti-moral. The same is true where people's feelings are directed towards some saving of lives or reduction of illness or suffering, but where the feelings dictate actions that in fact lead to more loss of life or more suffering than they prevent.

This is why however good or worthy people believe their feelings to be and however strongly they are felt, we must always scrutinise them not only to see whether they are in fact capable of generating policies or practices that would plausibly and coherently make the world a better place, but also whether they in fact tend to make the world better than would alternative policies which are not so strongly endorsed or indicated by the feelings that people just happen to have. In other words, we can and should educate our feelings in the light of our moral objectives rather than merely allowing our feelings to dictate our moral objectives.

Warnock, however, treats people's expressions of strong feelings as moral, whatever sort of world they are likely to produce. They are moral apparently simply because they are feelings expressed sincerely about morally important matters.[43] But sincerity is not enough. People may be sincerely and passionately prejudiced, their sincerely held strong feelings may be just the sort of feelings that we ought, morally speaking, to ignore or combat, not 'take seriously' and respect. We should in short only respect feelings that are respectable.

Now Warnock takes comfort from the fact that although the feelings expressed about these important issues differ, and although what people want done differs also, they do at least all want barriers to be erected. And Warnock concludes that the provisions of *some* barriers is what the very existence of morality depends on. But it is one thing to conclude that morality depends on barriers, and quite another to assume that barriers make for morality. For, as with reasons and feelings, while any morality involves barriers and while some barriers are constitutive of morality, not any old barriers are! Warnock is aware of this. For Warnock the test of where the barriers should be placed must 'ultimately be what kind of society can we praise or admire? In what sort of society can we live with our conscience clear?' But exactly what this means becomes of crucial importance. It might simply be that we would praise a society in which nothing happened to arouse our feelings of indignation and that our consciences would remain clear if our feelings were not ruffled. This view of the relationship of feelings to morality regards our feelings as reliable indicators of the moral qualities of actions or circumstances. On this view if our feelings of indignation are aroused or our consciences are troubled, this is always both good evidence that there is something morally wrong afoot and also the sort of evidence we are bound to take notice of. This is I'm sure the view taken by Warnock, as I hope will be clear in what follows in this and the next chapter. But this is I think a false and a dangerous view. As we have repeatedly seen in the course of our discussion, we may find that we have all sorts of primitive feelings which on examination prove dangerous and destructive. If we wish for a better world we would do well to look on such feelings with profound suspicion, rather than embrace them as the true guardians of morality. It may be that we would be better to suppress rather than indulge such feelings. In any event, anyone serious about wanting to act morally must be curious about whether their feelings are of the best. And this means, at the very least, examining them to see where giving them sway leads and what sort of world it is likely to produce.

To remind ourselves of just one example from the discussion so far, where someone feels that they must in no circumstances kill an innocent person but where refusing to do so cannot prevent the death of the individual concerned but means that it will be a lingering and painful one rather than a short and painless end; or where such a person's refusal to kill one such person means that many more equally innocent people will surely die, then in either case such feelings are both self-defeating and morally indefensible.

The Warnock proposals

So far I have set out what I take to be the main issues raised by *in vitro* embryology and have argued that the concept of the person developed in Chapter 1 gives us good reasons to permit work on human non-persons which does not involve either pain or suffering to such beings and which would be of palpable benefit to persons whether human or indeed of any other kind. We should, however, look at one or two points made by Warnock which either raise issues so far not covered, or which draw very different conclusions from those already reached here.

The main conclusion of Warnock as it affects the arguments of this chapter is that 'the embryo of the human species should be afforded some protection in law'[44] and that the protection it should be afforded should be first, that anyone handling or doing research on embryos should be licensed (such unlicensed work to be a criminal offence);[45] and second, that such handling, research and experimentation as is licensed should not be permitted beyond fourteen days after fertilisation.[46]

Now the Warnock Committee deliberately declines to address the question of whether or not the embryo is a person and what it might mean to claim that an individual is a person, and moves directly to the question of '*how it is right to treat the human embryo*'.[47] This is in a sense just an evasion because, for example, the discussion of the concept of the person developed in this book just is, among other things, a discussion of how it is right to treat the human embryo. However, Warnock makes no serious attempt to discuss how it is right to treat the human embryo. Only two considerations play any part at all in the conclusions at which the Warnock Committee arrives. The first is that apparently overwhelming consideration that 'some precise decision must be taken, in order to allay public anxiety'.[48] And the second is the objection to all research on human embryos, never refuted or even argued against in Warnock, that the human embryo is a potential human being.

The only positive reason given by Warnock for setting the limit on research at fourteen days is that it is at this point that the primitive streak occurs and this is 'the latest stage at which identical twins occur'[49] and hence is the first point at which it is clear that the number of potential human beings present are either one or more than one. However, this point must be irrelevant in any event. For if the potentiality argument is sound, then human potential is present as much before the development of the primitive streak as afterwards.[50] The development of the primitive streak does not affect the fact that the potential for one or more human beings exists, it just makes clear how many potential human beings are present. And of course if, as I argued earlier, the potentiality argument is unsound, then some other reasons must be adduced for protecting the human embryo, and these Warnock never provides.

So, if the potentiality argument is good, it is good against all non-actualisation of human potential and it is an argument against research on the embryo at any stage and against research on human eggs and sperm separately if they could be combined. It is also an argument in favour of unlimited and maximal procreation. If, on the other hand, it is not good then we are left without any account of 'how it is right to treat the human embryo' or rather without any justification for the account that Warnock gives. What is thus needed and what Warnock declines to give is some account of just what it is that is so valuable about adult human beings and other persons and of how and to what extent the features that make us valuable are present in the embryo. Without such an account we have no reason to think it is wrong to treat the embryo in any way that avoids suffering. When we know that research on the human embryo might save the lives of actual human persons, children and adults (which beings Warnock admits to be more valuable than embryos) we are owed some account of what justifies the prevention of such research. And to this end Warnock offers absolutely nothing that could be of an importance comparable to the good moral reasons for doing the research.[51]

7 Whose body is it anyway?

The discussion of the dilemmas presented by the development of techniques for *in vitro* fertilisation has raised and left unresolved a number of problems about our control over our own bodies and of what happens in and to them. Some of these problems concern the ways in which our claims to control our own bodies are in fact also claims to determine what should happen to others, and quite literally to settle how they should turn out and what they should turn out to be. Other problems concern the ways in which society sometimes claims control over us.

All the problems we shall consider here form a family, albeit an extended family. Many of them are not, however, very obviously related to one another. Most of them are indeed about the family, about parents and children and the ability to bear children or about claims that it is right or wrong to do so and about our responsibility for so doing. Many of these problems are also in a sense peculiarly problems that concern women. In this chapter we will consider two broad collections of problems. The first group concerns real mothers, surrogate mothers and what sort of children it is or is not morally permissible to have. The second group of problems concerns what might constitute a good parent or a good reason to be a parent.

In the next chapter we will turn to the related issues of the morality of choosing to have or not to have children at all, at the issues of abortion and birth control, determining the sex of children and at the issue of women's control over these matters.

1 Who's mother whose baby?

Egg or embryo donation and womb leasing or lending

The techniques of *in vitro* fertilisation have made possible 'egg or embryo donation' and 'womb leasing or lending'. In the first case a woman will donate an egg or embryo so that another woman may carry, give birth to and bring up a child of her 'own'. In this case the egg will usually be fertilised externally by the second woman's partner, and then be implanted in her uterus so that her pregnancy can then proceed normally. 'Womb leasing or lending', on the other hand, may be attractive where a woman cannot herself undergo either pregnancy or childbirth, but is able to produce eggs. These she can have fertilised, usually externally, by her own partner and the resulting embryo will be implanted in the lessor or lender, to be carried and given birth by her with the object of returning the baby to the donor of the embryo at some time after birth.

The assumptions behind each procedure will be different. In the case of egg or embryo donation it will be assumed, and there may be a contract (whether formal or not) which provides, that the resulting baby will belong to the recipient of the egg. Womb leasing or lending, on the other hand, implies (and again there may be some sort of contract to the same effect) that the womb is leased or lent to the donor of the egg and that the resulting baby will be returned to the donor after birth. All of these possibilities can be called 'surrogate motherhood' and are sometimes lumped together, although there are important differences between them. I shall concentrate on womb leasing or lending as the more extreme and dramatic form of surrogacy. I shall try to show that there is no reason to object to this, nor indeed to any form of surrogate motherhood despite the horror with which these practices are sometimes viewed, and indeed were viewed by the Warnock Committee.

Amateurs and professionals

The horror that the idea of womb leasing or lending very often engenders is hard to account for. It seems to arise from a combination of two very deep-rooted views about the evils of what might be called 'professionalism' in matters of this sort. One source of this attitude can I think be found in commonly held views about prostitution and the moral character of prostitutes. It is somehow felt that a woman who would 'sell' her body, whether for sex or for child-nurture, has somehow fallen below the threshold of moral consideration. The evils of prostitution, however, have nothing to do with the formal features of the transaction involved, namely that sex is sold in some way. They have rather everything to do with the side-effects and perhaps also the causes of prostitution. There is nothing wrong with receiving financial or material, as well as physical and emotional, rewards for participating in sexual activity with others. What is wrong is that people should be forced by economic, social or personal pressure, to engage in such activity against their will, or that they should unwillingly run risks of infection or injury. We will be discussing the basis of our ideas about sexual morality in Chapter 9, but for the moment I shall assume that moral objections to prostitution *per se* are without foundation and that the primitive reaction against it has somehow 'rubbed off' on our attitudes to the practice or possibility of womb leasing or lending.

The second of these deep-rooted objections is perhaps more characteristically British. It stems from the idea that there are people who do things for the love of the activity itself, with no thought or hope of reward—the amateur—and those who require to be paid—the professional. The amateur is often thought superior, not in ability, of course, but certainly in character. Nowhere more so than in matters personal. This is perhaps also part of the hostility to prostitution, that matters so personal and important must be done for love, or are best not done at all.

Whatever our personal preferences about these things, it is important to be clear that the fact that we ourselves would perhaps never dream of doing such a thing for money (although of course we all do them in a sense for reward) is not of itself an argument for the wrongness of such conduct. If we judge that certain things are so important or so personal that only love, or perhaps conviction, should play a part in our decision to do them, then well and good for us. But if others take a different view we should not object.

What other more defensible objections can be made to such practices as womb leasing and lending we will discover as the argument progresses. We must now turn to some initial problems that may arise if the practice of surrogate motherhood becomes established.

Real mothers

Where someone has actually embarked on the role of surrogate, despite the very clearest of assumptions or the most careful of contracts, disputes can arise. Suppose the donor of the egg decides that she cannot bear the idea of her baby, the child that carries her genetic make-up and that is the fruit of her womb, being brought up by another, and claims her own child back? She is likely to argue that she is the real mother and that the surrogate, to whom she mistakenly donated an egg, has a claim which must be subordinated to that of the real mother.

For the sake of simplicity we will assume that the father in each case was not the partner of either of the women but a strange and anonymous sperm donor with no further interest in the matter. Suppose the surrogate mother replies that she on the contrary is more of a mother. She has after all undergone the pains and risks of pregnancy and childbirth. She has nurtured and protected the embryo and that while not sharing her genetic make-up it is in a more literal sense flesh of her flesh. An analogous argument might be made by the surrogate mother who has leased or leant her womb, but now wishes to keep the child to whom she has given birth.

The donor of the egg is likely to want to call herself the real mother, to distinguish herself from mere surrogates. The surrogate mother, on the other hand, is likely to reject such a title if she wishes to keep the child, and argue that her claim to be the real mother is the stronger. How can we resolve the dispute between the rival genetic and surrogate mothers?

There are a number of considerations which we might judge important in trying to decide which woman should be permitted to bring up the disputed child but the question of whether the genetic or the surrogate mother has the better claim to the title 'mother' or 'real mother' is not one of them. This is because the possibilities opened up by these recent developments in embryology have split our traditional and commonsense conceptions of motherhood, and neither of the resulting twins has a better claim to be the heir to the title than has the other. The claims 'I'm your mother, you grew from my egg and carry my genetic make-up within you' and 'I'm you're mother because I carried you in my womb, nurtured and gave birth to you' seem equally strong claims to motherhood, and arguments that one is better or more authentic than the other seem well calculated to be both sterile and insoluble.

However, while the question of whether the genetic or the surrogate mother is the real mother may be insoluble, the question of which should keep the child in cases of dispute is both more practical and more pressing. The issue may of course be very complex, but the sorts of consideration relevant to a decision fall into two broad groups. The first concerns the question of which of the two women has the better claim to keep the child, and the second looks more to the interests of the child and asks which of the two women would make the better mother.

The claims of a surrogate mother

A woman might undertake the gestation of an embryo whose genetic make-up was entirely derived from other people, either as an act of altruism to help another woman to produce 'her own' child or as a commercial venture with the same object but where the rewards were not simply the satisfactions of helping fellow creatures.

Whether or not the motives of the surrogate mother were altruistic or commercial, it is likely that she would enter into a formal or informal contract which, whatever else its conditions, would provide at least: (1) that she return the baby to its genetic parents at some reasonable period after birth, (2) that she does carry the embryo to term and refrains from abortion, and (3) that she avoids actions likely to harm the growing embryo—like smoking, drinking alcohol or taking harmful drugs, etc.

Whatever the nature of the contract or the motives for entering into it, there would be major difficulties in the way of effective enforcement. Suppose the surrogate mother changed her mind and opted for early and legal abortion? If a normal mother was entitled to such an abortion, it would be difficult to deny an abortion to the surrogate mother. And what would be the alternative? To force her to go through with a birth with its usual attendant pains and dangers? It would seem to be literally impossible and morally repugnant to attempt to force a woman to go through with a pregnancy that she would be entitled to terminate were she a normal rather than a surrogate mother. And the alternative of making an award against her that she financially compensate the genetic mother would be no consolation to the injured party who wished only to have a child, and might in any event prove a useless expedient if the surrogate was impecunious. This would be particularly likely to be the case if the arrangement was commercial, since it would then be highly probable that genetic mothers would be drawn from members of high-income groups, while surrogate mothers would be likely to be driven to volunteer by poverty.

If, rather than opting for abortion, the surrogate mother wished after all to keep the child to which she had given birth, the dilemma would be equally great. Whatever the actual or implied contract the surrogate mother's claim to keep a child which she had nurtured and for whom she had undergone the pains, inconvenience and risks of pregnancy and childbirth, would be hard to answer. Disputes about any of these issues would be likely to be bitter and intractable, and any contractual safeguards more than likely to prove worse than useless.

The difficulties of framing legislation which would be sufficiently subtle and humane to cover the different sorts of cases that might arise in this area are formidable. The Warnock Report recommends that in every case in which surrogacy is permitted, the woman giving birth should have the legal right to custody of the resulting child. This is a tempting line to take, but I am not so pessimistic as Warnock about the possibilities of resolving disputes in each case on their merits. It is, however, beyond the scope of our interests in these problems to try to sketch a framework for such legislation. We should bear in mind that there is no reason to suppose that disputes in this area will be the norm, nor indeed that they would be any more numerous or intractable than other disputes in family law, none of which have ever been sufficiently grave as to provide reasons for outlawing marriage or childbearing for fear of the difficulty of the disputes that permitting such practices might engender.

Is there anything wrong with surrogacy?

The Warnock Committee set its face firmly against womb leasing or lending, but thought on balance that egg or embryo donation should be permitted provided that the woman giving birth should in all cases be regarded in law as the mother of the resulting child.[1] It is not clear from the report how Warnock could justify the distinction between egg or embryo donation on the one hand, and womb leasing or lending on the other. The reasons that Warnock gives for objecting absolutely to womb leasing or lending (which Warnock terms 'surrogacy' to distinguish it from egg or embryo donation) seem too weak to justify the blanket restriction and the taint of criminality that Warnock would impose on the practice of 'surrogacy'. They also seem inadequate, as we shall see, to support the distinction drawn between egg and embryo donation on the one hand and womb leasing on the other.

The Warnock objections

In addition to giving its own views, Warnock here, as elsewhere in the Report, lists the main objections[2] to surrogacy. Since Warnock's own view in this case echoes some of the main objections listed, I will first summarise these and then go on to Warnock's statement of its own position. The four main objections that seem to weigh with Warnock are:

(1) it is inconsistent with human dignity that a woman should use her uterus for financial profit and treat it as an incubator for someone else's child.[3]

(2) the relationship between mother and child is itself distorted by surrogacy. For in such an arrangement a woman deliberately allows herself to become pregnant with the intention of giving up the child to which she will give birth, and that this is the wrong way to approach pregnancy.[4]

(3) it is felt that a surrogacy agreement is degrading to the child who is to be the outcome of it, since, for all practical purposes, the child will have been bought for money.[5]

(4) since there are some risks attached to pregnancy, no woman ought to be asked to undertake pregnancy for another in order to earn money.[6]

The Warnock Inquiry recommends that the creation of agencies, whether for profit or not, for procuring surrogate pregnancies be rendered criminal, as would the actions of anyone at all who knowingly assisted in the establishment of a surrogate pregnancy.[7] The justifications they give for these drastic proposals are as follows:

> that surrogacy for convenience alone that is, where a woman is physically capable of bearing a child but does not wish to undergo pregnancy, is totally ethically unacceptable. Even in compelling medical circumstances the danger of exploitation of one human being by another appears to the majority of us far to outweigh the potential benefits, in almost every case. That people should treat others as a means to their own ends, however desirable the consequences, must always be liable to moral objection. Such treatment of one person by another becomes positively exploitative when financial interests are involved.[8]

Let's consider the Inquiry's own reasons first. The reasons why surrogacy for convenience is 'totally ethically unacceptable' are not given. Presumably it is felt that this is obvious, but is it? We have already considered the rather primitive objection to professionalism in matters of the body, but what else could be wrong with surrogacy for convenience? Maybe there is some idea that no woman should receive the benefits of motherhood without also suffering the pains, risks and inconvenience of pregnancy and birth? We could only test this hypothesis by knowing Warnock's reaction to the possibility of gestation for convenience in a completely artificial womb—a possibility as yet too far in the future for Warnock to have considered. But perhaps this is an unworthy thought since the chief reason actually given by Warnock is the danger of exploitation. However, the identification of exploitation is a difficult and complex matter and the speed with which Warnock is ready to infer its presence is disturbing. For example, it by no means follows, as Warnock claims, that where people treat others as means to their own ends there is automatically exploitation. We all do this perfectly innocuously much of the time. In medical contexts, anyone who receives a blood tranfusion has used the blood donor as a means to their own ends and the same is true of artificial insemination, and of egg or embryo donation, all of which Warnock is prepared to permit.

The idea of exploitation usually implies that the exploiter is able to apply some coercive pressure that those whom she exploits are unable, or ill equipped, to resist. Warnock produces no evidence that this is necessarily the case (or even likely to be the case) here. The suggestion that financial interests always make the use of one person as a means to another's ends 'positively exploitative' needs to be argued. Again, the suggestion must be that the financial interests add the required degree of coercive pressure. But this is not true in the everyday sale of goods or services. It must be here that there is some unstated and assumed suggestion that in the special case of surrogacy, that the service is one so naturally abhorrent that no morally respectable person would undertake it *unless* they were the victim of coercion. But again it is far from clear that this is so. Many people would and do regard the chance to carry a child for another as an act of altruism, whether or not they are paid or otherwise recompensed for the danger and inconvenience involved. In the case of bone marrow transplants, for example, we do not outlaw the practice for fear of exploitation. It is possible to guard against exploitation, if that is the fear, without banning the practice altogether.

We do not, for example, regard firemen or members of other rescue services as exploited either because those they rescue are in a sense using them as means to their ends, or because they are paid to run risks on our behalf. They *may* be exploited if the remuneration they receive is not commensurate with the risks they run, or if certain people or classes of people are pressured into becoming firemen. But that is another matter—and one against which we can legislate separately, that is, without banning the fire service altogether.

It looks very much as though the Warnock Committee have allowed themselves to succumb to something like taboos about the body and its natural functions, rather than think through clearly the issues involved and what might be involved in the exploitation of one person by another. If we look back to the more general objections listed by Warnock, the problem of finding a consideration which would justify the banning of surrogacy but which would not also require the outlawing of many other services we value and require is equally hard.

It is claimed, for example, that it is inconsistent with human dignity to use the uterus for profit. But why the uterus? We most of us use our hands and our brains for profit. Hair, blood and other tissue is often donated or sold, what is so special about the uterus? Why is human dignity seen as attaching to this part of the body rather than to the body as a whole. Is it the connexion with sexuality? Prostitutes for example are said to 'sell their bodies' for sex but not professional athletes for sport. Medical students sell their bodies so that drugs may undergo clinical trial but the same opprobrium is somehow absent—why? If no general principle about the sale or use of the human body in whole or in part emerges we are entitled to ask why in this special case human dignity is said to be violated. In the absence of a more general account, and in the presence of such selective use of the idea of violation of dignity as attaching to sale of the body or bits of it, we are entitled to see this claim as a rationalisation and not a reason and dismiss it out of hand.

The second suggestion, that some ways to approach pregnancy are proper and that others are not again needs argument. It is not clear, for example, that many (or any?) people approach pregnancy or the act that leads to it in anything like the sort of frame of mind that would stand much public scrutiny. Here at the very least we need some account of what the proper way to approach pregnancy is, why it is proper and why the need for a proper attitude is so great that people without such an attitude may be prevented by law from approaching pregnancy at all.

It is suggested that the surrogacy agreement is degrading to the child that will result. But is this worse for that child than not being born at all? We will return to this point later in the discussion. The issue here is simply whether the supposed handicap for the child is so great that a civilised society would not allow it to be imposed on children. Anticipating the argument to come, it is surely doubtful if such a taint, if taint it is, would be of such an order, particularly when the other arguments against surrogacy are seen to be so weak.

Before turning to objections to the practice of *in vitro* fertilisation, or indeed to surrogate mothers, which turn on the supposed fitness of the parents to rear children, we must consider two other objections to these procedures which are based on their supposed deleterious effects on society itself.

Harmful social effects
G.D. Mitchell has advanced two main reasons

> why receiving donated sperm and oocytes is deleterious to society. Firstly, a donation is frequently shrouded in secrecy and of a kind that leads members of families to be deceitful. Secondly, it gives rise to births of children who are denied adequate, or at least normal, knowledge of their genetic origins.[9]

Mitchell produces a standard argument for the general utility of truth-telling for society and argues that secrecy over donations of semen or embryos attacks the whole practice of truth-telling on which society and our 'daily commerce' with one another depends. While accepting that we should promote the useful and virtuous social practices of truthfulness and trust, we must bear two obvious points in mind. The first is that deceit and secrecy are not necessary concomitants of sperm and oocyte donation. It is perfectly possible for there to be complete frankness and free information about the entire transaction. But we should also bear in mind that isolated and particular instances in which people are less than frank with one another do not threaten society, nor do they significantly weaken the general disposition to truthfulness on which society may depend. Mitchell paints a picture of a society in which children can never trust what they are told about their origins because the mere existence of artificial insemination and oocyte donation, which are *sometimes* undeclared, means that 'children in normal families can never be sure of any answer they are given'.[10] This fear surely borders on paranoia. The fact that we know that lying exists does not lead to a general fear that any particular statement may be a lie. But again, at its strongest Mitchell's objection can only be a demand to remove deceit from these practices, not an objection to them as such.

Mitchell's second point is that it cannot be right 'to support processes which may well lead to the creation of children suffering some kind of deprivation which children born in the usual way may not expect to endure?' and that this deprivation just is ignorance of genetic origin. This, according to Mitchell,

> is knowledge which helps a child acquire an identity; he knows where he belongs. Not to have this knowledge may be said to deprive him of a natural right. So should we, as a society, and the profession of medicine in particular, connive at producing children who begin life with a disadvantage.[11]

This is a large and very general question with an importance far beyond our immediate concerns. We should note again before tackling it, however, that there is no necessity for the children whom Mitchell envisages to be kept in ignorance of their genetic origins any more than there is in the case of fostered or adopted children.

Should disadvantaged children be born?

Let's take Mitchell's worst case and suppose that the children of whom we have been speaking must for some reason be kept in ignorance of their genetic origins. Is this a disadvantage so great that we as a society should not connive at producing children thus disadvantaged? There are two ways of looking at this question, one is from the point of view of the potential child and the other is from our, from society's, point of view. From this latter point of view we must ask whether the deprivation in question is so great that it would be better if such children had never been born rather than that they should come into the world so disadvantaged? If, on the other hand, we look at things from the child's point of view 'the options are either no life at all, or life with the disadvantage of not knowing one's genetic parents.'[12] In the present case both points of view seem to yield the same answer. Parents and the wider society, who thought that it would be morally wrong to impose such a disability (when they had no alternative in the sense that these parents could only give life to children thus disabled or to none) would surely be placing too great an importance on one relatively minor disadvantage. From the children's point of view the issue seems just as clear. We can be confident that no such children would think that it was better that they had never been born rather than be born so terribly disadvantaged.

However, in other cases the two points of view can yield different answers. Suppose, say, through genetic screening, that parents knew they would have a very badly physically disabled child, or say that their child would have Huntington's Chorea which would mean that their offspring would die prematurely (probably before their fortieth year) of an incurable and very unpleasant disorder. Should such parents give birth in these circumstances and should we judge them wrong if they did so?

Looked at from the point of view of the child born with such a disorder, we might imagine that, handicapped severely though they were, such a life was still worth having, still better than no life at all. Similarly with Huntington's chorea, sufferers may (and do) judge that even a life inevitably foreshortened, and with an unpleasant and premature death looming, is still better than no life at all.

And of course, where such people actually exist there can be, as we have seen, no question of preferring our judgment to their own on the vital question of whether or not their lives are worth living. But where screening has revealed in advance a very high probability that children born to certain parents or at certain times will be severely disadvantaged, then parents must face the question of whether or not it would be right to bring into existence people whose lives would be so severely blighted.

Clearly taking such a decision would be a very weighty matter indeed. We would in effect be deciding that the foreseen disadvantage would be so great that it would be wrong of us to inflict such a disadvantage on someone by bringing them into existence. For this conclusion to be inescapable the disadvantage would have to be severe indeed, and of a very high degree of probability. But if it was, we might think it wrong to conceive people so disadvantaged or allow them to be born even though we might guess that, were they to come into existence, they might think almost any existence, including one like theirs, would be preferable to none at all.

Happy oblivion?
It is sometimes said that certain kinds of handicap, particularly
severe mental handicap, leave their victims dependent but happy.
They perhaps do not understand much of the world, but are
capable of enjoying and do enjoy a wide range of physical pleasures and seem to be happy and content with their lives. It is
argued that 'viewed from the inside' so to speak, their existence
is happy, so how, it is asked, can it be that they are in any way
disadvantaged or have lives that are not worth living?

We can of course judge such a condition to be a terrible disadvantage and handicap by reference to our own lives. If we judge
that it would be a tragedy for us to have an accident which left us
in such a condition, even though we would not know anything
about it or be capable of 'missing' the life which we had formerly
led, then it *is* a terrible tragedy. Similarly and for the same
reasons, if we would regard it as a tragedy if our own children
were to be born with such irrevocable brain damage that they
would be stuck with, say, a mental age of two years, and would
regard such an event as something to be avoided if at all possible,
then again we can see why such a condition is a real and terrible
affliction. And we can see this even though those so afflicted
cannot know that they are in any way disadvantaged or know
what they are missing.

Suppose that would-be parents could have a simple and risk-
free test which would show whether or not, were they to conceive,
their baby would be thus handicapped. If the test were positive
they could postpone pregnancy, undergo reliable treatment and
conceive a normal baby later. For someone to believe that the
condition we have described was not in any way a tragedy or a
handicap, they would have to accept that there was no reason at
all to have such a test, nor to postpone pregnancy if the test
proved positive.

Is it wrong to give birth to disadvantaged children?
In the case we have just imagined it seems right to postpone
pregnancy until the risk of disadvantage has been removed. But
suppose our imaginary parents discovered that, in their case, the
condition was irremediable and they could never have normal
children. Would their reasons for avoiding pregnancy then cease
to have any force? The answer would of course depend on the
expected level of handicap, but where the handicap was expected
to be severe, the reasons for thinking it better to avoid inflicting

such a handicap on individuals by bringing them into existence would remain.

There may then be many cases where it would be wrong knowingly to bring an individual into the world who would inevitably suffer an extremely severe handicap or other disadvantage. And our judgment that it would be wrong to bring such an individual into the world would not be shaken by our guess that were such a person to exist and be asked whether despite their terrible handicap they would judge their life to be preferable to no life at all, they might well prefer to go on living. It is one thing to contemplate the extinction of the life of someone who, despite terrible disadvantages, has formed plans and hopes for the future, has discovered ways of coping with a restricted life, and wants to live it. Quite another to decide gratuitously to *create* a life of pain and suffering.[13]

It is for this reason that it seems preferable to adopt as a test not what the disadvantaged person herself might be expected to say if asked whether, having started such a life and learned to cope with it, she would wish to go on living (or even is on balance pleased to have lived) but rather to ask what a compassionate parent ought to do or what a compassionate and moral society ought to think it right to have done.

Is it wrong to produce gifted children?

The corollary to our answer to the last question seems obvious enough and yet many would regard it as very wrong deliberately to set out to produce gifted children. The methods by which this might be achieved are growing steadily. For a long time eugenics appeared to be the only available method but new techniques have opened up the possibility of changing individuals by methods of genetic engineering and other ways of altering externally grown embryos.

The horror that the idea of super-beings usually provokes stems perhaps from its overtones of master-racism. But there is no reason why improvements to the human race as such, nor yet to individuals, should lead to a master-race at least in the sense of a group of beings with an interest in or a tendency towards enslaving or exterminating the rest. There is no evidence, for example, that those of our existing fellows whom most of us would regard as exceptionally gifted in one way or another show a greater tendency to megalomania than other people.

Eugenics seems unacceptable because it implies a policy of state or some other centralised selection of sexual or mating partners and the consequent restrictions on mating by those not officially matched. However, if individual couples choose to procreate on these grounds, it is not obvious that views about the ideal variety of offspring that might be produced are worse than other reasons for choosing a mate or having children.

Genetic engineering[14] is much more likely to produce effective ways of altering humankind and we would naturally want to scrutinise very carefully any proposed changes. But suppose it appeared possible to increase human intelligence, or slow down the ageing process by twenty years, or improve the circulatory system so that it was less prone to thrombosis, it would be difficult to imagine what might be wrong with so doing. Indeed, bearing in mind the argument of Chapter 2, to fail to make such improvements if they proved possible would be to take responsibility for the disadvantages that those born without benefit of such engineering would then have to endure. It would be like inventing antibiotics but declining to put them into production.

Again, I must emphasise that we would want to look very carefully at any proposed changes and be satisfied that they could indeed produce the expected results and would not carry with them unlooked-for and disastrous side-effects. But the same is true of any manipulation of the human body or mind, whether to existing people via accepted therapies, or whether to future people via genetic engineering.

Indeed, if we conclude that it is right to minimise the disadvantages that our children might be born with, then we must think it right to maximise advantages.

II Morally unsound parents

We, society, have never taken any care to scrutinise the suitability of natural parents for the role, while we have, on the other hand, for some time taken care to satisfy ourselves, as a society, that adoptive or foster parents be fit and proper persons to bring up children. This is strange enough, since if it matters that parents be fit and proper parents then it matters. Since the vast majority of parents are not in fact of the adoptive or foster variety, it seems extravagantly careless to regard this latter and numerically comparatively insignificant group as the only one needing to be properly vetted before being permitted to bring up children.

If, on the other hand, as evidenced by our actual practice, we think that it matters so little that natural parents be fit to be parents, then why do we pick on adoptive and foster parents and demand that they alone among parents establish their suitability in advance?

A consistent policy would either scrutinise all parents or none, it would either demand that even natural parents be examined in advance of conception and required to satisfy society that they, like adoptive and foster parents, were fit and proper candidates or, all parents would be allowed to have children first and only if they manifestly disqualified themselves later would their children be removed into the care of the community.

It is sometimes argued that the present mix of unbridled sexual parenthood and strictly controlled adoptive and foster parenthood, inconsistent though it is, constitutes the best available policy since we cannot as a matter of fact prevent people (let alone people judged to be undesirable or unsuitable) from procreating. This being the case, we should do as much as we can to see that children have proper and fit persons as parents and scrutinise only the potential parents of those children already in the community's care rather than attempting the impossible and trying to scrutinise all potential parents in the community.

But this is really a cop-out. It is no more impossible to attempt to prevent people from procreating illicitly than it is to attempt to prevent them from making whisky, or using drugs or avoiding tax illicitly. One can attach disincentives to the activity and penalise transgressors perhaps by taxation or some other financial disincentive. At the very least it would bring many more parents within the net of scrutiny. There are countries, for example, which are reasonably successful in preventing people from becoming parents before a particular age and in regulating the number of children born.[15]

There is much to be said for consistency here as in other areas of social policy, and before returning to the question of whether a policy of scrutinising all parents or one of scrutinising none would in fact be preferable, it is instructive to look at some moves that are being made in the direction of increasing the scrutiny of potential parents.

In the case of candidates for *in vitro* fertilisation, it is quite common for centres to require that candidates be either married or in a stable heterosexual relationship of at least three years standing before they will be considered for help.[16] Developments in medical technology have also highlighted a problem for homo-sexual parents and particularly for Lesbian mothers.[17] For while it has always been possible for gay women to have children in the normal way, techniques of artificial insemination and *in vitro* fer-tilisation have enabled such women to have their own children without any need for sexual intercourse with men.

Gay and single parents

Many people are disturbed by the idea of homosexual parents giving birth to and bringing up children either alone or in the context of homosexual rather than heterosexual relationships. Why this should be is entirely opaque. Many people object because they regard homosexuality as immoral and think that we should not permit those of morally unsound character to rear children. We shall see in Chapter 9 that there is absolutely no foundation for the view that there is anything immoral about homosexuality.[18] Moreover, any attempt to prevent Lesbian or in-deed single women from bearing and rearing children would wrong them in three important and separate ways.

Firstly and most importantly, anyone denied the opportunity to have children which they want to have is denied something almost universally acknowledged to be one of the most worth-while experiences and important benefits of life: in the woman's case the opportunity to become pregnant, give birth to and bring up children; in the man's, that of fathering and rearing his own children. To deny anyone this opportunity when they want it is to do them substantial wrong.

A second and separate wrong is done to people who are singled out as a class of second-class citizens or inferior beings, namely those deemed unfit to have children. For it to be known that gays or single people are not to be permitted to be candidates for *in vitro* fertilisation, artificial insemination or adoption is to label such people as unfit for one of the most important roles in life.

Finally, when and if such people do manage to have children despite society's very best endeavours to prevent them, they are usually subjected to more careful and conspicuous scrutiny than are more 'normal' parents. This again does them a separate, sig-nificant and identifiable wrong.

To subject an individual or group of people to these wrongs and injuries without the weightiest and clearest of justifications for so doing is clearly unjustifiable. I know of no evidence to show that homosexuals are or are likely to be worse parents than any other sort of person. Nor in the case of single parents is there any reason to suppose that the disadvantages for a child of being reared by a single parent approach anything like the significance or importance that would justify our preventing single people from rearing children. We do not, after all, compulsorily remove children from the care of a surviving parent when one partner has died. Nor do we, in the case of divorce or separation, award custody to third parties who are couples rather than to one (or both in turn) of the estranged partners.

To attempt to place restrictions on single or gay parents when it cannot be shown that there is anything morally wrong with being either single or gay and when there is no evidence that children are or might be disadvantaged by being reared by either group would clearly be without justification. The hypocrisy of so doing is, however, highlighted when we remember that no restrictions at all are put in the way of the vast majority of parents who do not need assistance with procreation.

One way in which we could remedy this imbalance would of course be to implement a policy of regulating all parents by screening would-be parents in advance.

Disadvantages of screening parents

A major problem in the way of screening all would-be parents, and perhaps licensing[19] only those judged fit and proper persons to be parents, is that we have no clear idea of what it takes to be a fit and proper parent. It may be easy to see that a particular child has been neglected or maltreated in some way but there is no clear evidence available as to the sort of person or types of people that are likely to neglect or mistreat their children. When general criteria are formulated they are often hopelessly unrealistic. A recent discussion of the problems facing a mentally handicapped pregnant girl concluded:

> here was an unsupported, mentally handicapped girl, who had become pregnant unwittingly, staying with an elderly couple in appalling housing conditions. Under those circumstances it seemed impossible that Mary would be able to look after her baby and it was likely that it would be taken into care.[20]

If appalling housing conditions, low intelligence and lack of support were established as general criteria for disqualifying parents the world would soon become depopulated. This might well be a good thing, but it would be so quite independently of any palpable deficiencies as parents in those who were thus disqualified.

If the screening of parents became a reality we might well want to examine an individual's reasons for wanting a child. What would be a good reason for having a child? It is difficult to think of reasons for having children commensurate with the importance and significance of the event itself. The prospect of creating another individual, helping him or her develop into a person and taking the responsibility for bringing that person into a world like ours is so massively momentous that the sorts of reasons parents usually have (or don't have) for doing such a thing seem pathetically inadequate. In our society it is more usual to ask people why they are not having children than to ask them why they are. However, if we assume that to be alive and to become a person is and will continue to be usually as good as to be a person is now, then perhaps *any* reason for having a child is a good reason. If this is so we have a further reason for placing no restrictions in the way of those people so generous as to undertake all the necessary labour and expense just so that another person might come to be.

A second major difficulty in the way of screening all potential parents would be the injustice of such a procedure. The injustice would be that of inflicting substantial punishments on people in advance and in lieu of their deserving them. We have examined the separate wrongs that would be done to people judged unfit to breed or to be parents. Those who failed the screening tests would be subjected to these disadvantages without having done anything to deserve them. This, coupled with the fact that we have no reliable ways of predicting which people or types of people might make bad parents, would make the injustice of operating such a scheme arguably worse than any cruelty to children its operation might be expected to prevent.

More practical arguments against a comprehensive system of parental control would be the undesirability of creating the massive apparatus of state-control that would be required for the operation of such a scheme and the difficulty of knowing how to cope with the likely persistent offenders who could not be further deterred by financial means.

All in all it seems far preferable to move towards a policy of permitting unrestricted parenthood and freely permitting artificial insemination and fertilisation as well as adoption and fostering and all types of surrogate motherhood in a context in which parents would be deprived of the custody of their children only if they severely mistreated or neglected them.

Two points remain to be considered. The first is the question of posthumous parents and the second is that of the commercial versus the altruistic use of the procedures we have been considering.

Posthumous parents

The possibilities we considered earlier of freezing and storing sperm and embryos make possible the birth of children long after one or both of their parents have died. The Warnock Committee feel that the possibility of a woman being inseminated with the sperm of her dead partner is one that should be actively discouraged.[21] Why this should be so is unclear. Warnock makes vague reference to the possibility of 'profound psychological problems for the child and the mother''[22] but does not consider the possibility of equally grave psychological problems for the mother if frustrated in her wish to bear her dead husband's child when she knows that his sperm is still 'alive' and could be used.

The motives for unfreezing and finding a surrogate for a frozen embryo, once both its genetic parents were dead, might be more suspect. If it was simply to be 'donated' to a mother who needed an embryo donation in order to have 'her own' child, there could be no objection. However, if it was used as a ploy to attach some part of the estate of the deceased parents we might be less sympathetic. Here it would be easy to prevent this by adopting and adapting Warnock's recommendations so that any child born following artificial insemination or embryo transfer that was not *in utero* at the time of the death of its last surviving genetic parent should be disregarded for the purposes of inheritance. This would have the added advantage of giving certainty to inheritance and succession.

Commerce versus altruism

I have argued that there is nothing necessarily wrong with the practice of womb leasing as opposed to lending and that the presence of some element of remuneration does not necessarily indicate that there is exploitation. We might, however, prefer to live in a society which operated with an ethic of altruism rather than of commercialism. The parallel that is usually drawn here is that of the merits of a non-commercial and volunteer blood transfusion service of the type operated in the United Kingdom over that of a commercial blood transfusion service as operated in the United States and elsewhere.

The merits of these rival ways of operating a blood transfusion service have been well examined elsewhere.[23] It is not clear, however, in the present case whether we are or would be in a position to choose between the commercial and the non-commercial approach to surrogacy. For while it is reasonable to suppose, and indeed experience has shown, that people would be quite willing to part with their blood and undergo the relatively simple and risk-free procedure involved in blood donation out of nothing more than the goodness of their hearts, it is less clear that a woman (or enough women) would be prepared to undergo pregnancy on those terms. So that if we were to permit only womb lending but not womb leasing we might effectively foreclose this option for most people. While, as we have seen, payment is not necessarily exploitative, it might be more likely to become so if vast sums lured otherwise unwilling mothers to undergo surrogate pregnancy. If we set statutory limits on the amount of money that could be paid for surrogacy we might reduce to vanishing point the chance of exploitation and also prevent this possibility from being put beyond the reach of the poorer candidates.

While the merits of the rival commercial and non-commercial schemes will doubtless continue to be debated, we can conclude that there is nothing *eo ipso* wrong with either womb leasing or lending whether for convenience or for more dramatic reasons and that we should be very clear about any alleged dangers or immorality before outlawing this or indeed any other new practice.

8 A woman's right to choose?

In the last chapter we considered many different types of parents and the issues surrounding whether or not it is possible to decide in advance who is fit to be a parent. The good reasons for rejecting a policy of screening all would-be parents in advance of their giving birth left open the way for people to choose freely whether to become parents. The decision was for each person to take herself, although of course this does not mean that there might not be very good reasons why particular parents should not judge that there were in their own case very good reasons why they should not in fact have children or have a particular child. We must now turn to the question of whether and when it is right to choose not to have children and then to some issues concerning other sorts of choice about what children to have.

I To be or not to be—a mother

It's my body
The women's campaign slogan 'a woman's right to choose' is nicely ambiguous. It seems to claim both that a woman has a right to choose and that she is right to do so. It is sometimes claimed that both this right and its rightness stem from the woman's ownership of her own body. She may abort her own foetus if she chooses, precisely because it is in a very real sense her own—to dispose of as she wishes. A prominent philosophical defence of this view claims, not implausibly, that 'if a human being has any just prior claim to anything at all, he has a just prior claim to his own body.'[1] This talk of 'prior claims' just means that the claim to ownership is not based on anything like sale or exchange but is the sort of claim from which all other sorts

of claim to ownership must stem. However, not all claims to ownership, even if they are undisputed *as* claims to ownership, carry with them the automatic right to dispose of the property in question in any way at all.

Suppose that I own a dose of a life-saving drug. I own it both in the sense that I bought and paid for everything that went into it, but also let's suppose because I invented it. It's been tested and proved and is now widely available. However, the only dose that can reach you in time to save your life is the one I own. I have nothing as important as saving a life in mind for this particular dose, but it is mine and I wish to keep it on my shelf rather than use it for saving your life. I don't suppose there will be many people who think, even without the arguments of Chapter 2, that I am morally entitled to keep the drug and sacrifice your life, whatever the legal position may or may not be.

Or, say I own a priceless painting, a fine work from a major master, or perhaps a fine old house, a unique example. May I burn either of these down if I choose? I may own them, but they are also public property in a sense, they are part of our culture; we, society, value them. I may be said to be more in the nature of a custodian or a guardian than an owner, despite my title deeds and receipts.

One way of characterising this tension is to say that while I have a right to keep my dose, or burn my painting if I choose, it would be wrong of me to exercise that right.[2] It could thus be the case that a woman had a right to choose, but that it would be wrong of her to exercise that right. However, given the sorts of thing at stake here, it does not seem plausible to claim that I have even a formal right to retain my dose of the life-saving drug in the circumstances described. It may be that the law is not sufficiently subtle to accommodate such cases, and that my legal title would remain intact; but it is difficult to retain any grasp on the idea that I might have any sort of a moral right to keep the dose at the cost of your life.

Of course the cases are not parallel with that of a pregnant woman claiming the right to do what she chooses with her body and everything that therein is, but they do show that we do not respect ownership as an absolute entitlement. The question in each case is: what is at stake if ownership is violated? Are the values of ownership more important than the values that would be threatened by an insistence on respect for ownership in this case?

Even the archest of conservatives and the most fierce defenders of private property are usually able to come to terms with the idea of, say, 'commandeering' property, both personal and real, but also lives themselves. When war or national interest are the justification, people and property are seized without ceremony. However, war and national interest, narrowly defined in military terms, are not the only causes in pursuit of which sacrifices, including sacrifices of property, may reasonably be demanded from citizens.

The point is simply that, even if the foetus were beyond a peradventure the property of its mother, she would only be entitled to do with it what she chose (and even end its life) if there were no independent grounds for valuing it more than as an item of her property. If the life of the foetus is valuable, then it should not be ended unless the reasons for so doing are more important than its life. The fact that someone has a claim to ownership is not a feature of comparable importance to the value of life. If a woman is right to choose, she is right not because she has a claim to ownership of the foetus, or because it is in her body, she is right because the moral reasons for respecting its life are less important than the moral reasons for respecting her decision to end its life.

Abortion and the concept of the person

A woman is in fact right to choose if she wants to. The rightness of this choice stems from our examination of the concept of the person in Chapter 1. The foetus is not a person and therefore cannot be wronged if its life is ended prematurely. It can of course be wronged in other ways, if it is caused any pain, for example. So that it is important to ensure that abortion is a painless process for the foetus. However, if this is done, then a woman may choose to have or not to have children freely, and may choose methods of contraception that are in fact methods of early abortion and she may also choose to have abortions much later in pregnancy. But are her wishes in this matter the only relevant ones? What of the wishes of the father of the foetus or of any other interested parties?

Who's right to choose?

We can now see that the fact that the foetus 'belongs' to, and is in the body of, a particular woman is not entirely irrelevant to the issue of the right to choose. It bears vitally on the question, not of the justification for abortion, but rather of *whose* wish for abortion, or whose wish not to abort, is relevant. If this woman wants an abortion, then it is her wish and her wish alone that has to be balanced against whatever value it is that the life of the foetus possesses. But it is one thing to conclude that it is the mother's wishes that are relevant to the issue of abortion, and quite another to conclude that they are decisive. It is this distinction that the slogan 'a woman's right to choose' conflates. When the distinction is made clear, we can see that a woman is only right to choose if the life of the foetus is judged sacrificeable to her choice. But why is it the choice of this woman, whose body and whose foetus it is, and this woman alone?

Father's liberation: an hypothesis?
Certainly the father of the foetus has an interest in its survival. The foetus shares his genetic make-up, and he may wish to have this foetus turn into a child and to bring it up. If we suppose that the father's views are to be taken into account, what follows? If he and the mother agree, of course there is no problem, and certainly he is entitled to make his views known. But suppose they disagree. If the father's wishes are at least as important as the mother's then perhaps we should spin a coin. And if they are more important, then his views should prevail. But in either case, if it is the wishes of the father that are to be operative, the consequences for the mother are grave indeed. She would presumably be forced to bear and give birth to a child she does not want, and have to endure the pain, inconvenience and risks of pregnancy and childbirth against her will. This would certainly constitute a grave physical assault upon the mother and her involuntary subjection to the risk of injury or even death. However much we can see that the father has a legitimate interest in the fate of the foetus, it would seem implausible to suppose that that interest was of an importance to justify such grave assaults upon the mother. And the same is of course true in the reverse circumstances in which a mother wanted to have her child and the father wanted an abortion. For his preference to prevail here would again involve a dangerous physical assault upon the mother. It would indeed be both a person and a society that had scant respect for women that could think of exposing her to such assault and danger against her will, and for the sake simply of another's wish to father children upon her.

Ultimately it is a question of rape. If a man is not entitled to violate a woman for the purposes of impregnating her, then he cannot violate her at a later stage, for the purposes of forcing her to give birth (or to abort). The suggestion that is often made, that by agreeing to sex with this man, or by agreeing to marriage with him, a woman tacitly agrees also to have his children, is irrelevant even if it were true. She may, and she is entitled to, change her mind. Suppose a woman enters into a solemn contract, drawn up by a lawyer, to have sexual intercourse with a man in nine months' time.[3] When the day comes she informs him that she has changed her mind. If he tries to enforce what the law calls 'specific performance' of the contract, it will be rape or attempted rape, and few would judge otherwise. Why people are tempted to think differently in the case of childbirth I cannot imagine—unless of course they judge that the wrong done to the foetus is greater than that done to the woman. But this judgment is, we have argued, implausible.

Contracts with embryos

A version of this argument is sometimes used to establish the impermissibility of abortion. The argument here is that by engaging in sexual intercourse a woman voluntarily engages in some risk of pregnancy however remote, because of the usual effectiveness or ineffectiveness of her method of contraception. If the remote chance occurs and she becomes pregnant, then the fact that it results from a voluntary decision on her part means that she is at least partially responsible for the existence of the foetus in the first place. Hence, since she is responsible for its being there to need her to carry it to term and nourish it, she has an obligation so to do.

Michael Tooley[4] suggests that her situation parallels the following sort of case:

> There is a pleasurable activity that I like to engage in. I know that in some cases this activity will have the unhappy side effect of destroying someone's food supply. This will not cause the person any discomfort provided that I supply him with food, which I can do, albeit at considerable trouble and expense. Now it seems to me that if I arrange things so that the probability that the activity will have the unfortunate effect is as small as possible, I am still responsible for the person's being in the situation of needing food on those few occasions when things go wrong, and thus am under an obligation to supply him with what he needs.[5]

If this is right, then only a concept of the person which can exclude the foetus *and* show why the foetus is of less value than the preferences of people, can rescue the mother from this sort of obligation. Indeed, the argument of Chapter 2 suggests that she might, save only for the argument of Chapter 1, have this responsibility even were she not partially responsible for the existence of the foetus!

The value of consistency

Those people who still do not accept the concept of the person developed in this book, or who are as yet unsure whether or not to accept it, will have severe problems about the justification of abortion.[6] If they hold that the life of the foetus is importantly valuable, two problems in particular will remain about the justification of abortion. The first concerns the problem of what follows from judging the foetus to be valuable.

If we remind ourselves that whatever value the embryo has (it may after all be only a few cells) derives not from what it is but rather from the fact that it has the potential to become a person, then one problem that we have already considered becomes clear—that if this is the source of its value, then we must value everything with that potential in that way—which means taking the same view of birth control as we take of abortion, and taking the same view of failure to procreate as we take of birth control! Moreover, since this view involves a clear moral imperative directing us to actualise all human potential, it also involves the sort of license for rape that we have just rejected.[7]

The second problem is more subtle. Those who reject abortion on the grounds of the value of the life of the foetus usually feel that exceptions should be made in a number of important cases. The chief among them are those methods of birth control that are effectively methods of very early abortion, like the coil and some contraceptive pills, which prevent implantation of the fertilised egg. Other exceptions include the permissibility of victims of rape being granted abortions as well as women whose own life or health would be at risk if they gave birth or continued their pregnancy. Finally, many who disapprove in general of abortion think that it is permissible to abort deformed or defective foetuses.

In the first three sorts of case it is clear that the factors which justify abortion have no effect at all on the moral status of the foetus. It cannot plausibly be claimed that the value of its life, whatever that value is, is in any way diminished by the fact that its mother has been raped, or is in danger, or has chosen a contraceptive method which gives it minimal life expectancy. What would be needed in these cases, and what is conspicuously absent, is an argument which could show how any of these factors affect the value of the life of the foetus. If it is valuable because it is human, it is no less human because its mother has been raped or because she is in danger. Of course we can understand why the victim of rape, or the woman whose life is literally threatened by her foetus, might not want to give it birth. But where is the argument that would show why these wants are suddenly more important than the life of the foetus, when in other cases equally strong desires to terminate pregnancy are not?

The case is only marginally different in the case of deformed or otherwise defective embryos. It seems that they might be less valuable because of the defects, but this is an illusion. If their value is that of other members of the human species, then they are none-the-less *that* for having some defects. We do not treat handicapped or injured adults, or even children, as if their very lives were of less value; and we would be wrong if we did. But this is of course because they are all equally beings capable of valuing their own lives. This factor is not available to bolster the argument of those who wish to distinguish defective embryos from sound ones, for it is a feature that they share. Again, what is needed is an argument that would account for the difference in the value of the embryo, and again this is conspicuously absent.

It is precisely because these distinctions cannot consistently be sustained that we are driven towards some overarching principle that will both explain and direct our intuitions. The concept of the person outlined in Chapter 1 attempts to do just this. Those who reject that view must find some other principle that explains and directs the distinctions they make between living beings. Those who find convincing the arguments for accepting that the life of the embryo is as important as any other life-form must reject all abortions and encourage all chances of conception.

The argument from vindictiveness

Those who wish to retain their view that abortions are wrong because of the value of the life of the embryo, but who wish to allow the exceptions we have been considering, should be worried about how these distinctions are to be explained. The most plausible explanation I have seen offered is that advanced by Janet

Radcliffe Richards. She argues that there is only one explanation that fits the facts:

> Since abortions are allowed in the case of rape, the foetus cannot be regarded as a full human being. If, then, pregnancy is forced on other unwilling mothers, it is not because the child is a human being whose life is sacrosanct. Why then are such mothers not automatically allowed to have abortions? One plausible explanation is that the child is being used as an instrument of punishment to the mother, and that talk of the sanctity of life is being used to disguise the fact.[8]

If we go on to ask what the mother is being punished for, Janet Radcliffe Richards has an answer to that too:

> It looks as though the only thing which the woman who conceives accidentally has done to differentiate herself from (other mothers) is to have indulged willingly in sex without being willing to bear a child. .... Can it be that you are morally right if you put up with sex if you see it as a means to an acceptable end (having a child) or if it is forced on you against your will, but not if you actually *want* it?[9]

Those who dislike this conclusion but who wish to maintain the distinctions which it explains, must find a more palatable explanation for their attitudes.

II Doing it my way

We have concentrated on the legitimacy of abortion and hence on the justifications for ending the life of the embryo. However, for those who want their children the important decision is not so much whether or not to have children—that decision has been taken—rather it is the decision about how, when, and where to have their child that is important. Childbirth is just one of very many areas of health care in which patients and clients find that their choices and preferences are effectively controlled by the professionals.

In pregnancy and childbirth this control may be pervasive indeed. From the numerous pre- and post-natal clinics and visits, to the circumstances of the birth itself, the control can be comprehensive. There has been an increasing demand by parents both for more freedom of choice in these matters and, particularly, for a less clinical and more personal environment in which to have children. Many mothers would prefer home delivery to the almost standard institutional delivery in industrialised nations. Many mothers would also prefer to exercise greater control over the manner and conditions of giving birth. They want to choose whether or not they are given drugs, or caesarians or have the birth of their baby induced. They don't want to be treated as patients, as in some way ill; they want to replace a clinical and sterile environment[10] with a warm, friendly and homely one.

What is against satisfying parental preferences in these matters? Those who have argued for hospital and 'high-tech' confinements have based their arguments on the belief that this is a safer form of obstetric practice. While this belief has been sharply challenged of late,[11] I do not want to enter this particular debate. Rather, let's assume for the sake of argument that what I call 'hospital high-tech' is incontrovertibly the safest method of giving birth in that it involves less risk to mother or baby than any proposed alternatives. Now this would be a good reason for parents to choose it. But they may have other priorities and be willing to accept less in the way of safety for more in the way of what might be called 'worthwhile experience'. If this is so, what is against their being permitted to exercise this choice?

The only argument against their being permitted to exercise free choice in this area is that they are either not entitled to risk their own lives or they are not entitled to risk the life of their baby. However, as we have seen, a mother is fully entitled to risk both of these if she chooses.

It should be not only respect for persons but also respect for the best standards of health care that indicate a responsiveness and sensitivity to the preferences of patients and clients. It is the professional's responsibility to know and advise patients and clients on the best ways to achieve what both desire, namely the promotion of health and the highest and safest standards of care. However, if patients have strong preferences for a style of care which is somewhat different to that favoured by the professionals, they will be able to decline treatment that is not in accord with their wishes and to make their own arrangements. It is in everyone's interests that a harmonious partnership be maintained between professionals and patients, and this can only be achieved on a basis of mutual respect. But, since it is not usually patients that are doing things to the professionals, the ultimate choice must lie with the patients as to whether or not they are prepared to accept what is offered.

III Final choice: the all-female world

We have seen that women's choice in the matter of child-bearing
is fairly comprehensive. They may freely choose to have or not to
have children and also very largely what sort of children to have.
One possibility of choice, remote as it may seem, will horrify
many and it is worth exploring both for what it tells us about the
proper limits of free choice for individuals, but also because of
the lessons we can learn from it about the limits of choice for a
society and perhaps even about the limits of choice for the world.

Suppose, taking up again the suggestion made in Chapter 6,
that methods of artificially inducing parthenogenesis in humans
were developed, so that women could reproduce easily without
any recourse to men, even for the donation of sperm. This would
create the possibility of a viable all-female society. This society
would be different, and not simply because of the absence of men.
It would not be like our own society with the men removed. For
one thing the females produced by this process would be near-
clones of their mothers, very alike genetically and so very alike
also in the noticeable respects—physical appearance, and probably also in ability and personality. However, we can also suppose
that techniques of genetic engineering have advanced sufficiently
for us to manipulate things so that greater diversity could be
obtained if that was desired.

Suppose, further, that these advances coincided with the resurgence of a particularly vigorous and militant feminism, a feminism which fervently believed that a good measure of the evils
of the world had been brought about both by the dominance of
men, and by the dominance of certain distinctively (though not
exclusively) male characteristics. Suppose they believed, as many
women do, that men were on the whole more egocentric, aggressive, competitive and intolerant than women, and that these
features made them in turn more violent, insensitive and perhaps
more callous. It might then seem a rational and progressive step
to attempt to create a society from which these disastrous characteristics, and the characters that possessed them, had been eliminated. It would not of course matter that these gender differences could be established beyond doubt, what would matter
would be (as we shall see in more detail shortly) that women on
the whole accepted the validity of these differences.

Suppose this resurgence of radical feminism was consequent
on, and perhaps partially prompted by, a series of catastrophies

or a gradual and severe worsening of the circumstances of life. Perhaps these catastrophies might be a series of wars or even civil wars or other internecine strife. Equally catastrophic might be the emergence of a society which was callous and unfeeling, in which survival depended on aggressive competitiveness and the ruthless exploitation of the weak, or of the populations of weaker societies. In this society weakness and vulnerability might have come to be thought of as self-inflicted wounds which lessons in self-sufficiency and self-reliance might remedy better than the cushions of social welfare legislation and emphasis on 'caring'. Here the weak going to the wall might be seen as a necessary condition for the future success of the society.[12]

Again the details of the sorts of social circumstances and history that might prompt, or appear to give substance to, the beliefs we are considering are not important to the argument. What matters for our purposes is that most women see the circumstances in which they find themselves as making both highly desirable and urgent the establishment of a radically new sort of society—a society in which the human defects that had led so apparently inexorably to disaster might be eliminated or at least minimised. It might well seem, both to feminists and perhaps to women generally, that it was men and male dominance that had brought these disasters to the world. If so, they might wish to create a society in which men had no part, not because, like women in the past, they would be relegated to the role of second-class citizens, but rather because they would simply not be there.

The rationale of this society might be the simple proposition that reform required not the development, acceptance and implementation of a new political and moral theory, but rather required a new type of citizen. And the society which produced such citizens would be founded on and embody, not a political so much as, say, a eugenic theory.

This might not be so bizarre or so crazy a view as might at first appear. One of the fears most commonly expressed about attempts to change the human personality by genetic engineering, so that more desirable features would become dominant is simply that we cannot predict what other undesirable changes would be consequent on such an attempt. This fear, particularly, characterised much of the discussion about the desirability of eliminating aggression from the human psyche. It was pointed out that, while aggression was undesirable, it might not be possible to eliminate such an emotion without also destroying the basis of other more desirable emotions, such as love. What would love be like if it did not involve some aggression towards anyone or anything that would destroy our loved ones, for example?[13] Now in proposing an all-female society, we would not be faced with quite the same problems. For one thing we know what women are like—we would not be contemplating the creation of new or radically altered human beings, merely the elimination of men.[14]

This knowledge of what women are like would give women a good reason to think that an all-female society would be an improvement, at least against the background of the social circumstances we have imagined. Feminists certainly might think, and feel justified in thinking, that the reduced aggressiveness and competitiveness which characterises females generally, gives good reason to hope and expect that a society of women would be able to manage affairs without creating the disastrous features of the society they wished to escape. Of course such a society would have its drawbacks. We may, however, be inclined to exaggerate these. The first and most obvious disadvantage is that the men wouldn't like it (which invites the obvious, and not entirely frivolous, retort, that the men aren't going to get it!). It is whether or not the women would like it that is the question at issue. I would like to think that they would miss us, and find the prospect of a society and a life without men wholly unappealing. But I wouldn't want to bet my life on it. Certainly women would in the future have to face the prospect of adapting their sexuality, and their breeding and child-rearing patterns, to substantially altered circumstances. But they might, and we'll suppose they will, find the prospect of the gains more alluring than the prospect of the losses is fearful, that what they'll lose on the swings is more than compensated for by the gains on the roundabouts.

Part of the viability of the emergence of an all-female society will depend on the way it is to be achieved. It would be hard to claim that the brave new world that would not have such people in it would have a good claim to the moral progress it was designed to achieve if it could only be brought about literally over the dead bodies of men. Let's imagine one way in which the women in our imagined circumstances might go about planning the creation of their new society. Let's also suppose that they are convinced and agreed that if a morally respectable plan can be worked out they will implement it.

The plan

First let's suppose that the women in our imagined society are as
sensitive, generous and morally scrupulous as their ideals lead us
to expect. They believe that the transition should be gradual, and
as painless to men (but not of course to male egos) as it is possible
to make it. They resolve that the best way of achieving the new
society is simply to let men gradually die out. Until they become
extinct through non-replacement, the women will go on treating
them exactly as before. They will continue to associate with men
on the same basis, everything will be as it was, except that women
will resolutely refuse to allow children to be born other than by
artificial parthenogenesis. In the transition period men will
initially notice no change. The women, being both exceptionally
resolute and exceptionally kind-hearted,[15] agree to maintain their
existing relationships with men and further agree that men can
go on ruling and managing and dominating and so on to their
hearts' content. There's no reason why the women should not, if
they wish, continue to sleep with men, and being kind-hearted
perhaps they will (as a sort of consolation prize awarded to men
to help them bear the thought of their final redundancy?). In this
way their plan will not be in any way dependent on the goodwill
of men. Men can do everything they used to do except father
children. And of course they never had a moral nor yet even a
legal right to do this against the wishes of women. In this respect
also things will be as they always were.

One problem in particular troubles the deliberations of the
council of women, who are charged with the evolution of the plan
for transition to the new society. That is the question of whether
they have an obligation to ensure that there be as many citizens
in the new society as there were in the old. Certainly they are
anxious that the benefits of the new society be enjoyed by as many
as possible. They are also anxious that their proposal does not
lose some of its moral force by being open to the charge that as
a consequence of its implementation fewer people who might have
lived happy and useful lives will be born. For this reason they
agree to maintain or even increase upon existing population levels
in the society. In this way, no one can say that the world will
contain fewer people whose lives will be worthwhile as a result of
their policy.

Of course the people born into the new society will not be the
same ones that would have been born had the idea never been

floated, but this will be true of any society in which people vary their breeding habits from generation to generation. If, for example, people begin to breed later rather than sooner, then the children born will not be those who would have been born had this change not taken place. And of course choices of partner and of month of conception also create different people than those who would have been born had these factors been different.

As men die out and the feminist millennium approaches, women will gradually take over all positions previously occupied by men. Traditional family life will change. It may cease altogether and be replaced by collective child-rearing and extended families. Some women will certainly set up homosexual partnerships, and rear children in the traditional two-'parent' unit. Some others will find the possibility of having children without sexual relationships a distinct plus. Others presumably will find the loss of heterosexual relationships a severe source of unhappiness. However, all agree that this prospect, however bleak, is distinctly preferable to the alternative, the old male-dominated and disaster-prone society, and agree that the prospective gains are well worth the foreseen losses.

The new society would of course have to close its frontiers to men, but many relatively closed societies have existed and continue to exist without severe difficulty. However, and of course, the ultimate aim of the women in our imagined society would be to persuade their sisters of the advantages of the scheme and to aim for an all-female world.

The all-female world

This could be achieved in the same way and for the same reasons as the all-female society. Indeed it would have to be the ultimate aim if international as well as internecine warfare were to be eliminated. The women of the world might of course want to put out a safety net in case their prognosis proved doubtful, and the new world proved to be not quite so brave as they had hoped. This they might do by 'banking' large quantities of sperm or even large numbers of male embryos achieved by *in vitro* fertilisation in the transition period.

Suppose that interplanetary travel eventually revealed to us a world very much like our own, inhabited by beings of one gender who reproduced parthenogenetically. Suppose further that they were very like female human beings. If their world proved to be one in which wars and violence were unknown, in which the people co-existed without the need for competition and aggression and were reasonably happy and contented into the bargain, it is not obvious that we would find their world wholly deplorable nor manifestly inferior to our own. If on further enquiry we found that they did have pleasurable physical, as well as emotional, relationships with one another, we might well even come to admire their world and wish, wistfully, that we were able to emulate it. It might well be not unreasonable or fanciful to conclude that the gains might well be worth the losses, if only we could repeat the experiment here.

Why not do so?

There is no doubt that the all-female world would be a drastic attempted solution to our problems. But perhaps drastic solutions are required. Even without the recent history of specific disasters that we have imagined as giving rise to the resurgence of the very radical feminism which motivates the all-female world, something drastic is needed. Advocating the serious consideration of genetic engineering or other bio-technological manipulation of the human make-up, Jonathan Glover recently reminded us that:

> Our emotional and imaginative limitations are especially apparent when we consider the psychology of war. We all know how here our technology has grown faster than we have. It is not clear that we will survive at all. Our arrangements for avoiding war are so flimsy, and we have not yet developed the sense or urgency appropriate to our precarious position.[16]

This same precariousness, in which we stand between balance of terror and complete annihilation, might lead even rational men to judge that the all-female world is infinitely preferable to no world at all. Particularly when the prognosis for peace in such a world is at least as good, and in many ways far less problematic, than would be the prognosis consequent on bio-technological manipulation.

One feature of the all-female world that renders the prospect of it unattractive to many is the reduction in human variety that it would involve. Here again, it is true that all varieties of men would be missing, but there is no reason to suppose that the variegation of females could not eventually make up for this. Again, the loss of variety might well be less than would be consequent upon attempts to remove the defects in sympathy and imagination that make disaster so probable.

For myself, I would like to find a way of preserving mankind (in the post-feminist understanding of that term). I am not fully convinced that women, left to themselves, would not prove to be as disastrously aggressive as men. And I am fully convinced that a world in which men and women found a way of living peacefully and non-exploitatively together would be vastly preferable to the all-female world, even if that were also peaceful and non-exploitative. However, I am not so much concerned here with what we should do to make our species less disaster-prone, though I am clear that we should try to do *something*. What I want to consider is whether there are any good moral reasons for preventing the realisation of the all-female world if women become and remain convinced that that is the best chance for avoiding the disasters that are consequent upon defects in the human personality and in preventing the ultimate catastrophe of nuclear war.

Suppose all women decide that they'd like to realise the all-female world, would men be right to try to stop them?

The final solution

Well, men would certainly be right to try to *persuade* women against taking so drastic a step. And the shock that the prospect of such a step would give men might of itself have a very salutary effect on their complacency.[17] However, the shock might equally well drive men to a different extreme. If persuasion failed, would men be justified in *preventing* the realisation of the all-female world?

It should be clear that the only way in which this could certainly be achieved would be either by rape or by the forcible prevention of abortion in a case where a pregnancy had accidentally resulted from voluntary sexual relations in the transition period. The question we must ask is, is it so certain that the all-female world would be a disaster of such proportions that rape would be justified in order to prevent it? I assume that rape could in theory be justified if it was the only way to prevent a much greater evil, just as killing and even murder could be similarly justified.

Although the female world would be a disaster for men, it is far from clear that it would be a disaster for humankind. Moreover, it would not be a disaster for any man now living if the transition arrangements we have discussed were adhered to. No man would have his own life threatened, each would live on as before, the principal difference would be that no man would be a father. This, while a genuine tragedy for many, would not be a disaster of the order of magnitude that would justify rape as a method of redeeming the situation.[18] For men have never had a right to father children nor to produce heirs for themselves at such a cost.[19] While their preference might well be, and might well rationally be, for the continuance of a mixed world, the disadvantages and dangers of the alternative would hardly be such as to justify the only effective method of preventing its occurrence.

A woman's right to choose?

The chances of all women uniting on any issue, let alone uniting on the issue of an all-female world, may be remote.[20] Whether we should heave an immense sigh of relief that this is so or whether we should treat it as a matter for profound regret seems to me to be less clear. Consideration of this radical possibility, however, serves to remind us of three important things.

The first is that if we can find no reasons adequate to persuade us that we are entitled to resist the all-female society, how much less can we object to parents choosing the sex of their own children if this becomes possible and it is what they wish to do.

The second is that medical science has always and will continue to open up new, exciting and daunting possibilities for us and our world. The control of these possibilities belongs to us all, and the wider the consideration and discussion of how to use them for the best, the safer we will all be.

The final important fact to bear in mind is that medical science and the professionals who employ its products are not simply in the business of restoring and preserving our health. Many of the things they do can and do profoundly affect the course of individuals' lives and indeed the nature of society and of the world. In addition to the dimensions of such influence with which we are familiar, new techniques will increasingly make possible the changing of our very nature and consequently of the nature of human destiny. This power is ours to use or not as we choose. If we are to survive the dangers brought about by similarly dramatic progress in our capacity to destroy ourselves and our world, it may be very important to use these techniques sooner rather than later.

9 Sexual morality and the natural

Immorality and sex have enjoyed a long and intimate relationship and they are now as hotly and as frequently conjoined as ever they were. But is this coupling permissible? When moral standards become an issue or when examples of immorality are sought it is often sexual practices, or the publicity of sexual practices, that occupy the centre of the stage. A newspaper headline announcing 'doctor struck off for immoral conduct' promises sexual revelations, and even parliament,[1] when speaking of 'immoral conduct', assumes this conduct to be sexual. Popular appeal keeps these issues in the permanent repertoire of our moral concern; but are there any good reasons why 'sex' should be employed in the legitimate moral theatre? In short, is there such a thing as sexual morality?

The answer to this question is of more than prurient interest, since a number of very important areas of social policy as well as of medical practice presuppose the existence of such a morality. First, the general criminal law legislates against a large range of sexual behaviour which could not possibly be regarded as wrongful, unless it was accepted that there were good grounds for regarding the behaviour as seriously immoral. Sodomy or buggery, for example, between a consenting man and woman, including a husband and wife, is a crime punishable by lffe imprisonment in the United Kingdom.

In education, sex education is widely accepted as a part (perhaps the most important part) of moral education, and parents expect standards of sexual morality to be upheld and communicated in schools. In public life, officials and celebrities of various sorts are expected to uphold standards of sexual morality by avoiding sexual practices and liaisons common in society at large.

Nearer to our present concerns, there is a wide range of areas and of practices which presuppose the existence of such a morality. We have already noticed the 'moral' disapproval of and objections to homosexual parents, and seen that assumptions about the morality of the gay life can lead to restrictions being placed on the freedom of gay people to procreate and to bring up children. In the field of provision for, and care of, the mentally and physically handicapped, moral judgments about sexuality are no less important. Many handicapped people are effectively prevented from having any sex life at all, when those on whom they depend think that morality requires that masturbation, 'petting' and other sexual contact be prevented or discouraged. The same result is also achieved when no special provision for sexual contact, or education in methods of achieving it, is made. If it were clear that sex has nothing to do with morality many of the supposed reasons for such restrictions would disappear.[2]

In this chapter I want to try to kill two related birds with one line of argument. I want to show that there is no such thing as sexual morality and, in doing so, to demolish the very tenacious idea that there is something good, or at least morally respectable, about things or practices or even inclinations that can be thought of as being, in some sense, natural. And likewise the corollary, that there is something bad about things unnatural or perverted.

Although it will, I hope, be by now clear that the whole practice of medicine is dedicated to frustrating and corrupting the ordinary course of nature at every turn, the idea that the natural is somehow none-the-less a virtue is hard to eradicate. Because it is perhaps buried deepest in our assumptions about sex, I have reserved until now a more detailed look at this troublesome idea.

Sexual morality

To ask whether there is any such thing as sexual morality seems itself somewhat perverse, since we all know that there is. Certainly there is, if what is meant is a set of rules or social norms governing sexual behaviour and its protrayal. But our question is quite simply whether these rules are *moral* rules or merely legislated prejudice. So that to take our question seriously is to ask whether there is anything about sex or about particular sexual practices which is wrong because of the nature of sex itself, or because of something about the sexuality of the practices. We cannot give an affirmative answer to our question merely because some sexual acts have features which would make them immoral even if they had no sexual element in them at all. For example, rape would be a paradigm of an immoral act which involves a sexual element. But rape is immoral because it has features that would make any act at all which involved those features immoral quite regardless of whether it contained any sexual element. The immorality of rape derives from its involving assault, violation, the unwanted and involuntary infliction of distressing bodily contact, and possibly of fear, pain and humiliation. It may also involve a real danger to the victim's physical and mental health, and to her prospects of future happiness. These features would make any practice which involved them immoral, whether or not it also involved sex in some way.

If we now contrast rape with a whole range of sexual practices commonly thought to be immoral, a clear distinction emerges. For these practices are regarded as immoral even though they contain no elements which would be immoral if they were not also sexual.

For example, buggery between consenting adults including husbands and wives, sexual acts with inanimate objects (fetishism) or with animals (bestiality) or with dead bodies (necrophilia) are all commonly regarded as immoral, although one is hard put to say what is wrong with them except that they are acts of buggery, fetishism, bestiality, or necrophilia.

If we assume, for example, that the animals either enjoy themselves or do not find sex more repulsive than other human contact that they have, the only thing wrong with bestiality would be any possibly harmful effects on the human agent. I know of no evidence for the harmful effects of bestiality, but any that there may be would have to be worse than depriving animal lovers of sexual release and also worse than the many things (like smoking) that we permit human beings to do to themselves without significant restraint.

If we assume, on the other hand, that animals do not much like sex with humans, we must still ask whether a rational animal would find sex preferable to the standard alternative, which is to be caged, murdered and eaten. It is difficult to see a moral objection to bestiality from non-vegetarians which does not attach exclusively to the fact that the relationship in question is sexual rather than culinary. And we can safely disregard the moral sensibilities of shoes or other fetish objects. Moral objections to bestiality and fetishism tend to remain even where we can rule out any features of these practices that would make them what we

might call straightforwardly immoral; and where we can also rule
out straightforwardly immoral side-effects.

The same is true of that most reviled of all sexual practices,
necrophilia. What is most striking about reactions to these sorts
of practices is that the revulsion, and with it the sense of immorality, linger persistently even when there is nothing about the
practice that would make it immoral according to our usual criteria. Reflecting on our reasons for judging necrophilia immoral
we might well at first assume that even if the 'victim' dies of
'natural' causes (that is, was not murdered by the necrophiliac)
he or she would almost certainly not have wished his or her body
to be used for someone else's bizarre sexual gratification. We may
also confidently assume that relatives and friends of the deceased
would also be appalled by the idea. But all these features are
harmful side-effects of necrophilia since they are detachable.
What if the deceased wanted to help a lonely necrophiliac after
death and had bequeathed his or her body to be donated to 'nec-
rophiliacs anonymous' and had either no relatives, or no relatives
who would hear about the bequest? Most people who disapprove
of necrophilia, and believe they have moral grounds for their
disapproval, would be unmoved by the removal of the side-
effects. Their confidence in the immorality of necrophilia would
be undiminished. So what's so wrong with necrophilia? Well
clearly it's perverted, unnatural, obscene and disgusting.

Obscenity and disgust

We will not need to spend too long on obscenity and disgust.
Although many people are inclined to raise strong objections to
behaviour they regard as obscene and disgusting this is no evidence at all for its immorality. The mere fact that people strongly
object is of course no reason to come to any conclusion about the
morality of the object of their objections despite Lord Devlin's
strong views to the contrary.[3] Many things may disgust us that are
in no way immoral. We find the sight of an incontinent geriatric
disgusting where no questions of morality arise. We might also
be disgusted by the behaviour of the female jumping spider who
devours her mate after copulation, without making any judgment
about the morality of the reproduction of spiders, or about their
diet.

Obscenity is slightly more complex. It is defined in terms of
offence, either to modesty or decency or to the senses or the mind.[4]
Offence, like disgust, is of itself no evidence of immorality. We

may take offence at all sorts of thing, like deserved criticism, or accurate descriptions of our person or behaviour, which cut no moral ice at all. In terms of our present preoccupation with sexual morality, it is offence against modesty and decency which concerns us. Again it is unclear that indecent behaviour (or gestures) are in any sense immoral although they may be *impolite*. Indecency and modesty have much more to do with etiquette[5] than with morality and, while standards of decency may concern us greatly, even to the point where we wish to regulate them strictly, they are not, in the absence of an argument, *eo ipso* also standards of morality. One example must suffice. If I walk naked in the street or upon Brighton beach, my behaviour may be indecent (exposure?) but it is not immoral. No one is harmed by it, the fabric and structure of society are not threatened, and even quite young children will survive the experience undamaged, unless intimidated by the reactions of other adults. No violation of rights, breach of duty or trust is involved; so unless this behaviour can be shown to be perverted or unnatural, and unless these categories can be given moral content, then whatever objections you may have to my behaviour (aesthetic?) they are not moral objections.

Respecting norms and respecting other people

It is sometimes argued that there is a general moral obligation to respect the norms of one's own society, and that since there are clearly norms against behaviour that is obscene and disgusting, our duty to avoid the violation of society's norms requires us to abjure such behaviour. The immorality of indulging in such behaviour would thus be either simply the immorality of violating the norms of society or, more subtly, the immorality of failing to respect those people who share the norms. In this latter case the immorality would be that of failing to respect other people by flouting the norms they accept.

There are norms and norms. If the norms in question are moral norms, then the reasons we have for not flouting them are moral reasons and we should accept those reasons because we ought to act morally. However, behaviour, or dispositions to behaviour, is not immoral simply because it is obscene and disgusting, and in the case of the behaviour with which we are concerned, unless it can be shown to be perverted or unnatural and unless such categories can be given moral content, it will be impossible to convict fetishism and the like of immorality. Anticipating the argument to come, if it is, as I believe it to be, quite impossible to convict the practices themselves of any moral wrong, then any remaining claim that there are nevertheless moral reasons for respecting norms against such things must show either that the practices have immoral side-effects, or that there are moral reasons for respecting the prejudices or preferences of those who object to such practices.

To take the latter possibility first, when we are contemplating the enforcement of norms which prevent people, albeit a small minority in this case, from doing something which cannot be shown to be in any way harmful or immoral, simply on the grounds that others object, and that their objections should be respected, we must ask whether there are in fact good reasons to respect their objections. When no damage, danger, harm or other immorality can be shown to flow from the practice, objections to it must either be sheer prejudice, irrational and arbitrary, or they must be (more politely) matters of personal taste and preference. We must also remember that it is a central part of the morality which we all share that prejudices or irrational beliefs of one section of the community should not be forced upon other sections on such grounds alone. The claim that there could be any moral obligation to respect a rule that purported to do such a thing is entirely without foundation.

It is sometimes argued that the norm is required because the reverse is in fact the case, that the minority of sexual 'perverts' are attempting to impose their preferences and prejudices upon the 'decent' majority. Here we should remember that we are talking about the legitimacy of pursuing such practices and preferences in private, where no question of their being foisted on an unwilling majority arises. Nobody talks of respecting the norms against defecation or married-lovemaking, although we might well object to either taking place in public.

The alternative, that the practices in question have immoral side-effects, must I think reduce to the claim that they are harmful to society, and that norms against them are required either to prevent such harm or because they define some ideal conception of society which cannot be realised, let alone approached if such norms are flouted.

There seems to be no more evidence that these unpopular practices would damage society than there is that they might damage their devotees in some way. Claims (or hopes?) that such evidence will emerge must, in the absence of any evidence, be treated with suspicion. Of course society would be different if such practices were permitted. For one thing it would be that much more tolerant a society than it is at the moment. But society cannot claim any general right to insulate itself against all change, including change that a majority regards as change for the worse, when such change can only be prevented at a high moral cost—the cost of suppressing the innocent (though unsavoury?) sexual preferences of a minority. Indeed, we can ask whether a society which permits such suppression can indeed claim to be a better society than its more tolerant alternative.

Perhaps a society which contains people who indulge in such practices is less attractive than one which does not. And those who practise such perversions may have more unsatisfactory lives than those who do not. These are points to which we will return. But it is a long way from these rather mild claims to one which would outlaw such practices on the grounds that their acceptance would damage society's self-image. For one thing society does not have to approve of or even find them acceptable, it must simply recognise that, while perhaps unattractive and unsatisfactory, they are in no way wrong and there is no justification for their prohibition.

Indeed, society can maintain norms against such practices if it wishes. But these must be norms of the same sort as those against a dirty appearance and bad table manners. We don't have to approve of such things, or associate with those who do. What we do have to do is recognise that they are in no way immoral and that people who prefer to live with such practices owe us no more respect than we owe them.

We must now turn to the related categories of the perverse and the unnatural, and ask what moral significance attaches to behaviour in either of these categories. To do so we will look in some detail at some recent philosophical work on these twin categories which sheds light on many of the assumptions made in health care.

Perversion and the unnatural

One of the most interesting of the many recent attempts to grapple with this problem is Tom Nagel's essay on 'Sexual Perversion' [6] Nagel begins by outlining the general conditions that any concept of perversion would have to meet.

First, if there are any sexual perversions, they will have to be sexual desires or practices that are in some sense unnatural, though the explanation of this natural/unnatural distinction is of course the main problem.

Second, certain practices will be perversions if anything is, such as shoe fetishism, bestiality and sadism; other practices, such as unadorned sexual intercourse will not be; about still others there is controversy.

Third, if there are perversions, they will be unnatural sexual *inclinations* rather than just unnatural practices adopted not from inclination but for other reasons. Thus contraception, even if it is thought to be a deliberate perversion of the sexual and reproductive functions, cannot be significantly described as a *sexual* perversion. ... And although there might be a form of fetishism focused on the employment of contraceptive devices, this is not the usual explanation for their use.[7]

While Nagel's third condition solves the problem of contraception, his placing all the weight of his account on inclinations rather than on actions has equally unsatisfactory consequences. On this view, prostitutes or actors indulging in 'perversions' not from inclination but for money or to make a dramatic point[8] would, however perverse their practices, not be involved in perversions and no unnatural acts would have occurred.

There are two main problems with Nagel's account. The first is that despite his clear statement that the natural/unnatural distinction is the main problem, he goes almost no way to elucidating this distinction. The second is that the positive account that he offers of perversion, while subtle and interesting, gives perversion only partial, and ultimately very limited, moral content. Nagel is aware of this and seems content to provide an understanding of the idea of perversion and of why such a term might be a useful way of thinking about sexuality. It is very important to be clear, however, that despite the seductiveness and originality of Nagel's account, it does ultimately fail to give us any but the most limited and circumscribed of reasons for moral disapproval of perversions.

The account Nagel offers of the perverse focusses on an ideal of interpersonal relationships as involving a multi-layered 'reciprocal interpersonal sexual awareness'[9] which would typically involve 'a desire that one's partner be aroused by the recognition of one's desire that he or she be aroused'.[10] This is the requirement that in sex we do not treat our partners as sexual objects merely but as *partners*, the arousal and satisfaction of whose desires is as important as our own. Nagel's account is psychologically rich because it notes the way arousal breeds arousal and desire feeds on desire. Its moral content, though, is the simple Kantian imperative not to treat people merely as means but as ends in themselves. This is fine for interpersonal sex and gives a reason for thinking sexual practices which obey this imperative are morally preferable. However, it does not show why non-interpersonal sex, fetishism, bestiality and necrophilia, for example, are in any way immoral. For this we must rely on the natural/unnatural distinction drawn in such a way as to show why these are unnatural and also in a way that gives the distinction moral content.

Nagel suggests an account of this distinction, despite its acknowledged importance, in only the sketchiest of terms. He says: 'But if humans will tend to develop some version of reciprocal interpersonal sexual awareness unless prevented, then cases of blockage can be called unnatural or perverted.'[11] 'Blockage' here means 'that a normal sexual development has been turned aside by distorting influences'[12] and that any 'interference with the development of a capacity that is there potentially' will be unnatural and hence perverse. The plausibility of Nagel's account rests on our independent moral preference for 'reciprocal interpersonal sexual awareness'. I say 'independent', because this approval has nothing to do with the fact that it is *sexual* awareness of which we are speaking nor that such awareness is in some sense natural or unperverted. We approve of it because we accept that people should not be treated as objects merely. This is clear when we reflect that there are many things that human beings normally 'tend to develop', like heart disease, the common cold, a capacity for racial hatred and for war, which may well be 'natural' in some sense, but the blocking or distorting of which would not be regarded as perverse. Indeed, even if we confine our reflections to matters sexual the evidence such as it is would seem to confirm that men at least have a natural tendency to develop the capacity to treat women as mere sexual objects unless this tendency is blocked by some distorting influence like women's liberation.

Sarah Ruddick, in her reply to Nagel's arguments, finds no difficulty at all with the definition of the unnatural.

> The *ground* for classifying sexual acts into the natural and unnatural is that the former serve or could serve the evolutionary and biological function of sexuality—viz., reproduction. 'Natural'

> sexual desire has as its object living persons of the opposite sex
> and in particular their postpubertal genitals. The 'aim' of 'natural'
> sexual desire—that is, the act that 'naturally' completes it—is gen-
> ital intercourse. Perverse sex acts are deviations from the 'natural'
> object (for example, homosexuality, fetishism) or from the standard
> aim (for example, voyeurism, sadism). Among the variety of ob-
> jects and aims of sexual desire, I can see no other ground for
> selecting some as natural, except that they are of the type that can
> lead to reproduction.[13]

We should be clear at once that Ruddick does not attach any
moral importance[14] to the distinction between the natural and the
perverse. However and for the record, her way of drawing the
distinction creates more problems than it solves. Firstly, if the
question of whether or not sexual acts could lead to reproduction
is a question of fact, then sex with contraception, or in periods
other than of ovulation or between the sterile or the sterilised
could not in fact serve the interests of, or lead to, reproduction.
Ruddick is aware of this and insists that the important point is
that sexual desire is natural if 'it could lead to reproduction in
normal physiological circumstances'.[15] Whether normal physiological circumstances are such as to allow us to judge that sex in
such circumstances could lead to reproduction is doubtful. If we
bear in mind the comparatively short period of ovulation in any
cycle, combined with the chances of sex during such period actually leading to reproduction (when we know that around 70 per
cent of conceptions do not result in a live birth and it is unclear
what percentage of copulations result in conception) it begins to
seem eccentric to regard *normal* physiological conditions as of a
kind that could lead to reproduction. It is surely the *abnormal*
circumstances that lead to reproduction.

The corollary to Ruddick's position is even more eccentric. She
would have to regard as a natural sexual experience male masturbation followed by collection of semen which was then used to
fertilise, in a dish, an egg that had been collected by catheter from
the womb and that was subsequently implanted in the uterus of
a different woman who was unconnected with the donor of the
sperm. This, like rape, would be natural because in Ruddick's
sense of normal physiological circumstances it *could* lead to reproduction.

Although as we have noted, Ruddick does not believe that there
is much in the way of moral significance attached to the perverse,
she does think that there is some importance to maintaining the

idea of sexual morality. Before looking at what sexual morality might be founded on if not the natural/unnatural distinction, we must examine a recent and determined attempt to re-establish perversion and the unnatural as moral categories. Donald Levy[16] suggests 'that an unnatural act is one that denies a person (oneself or another) one or more of these basic goods without necessity, that is without having to do so in order to prevent losing some other basic human good.'[17] The basic goods Levy believes can be exhaustively defined as those goods which will be 'desired no matter whatever else will, insofar as they are necessary for the getting of any other human goods'.[18] Levy suggests that a 'rather complete' list of such goods is the following: 'life, health, control of one's bodily and psychic functions, the capacity for knowledge and love'.[19]

According to Levy perversions are a sub-class of the unnatural and can be identified as follows:

> When a person denies himself or another one of the basic human goods (or the capacity for it) and no other basic human good is seen as resulting thereby, and when pleasure is the motive of the denial, the act is perverted. When the pleasure is sexual, the perversion is sexual. It should be clear from this definition of perversion that pleasure is assumed not to be a basic human good. First because one can have too much of it—to see this consider the case of a person hooked up to a machine stimulating the pleasure center of the brain. Suppose he were unwilling to disconnect himself even long enough to obtain food and sustain life. He would have died for a bit of extra pleasure.[20]

Levy's arguments have two fatal flaws. The first is that his arguments for pleasure not being a basic good as he uses this term are inadequate. Levy's argument seems to be that pleasure can't be a basic good because you can have too much of it, the evidence being that too much is self-destructive as in his illustration above. But at least one of Levy's basic goods is also like this, namely love, and the same sort of evidence might be adduced. If I love someone so much that I can't bear to live without them and when they die I either pine away or kill myself, then it looks as though I did have too much love, in Levy's terms at least.[21] Levy's second argument against pleasure as a basic good is that 'a person can seek to minimize human pleasure quite generally (perhaps as an obstacle to the maximization of knowledge or other basic goods) without casting his humanity into doubt—a rather extreme puritan might illustrate this.'[22] Levy had earlier suggested that one way of identifying basic goods was as those which could be disvalued only by a non-human. But it's far from clear that someone could not seek to reduce human knowledge quite generally, perhaps because he thought it dangerous to life, seeing the hydrogen bomb as a product of too much knowledge. It's not obvious that such a person would be more inhuman or more dangerous than the extreme puritan.

The reason why it's important for Levy that pleasure be not a basic good is that one is permitted to deny oneself or another a basic good only if one thereby makes possible the enjoyment of another such good. But since pleasure is the motive of most perversions, and perversions are defined as the denial of basic goods without promotion of others, then if pleasure is a basic good there are no perversions at all.

The second flaw fatal to Levy's argument is that few of the acts or dispositions that most people, including Levy, would want to call sexual perversions do in fact constitute a denial either to the agent or others, of any of the basic goods. It is not clear that the fetishist, or the necrophiliac or the animal lover, for example, damage any basic goods either for themselves or for others. Their health, intelligence, capacity for love and control of bodily and psychic functions may be unimpaired—it's just the case that in addition to loving men, women and children they also have a fondness for shoes or sheep or the dear dead departed. Levy is just wrong when he says in a footnote that such people have 'lost the ability to love another human being sexually', although some of them may have. But even if they had, sexual love is not the only or even perhaps the most significant form or mode of expression for human love and so it is again far from clear that loss of this ability is destructive of a basic good. In the example that Levy discusses of 'the young girl sexually initiated by an older person', he claims 'that the fact that there is no way of undoing the harmful effects with the ease and certainty with which they were induced establishes the correctness of classifying the case as one of sexual perversion.' Here Levy has abandoned *all* his criteria. Although he claimed that denial of a basic good is a necessary condition of perversion, he now makes disparity between the ease of causing harm and the ease of its undoing a sufficient condition of perversion. But worse, there is no evidence that such sexual initiation is necessarily harmful. But if it is traumatic, as it is perhaps likely to be in present-day society, again there is no evidence (nor is it plausible to suppose) that the harm caused is such as to cut the girl off from any basic good or from the capacity for enjoying any basic good.

It is characteristic of discussions of sexual perversion that the inclination to classify and condemn certain actions or dispositions as perverse is so strong that it persists, as with Levy, even where it is inconsistent with his entire and carefully argued account.

One feature of all the accounts of the distinction between the natural and the unnatural that we have looked at is that they either have no moral force or if they do they fail to capture the paradigms like necrophilia, bestiality and fetishism. If we turn away from philosophers' accounts for the moment and look at what might be thought of as some common-sense ways of drawing the distinction, we find the same problem.

Popular ideas of the natural

It is a problem that seems to me to be intractable, for most of the phenomena or actions or even dispositions that would have to count as natural, on any but the most eccentric of definitions, are not only without moral force but are also thoroughly disastrous. 'The ordinary course of nature', for example, is characterised by disease, famine, flood, pestilence and the like and we human beings spend a good deal of our time and energy combating these 'natural' disasters. Even if we confine our idea of the natural to human nature we are little better off, for violence, brutality, rape, warfare and so on are all arguably quite natural for man (and most of them even for woman). Indeed, if one or other of the versions of natural selection describe a natural evolutionary progress for human beings, then again while it may be evolutionarily successful one could hardly describe the survival of the fittest and its corollary, the destruction of the weakest, as a humane (albeit a human) arrangement.

Similar problems arise for other commonsensical accounts of the natural. The temptation to define it in terms of 'how things usually or normally are' requires us to give some moral priority to the *status quo* and this, as H.L.A. Hart has pointed out,[23] leads to moral stagnation. Many popular ideas about the natural are just nutty (if charming). People seem almost instinctively to draw a distinction between the natural and the unnatural and can unerringly distinguish natural landscapes on the one hand, and can tell margarine from butter on the other. The problem here is of course the arbitrariness of it all. Natural landscapes tend to be

pre-industrial—but why not pre-glacial? Natural food products
are those that have not 'artificially' been tampered with, as if
freedom from harmful bacteria was not an artificiality!

Perhaps the most tenacious of all popular ideas about the
natural is the view that natural conditions are those which have
'not been interfered with by man or woman'. This depends upon
the suspect assumption that human beings are not themselves
natural, or at least as natural as anything else. It involves the idea
that there is a natural order which is only revealed when the
influence of human beings has been eliminated. Herodotus tells
a charming story that illustrates this view. The Egyptians in the
reign of Psammetichus wished to discover which was the original
language, the language that occurred naturally to people. To this
end the Pharoah caused two children to be brought up in isolat-
tion and commanded that no words were to be uttered in their
presence. The idea was that the first words that came to them
naturally would be those in the original language. Sure enough
the children eventually pronounced the word 'becos' and research
established that this was the Phrygian for 'bread'. So priority was
accorded to the Phrygians, the natural language for humankind
was discovered, and social science was born.[24]

One account of the natural that seems to have some moral force
is that proposed by Mary Midgley. She argues[25] that we must think
of 'nature in the fuller sense, not just as an assembly of parts, but
as an organised whole. They (the unnatural) are parts which will
ruin the shape of that whole if they are allowed in any sense to
take over.' Midgley's account, while attractive, seems either to
capture too much or too little. Many passions and preferences
would ruin the shape of a balanced life if they took over, but are
they unnatural if they don't take over or haven't taken over?

A passion for motor racing, or eating, or playing 'space-invad-
ers' or football or even philosophy might well ruin the shape of
any life that it took over. It might be sensible to describe such a
situation as unnatural. As unnatural at any rate as margarine,
Trafalgar Square or languages other than Phrygian. But whether
there would be strong moral objections to a life taken over by
philosophy or football is another matter.

We began by asking whether there was such a thing as sexual
morality in the sense that sexual practices might be considered to
be immoral in the absence of any features that would make them
immoral on any account of morality. It looked as though there
ought to be some such features because of the inclination to class

practices like necrophilia, bestiality and fetishism as immoral even
where harmful side-effects could be entirely ruled out. Despite
the absence of harmful consequences or side-effects, these practices remained obscene, disgusting, perverted and unnatural but,
as I hope is now clear, these categories can only be given moral
content at the cost of condemning much that is either morally
neutral or positively beneficial. There are, however, accounts of
what is morally wrong with perversions which do not depend on
the natural/unnatural distinction and to these we must now turn.

Good sex

Sarah Ruddick gives moral approval to what she calls 'complete
sex'. She concisely sums up her conclusions as follows:

> To say that complete sex is superior to less complete sex because
> it is conducive to psychological wellbeing, involves a particular
> type of respect for persons, and is frequently coincident with
> valued emotions which are productive of virtue.
>
> To say that complete sex is superior to incomplete sex is not to
> say that we should avoid incompleteness.[26]
>
> The pursuit of more pleasurable and more complete sex acts is
> only one among many Moral activities. Since our sexual lives are
> very important to us, this pursuit rightly engages our moral reflec-
> tions.[27]

There is much in what Ruddick says here. The burden of it seems
to be that, while there is such a thing as sexual morality, there is
no such thing as sexual immorality—good sex is good but bad sex
is merely less good, it is not to be avoided. Here her conclusion
is virtually the same as Nagel's that 'bad sex is generally better
than none at all'.[28] Her notions of 'completeness' in sex are also not
significantly different from Nagel's ideas of multilayered sexual
awareness. However, this is surely the most attenuated of moralities, in which to judge an act or a disposition to be immoral is
not to judge it either to be wicked or to be avoided. Both Nagel
and Ruddick seem to be committed to the rather odd moral in-
junction 'that's morally wrong but go ahead'. The moral force of
what they say is very near that contained in the old addage 'if a
thing's worth doing it's worth doing well' and it invites and
accepts precisely the same riposte 'but if a thing's worth doing it's
worth doing badly!'

Since the reasons for maintaining an exclusively sexual morality
seem so weak and since the view that sex is *eo ipso* of moral

concern is the occasion for so much unnecessary guilt, malice and repression, it would seem that the moral arguments available indicate that we should regard sexual behaviour and sexual preferences as outside morality unless they involve features, like the unwanted infliction of pain, suffering, harm, injury, and so on, that would bring them into the moral domain whatever dimension of life they came from.

One final set of reasons for thinking that there might be such a thing as sexual morality remain to be considered. They have to do with what might be called the function of sexual morality, and though there are numerous accounts of and sources for this type of view a not untypical account is that concisely summarised by Tony Honoré in his book on *Sex Law*.[29]

Anti-social sex

Honoré identifies four 'aims' for the traditional rules of what is called 'sexual morality'. By 'aims' Honoré means 'rational purposes which could account for the rules, even if the rules have not been consciously adopted or retained for these reasons'.[30] Honoré's four aims he sets out as follows:

> One is the need of groups in a hostile world to maintain and increase their numbers. This need makes for rules which forbid those forms of sex which cannot, or do not ordinarily lead to children being conceived. ... A second aim of traditional sexual morality is to strengthen the family as the unit within which children are to be reared and which gives society its main structure. ... A third strand ... is an ascetic one. It is best to abstain from sex altogether, or reduce it to a minimum. ... This ascetic strand merges with another which is specially prominent in protestant Christianity and Marxism. According to this view indulgence in sex should be minimised because it interferes with the production of material things, which is the main business of life.[31]

This is not the place to assess the rationality of these rationalisations; however, where rules are justified by the desirability of the goals they allegedly promote, we need to ask three sorts of questions. The first is whether the goals are more important than the cost of achieving them by the chosen route. For example, even if marriage were beyond a peradventure a desirable social unit, both as the context for child-rearing and as a contributor to social stability, we also accept other values and have other moral priorities. We believe that individual liberty and respect for persons is important; part of this belief is our acceptance of the wrongness of depriving someone of their liberty when what they propose is neither harmful nor immoral.[32] We might well conclude that social stability purchased at such a high cost in violation of rights had lost most of its attraction.[33] Secondly we would want to know whether the rules were in fact well calculated to achieve their objectives and were not rather better calculated to promote some other and less defensible objective. Rules against homosexuality and onanism, for example, seem better calculated to pacify bigots than to promote marriage and one is entitled to ask whether if protection of marriage is really the objective of such rules this end might not be better achieved in other ways, which is the third of our questions.

The tendentiousness of this style of defence for rules which discriminate against particular sections of society, and justify such discrimination in terms of its social utility, is highlighted by the history of the subjection of women. The spectre of the dissolution of marriage and the destruction of society were foremost among the many evils predicted upon the 'emancipation' of women. And here too, individual rights and liberties were held at naught when compared with the preservation of 'society' as perceived by men.

Conclusion

The tenacity of the idea that many sexual practices like, for example, fetishism, bestiality, necrophilia and perhaps also incest and homosexuality would remain morally wrong even where they could not be shown to have involved any harm, injury or pain and where no violation of rights or breach of duty or obligation occurred seemed to indicate that there must be a separate category of purely sexual morality divorced from our general criteria for judging of the rightness and wrongness of actions or dispositions to act. It looked as though this wrongness must consist in the fact that such acts were obscene, disgusting, perverted or unnatural. While they may be all of these things, examination of these categories does not allow us to conclude that any action or intention is to be judged morally wrong on these grounds alone. For even if a coherent account of the crucial categories of the perverse and the unnatural can be given there is no good reason to suppose that it will yield any morally relevant distinction.

There is then no reason to suppose that there is such a thing as sexual morality in the sense of a morality which provides grounds for moral judgments about sexual desires or practices which cannot be shown to be immoral in any of the ways which would make such practices immoral if they involved no sexual element at all. Of course, since sex and sexuality are very important to most human beings, sexual practices will continue to figure as important examples of general immorality where they involve violation, injury, exploitation and so on, and this will perhaps be particularly important in education where children's natural interest in sex can be relied upon to make discussions of 'good sex' in Nagel's and Ruddick's terms an important part of moral education. But we should be clear that it is part of moral education because respect for the feelings, wishes and desires of others is part of morality and not because sex *eo ipso* raises any moral issues at all.

There is nothing wrong with sex of any kind including fetishism, bestiality, necrophilia, buggery, incest, paedophilia and the variety approved of by missionaries. There is lots wrong with violation, exploitation, the infliction of harm, pain, suffering and so on. But that, as has been the argument of this chapter, is another story that has no necessary connexion with sex.

We can conclude therefore that the sexual preferences of health care professionals should not influence their treatment of those whose preferences differ. At the beginning of this chapter we reviewed a number of areas in which the belief that there was such a thing as sexual morality might well influence the treatment offered to, and the provision made for, various sorts of patients. I hope that it is now clear that such influence is entirely improper.

Of course we are entitled to prefer some sexual practices and attitudes to others, and we may have moral reasons for these preferences. Sexual attitudes which express love and respect for others are morally preferable to those which express hatred or contempt. But we are no more entitled to vary our health care provision or decline to make such provision for those who do not like their sexual partners or choose inanimate or non-human ones than we are to do the same for those who don't much care for doctors, or philosophers or any other group within society.

10 Respect for persons I

Persons are beings capable of valuing their own lives. We have noted the vast variety of different reasons that people have for valuing their lives, and the different ways in which they think it important to organise their lives and the societies in which they live. Many of these differences stem from, or are expressive of, moral differences between people and are thus likely to remain important. It was the very intractability of these differences that made it seem unlikely that any agreement could be reached on a list of the things that made life valuable, and which made it seem more promising to concentrate on the fact that persons would be the sorts of beings who had their own reasons or purposes for life, rather than on the content of those reasons or purposes.

The recognition of the fact that we are likely to differ, and to go on differing, from one another as to what is important and valuable about life, and that this ability is itself part of the peculiar value that people's lives usually have, occupies a special place in moral theory. Those who accept that all the many differences between people, important as they are, do not of themselves make the life of one person more valuable—more worthy of preservation—than the lives of any other, exhibit that basic attitude to their fellows which is often called 'respect for persons', and which is the starting point of morality.

It is the starting point because it involves recognising that other people matter and so also that how they live their lives, and the quality of their lives, matters as well. It is precisely because they are so important that what they believe is so important, and it is because both they and their beliefs are so important that morality matters so much. There would be little reason even to get as far as disagreeing with others morally, unless it was accepted that they and their beliefs mattered.

This book, like any work in ethics or in social or in political theory and also, of course in medicine, is written for those who accept that people are valuable, and who are prepared to exhibit 'respect for persons'. It cannot demonstrate that one *must* value life and show respect for persons, but it can say something about what these involve and about the consequences of accepting them. That their necessity cannot be unequivocally established is perhaps a matter of relatively small importance, since most people do in fact accept both that life is valuable and that they should in some sense show respect for persons.

We must now try to say something about what respect for persons involves and of its importance for some of the most poignant dilemmas that confront those involved in health care.

I Respect for persons

The attitude to others that we call 'respect for persons' has two essential elements. They are essential just in the sense that no one could coherently claim to respect others if their behaviour failed to exhibit both dimensions. Someone who has respect for persons will show both

(1) concern for their welfare,
   and
(2) respect for their wishes.

Normally these two dimensions of respect for persons are complementary, but there are many cases where there are some tensions between them, and it is at these points that some of the most acute dilemmas of medical ethics occur.

(1) Concern for the welfare of others

When health care professionals accept that their first duty is to act always in the best interests of their patients they are in effect saying that they are concerned for the welfare of their patients and that this is in no way inconsistent with manifesting 'respect for persons'. Welfare is not here used as a technical term—it means what it usually means, 'the state or condition of doing or being well',[1] which will include things like happiness, health and living standards.

An initial problem is that concern for the welfare of others is compatible both with paternalism and with moralism. Briefly,

paternalism is the belief that it can be right to order the lives of
others for their own good, irrespective of their own wishes or
judgments. The characteristic cry of the paternalist is 'Don't do
that, it isn't good for you.' *Moralism,* on the other hand, is the
belief that it can be right to order the lives of others so that
'morality' may be preserved. The characteristic cry of the moralist is 'Don't do that, it's wicked.'

Both the paternalist and the moralist are genuinely concerned
for the welfare of others. They argue that it cannot be in your
interests, nor can it be conducive to your being in a state of doing
or being well, if you either do what isn't good for you or act
immorally. Despite the genuineness of this moral concern, both
paternalism and moralism involve treating the agent as an incompetent. They deny the individual control over her own life and
moral destiny and treat her as incompetent to run her own life as
she chooses. While both involve genuine concern for the welfare
of others, neither can lay claim to demonstrating respect for their
wishes.

(2) Respect for the wishes of others

Respect for the wishes of others is central to any claim to accept
that their lives are valuable because, as we have seen, for each
individual life has unique value and that value is determined by
what the individual wants to do with his or her own life. Because
it is we who give our lives value, that value is in pawn to our
freedom to pursue our own objects in our own way. Unless the
value of our lives is to be undermined, the only constraint on our
freedom to do as we please should be the familiar proviso that
what we please to do does not harm others or does as little harm
to others as it is possible for us to do. If this were not so, respect
for the wishes of others would show them scant respect.

John Stuart Mill, with whom this extreme libertarianism is
most closely associated, had another argument to offer for the
freedom of individuals to pursue their own plans for their lives in
their own way. I have connected this freedom with the value of
life itself, but Mill connects it with a person's capacity to improve
himself and with the improvement of humankind:

> He who lets the world, or his own portion of it, choose his plan of
> life for him, has no need of any other faculty than the ape-like one
> of imitation. He who chooses his plan for himself, employs all his
> faculties. He must use observation to see, reasoning and judgement
> to foresee, activity to gather materials for decision, discrimination

to decide, and when he has decided, firmness and self control to
hold to his deliberate decision. And these qualities he requires and
exercises exactly in proportion as the part of his conduct which he
determines according to his own judgement and feelings is a large
one. It is possible that he might be guided in some good path, and
kept out of harm's way, without any of these things. But what will
be his comparative worth as a human being? It really is of importance, not only what men do, but also what manner of men they
are that do it. Among the works of man which human life is rightly
employed in perfecting and beautifying, the first in importance
surely is man himself.[2]

The problem for all who care about others just is how to reconcile respect for the free choices of others with real concern for
their welfare, when their choices are or appear to be self-destructive. Where, for example, someone wants to choose suicide or
heroin addiction, what should those who care about and respect
her do?

One classic way out of this dilemma has been for those who
care about people with self-destructive preferences to argue either
that the self-destructive preference is not a genuine preference,
or else that it is not genuinely autonomous and therefore that
its satisfaction is not *really* what the individual wants. For convenience we will examine both these possibilities under the
heading of autonomy.

II What is autonomy?

Autonomy is, strictly speaking 'self-government', and people are
said to be autonomous to the extent to which they are able to
control their own lives, and to some extent their own destiny, by
the exercise of their own faculties. Full autonomy and even fully
autonomous individual choices, are in a sense ideal notions, which
we can at best only hope to approach more or less closely. This
is because all sorts of things tend to undermine the individual's
capacity for autonomous choice. By examining some of the main
sorts of considerations which have this damaging effect, we shall
both approach a clearer understanding of autonomy and see more
clearly whether or not paternalistic interference in the lives of
others might be justified by imperfections in the autonomy of
people's choices.

I don't suppose it is possible to produce an exhaustive list of
the features that tend to diminish an individual's autonomy, but

we will consider what are often thought to be the main ones under four general headings. An individual's autonomy is apparently undermined and diminished by four different kinds of what we might call 'defects'. These are:

(1) defects in the individual's ability to control either her desires or her actions or both;
(2) defects in the individual's reasoning;
(3) defects in the information available to the individual, upon which she bases her choice;
(4) defects in the stability of the individual's own desires.

We shall examine each of these in turn.

(1) Defects in control

An individual's ability to control his own choices may be defective in a number of ways. He might, for example, have a mental illness which makes it implausible to regard him as in any sense in control of himself. If it is reasonable to conclude that the illness has such extreme effects on the individual's ability to control his life, then this will be a case in which preferences expressed while so comprehensively out of control must not be regarded as the genuine preferences of the individual in question. Such a conclusion, however, should not lightly be arrived at, and we must demand more in the way of evidence of comprehensive lack of control than the bare fact that the individual is displaying some of the symptoms (or even all of them) of a recognised mental illness. It would have to be shown either that the illness was such that none of the individual's choices could be taken as genuine, or that this particular choice could not be so taken.

More interesting for our present purposes are the circumstances in which an individual might find his behaviour controlled by desires which he does not wish to have. Drug addiction would be an obvious example. Where the addict wishes no longer to take heroin say, but still passionately desires another fix, there is a tension between the addict's first-order desire for drugs, and what might be described as a second-order desire not to be an addict. This problem of addiction can have milder manifestations, as where someone wishes to lose weight but cannot resist another cake. Their second-order desire to lose weight is controlled by a first-order desire for this delicious mouthful. We should note that addiction is not of itself destructive of autonomy, but is so only where the agent wishes not to be addicted. We are all more or less addicted to all sorts of things and are quite pleased to be so. When I sit down to dinner my wish for a good meal is in no way defective from the point of view of my autonomy, despite the fact that I, like everyone else, am addicted to food. Similarly when I choose to play squash or study philosophy, to both of which I am addicted fully voluntarily, my autonomous choice is in no way defective because, although I am conscious that I cannot give them up (or it would be exceedingly difficult for me to do so), I have no wish at all to do so.

(2) Defects in reasoning

There are a number of ways in which an individual's processes of reasoning may be defective in ways that vitiate, or partially vitiate, the choices which they purport to justify or explain. First, some examples. Someone who smokes cigarettes because 'there's no real harm in it', or who believes that it is safe to drive home after an evening's drinking because 'I can take my drink' is, if they genuinely believe what they say and act on the basis of that belief, operating under a substantial defect in reasoning. The same defects are characteristic of prejudice of all kinds. Where people allow received opinion or gut reaction to form the basis of their values, or when they form opinions based on manifestly implausible 'facts', their autonomy is undermined. If, for example, a woman were to accept a severely traditional conception of a woman's role, seeing her life in terms of the comfort and support of men, looking after the home and the children and leaving all decisions to men, because 'this is what women are created for', then her autonomy would be severely undermined. Such uncritical conformity to traditional values would render her less autonomous than her more liberated sisters. She might, of course, be more happy or contented, but that is another matter.

Three main rules for avoiding the sorts of defects in reasoning that can undermine autonomy might be formulated as follows.[3]

(a) That there should be no mere 'parroting' or blind acceptance of the views of others or of one's own society. This involves some active attempt to establish one's own views and to discover their truth or validity for oneself.

(b) That where my choices are based on my reasons for them, that these reasons should not be vitiated by something like blind prejudice. And where the choices are based on some factual premise or claim, that there be a commensurate re-

lationship between the strength of the evidence for those
facts and the strength of the beliefs they support.

(c) Where my choice is based on an inference from facts or
propositions, that the inference should be valid. So that
where, for example, I infer from the fact that my Aunt
Edwina lived to be 193 and smoked a hundred cigarettes
every day of her life, that I can do the same, or, that cigarettes are unlikely to harm me because 'she did all right on
them', my inferences will be defective in a way that under-
mines my autonomy. After all, I do want to live to be 193,
and I don't want cigarettes to spoil my chances of so doing,
so I don't want to smoke if these goals will thereby be
damaged.[4]

We should be clear that defects in reasoning will only damage
autonomy where the defects undermine or tend to undermine the
agent's capacity to make choices. Bad reasoning will always have
this tendency, of course, but we must remember that some stated
reasons are merely rationalisations and are known by the agent
himself to be 'non-operative'. Also, some genuine choices may be
'mere caprice' and none the less genuine for that.

(3) Defects in information

Where beliefs or choices are based on false or incomplete information, or depend on such information at any crucial point, they
will to that extent be less autonomous. So that where the agent
is misinformed, or only told part of the truth, or where he is kept
in total ignorance, his capacity to make the best choices he can
will be undermined. This can happen of course by others deliberately deceiving him, for whatever motives, or knowingly giving
only partial information, or it can happen by negligence or sheer
mischance. It may of course also be the agent's own
information-gathering (or lack of it) that is at fault. And finally
we should not rule out the possibility of the agent failing to
understand, or understand the significance of, the information he
obtains. Here too there is room for negligence, or deliberate
obfuscation on the part of those supplying the information, and
also for an unhappy and unwitting gulf between the medium of
the message, and the agent's ability to comprehend it.

(4) Defects in stability

We live in time and hopefully for a long time. This means that
our character, and with it what we value and like to do, is very

likely to change over time and to change considerably over long periods of time. It is therefore unsurprising that decisions made in one segment of life may come to seem absurd or embarrassing or just wrong, and may even be bitterly regretted later. This instability in our preferences is often cited as a justification for paternalism. People must be prevented from doing things they will come to regret—'I'm only doing this for your own good and one day you'll be grateful.' There is a fundamental incoherence in such arguments. I now regret many of the things I did and the priorities I had and the decisions I made when I was 18; but my current regret, or change of heart or mind is no evidence at all that the decisions made in my youth were wrong, irrational, or in any way open to paternalism. If decisions are wrong because there is good reason to suppose that the agent will at some later time come to regret them, or think differently about them, then no decisions can be made until, at best, extreme old age. Apart from the absurdity of this, it reveals a fundamental mistake about the nature of autonomy. Autonomy is the running of one's own life according to one's own lights. The fact that these lights change colour and intensity over time is no evidence at all that the later lights are either better or more 'one's own' than the earlier ones. They're just different. To be autonomous, self-determined, just is to be able to do as one wishes—not to be able to do as one will wish at some future time.

We must also bear in mind the point well made by Mill in the paragraph immediately preceding the one already quoted. Mill argues that self-determination improves not with time but with practice, and that one's later decisions only have a chance of being more self-determined than one's earlier ones if one is permitted to make the earlier ones, and learn from them, but that no such improvement can be consequent upon paternalistic intervention in our lives.

> The human faculties of perception, discriminative feeling, mental activity and even moral preference are exercised only in making a choice. ... The mental and moral, like the muscular powers, are improved only by being used. ... If the grounds of an opinion are not conclusive to the person's own reason, his reason cannot be strengthened but is likely to be weakened by his adopting it: and if the inducements to an act are not such as are cosentaneous to his own feelings and character ... it is so much done towards rendering his feelings and character inert and torpid, instead of active and energetic.[5]

Perfect autonomy then, decisions taken without any defect at all either of information or reasoning or of control, is, like any ideal, unattainable. But the fact that autonomy, like many important and desirable things, is a matter of degree does not make it any the less worth striving for, nor does it make it any the less important to have as much of it as possible. In this it is like health. One will be autonomous simply to the extent that one's decisions are one's own, unfettered by others and suffering as little from the various defects as is possible.

III Is paternalist interference justified?

The only thing that makes paternalism morally respectable is its claim to be an essential part of what it is to respect persons. In most cases our concern for the welfare of others poses no problems and is non-paternalist. For they are as concerned about their own welfare as we are. The problem arises where we and they disagree about what is conducive to their welfare or where we don't disagree but they happen not to want to maximise their own welfare. In these cases it seems that paternalist concern for the welfare of others cannot be consistent with respect for them as persons where the agent's choices are *maximally autonomous.*

This is because autonomy is, as we have seen, part of what it is to value life. For whatever it is that makes life worth living for us, and however much this differs from what makes life valuable for others, our life would cease to be of value to us to the extent that we were prevented from pursuing those things, whatever they are, that we want to pursue. And this will be true even in the limiting cases, where we either choose to lay down our lives for our values, or where, because we have ceased to value life, we wish to die. In both of these limiting cases the value of life just consists in our being able to lay it down for these reasons in these circumstances.

Maximally autonomous decisions

We have seen that there is no such thing as complete autonomy. An agent's decisions will, however, be maximally autonomous where they are as autonomous as they could reasonably be in all the circumstances. These circumstances will include considerations like how important to the agent the decision in question is (which will relate to how much time it is worth spending on the decision process), and the fact that with any decision, a law of diminishing returns will operate to cut short the decision process at some stage. However, we can say that an agent's decision will undoubtedly be maximally autonomous where:

(1) there are no apparent defects in control;
(2) there are no apparent defects in reasoning, or no defects in reasoning which would bear on the validity of the conclusions upon which the agent's decisions are based;
(3) there are no apparent defects in the information available to the agent and which are germain to the decision at hand.

If this is right some important conclusions follow. The first is that paternalism will never be justified where the would-be paternalist can show no defect in the autonomy of the decision in question. And this will be so whatever might be said about this agent's *general* ability to make autonomous decisions. Nor will paternalist intervention be justified where the paternalist can only show a defect in the decision process which is irrelevant to the merits of this particular decision—where, for example, a patient refuses therapy on the grounds that it is painful and there is only a 60 per cent chance of the therapy being successful, and in fact the more realistic figure is 50 per cent.

But perhaps even more importantly, the paternalism will only be justified for so long as it takes to apprise the agent of the defects in his decision. Once this has been done and the new information conveyed, or the invalid inference pointed out, and the agent still wishes to implement his decision, then the justification for paternalism ceases. An example of Mill's clearly illustrates this point.

> If either a public officer or anyone else saw a person attempting to cross a bridge which had been ascertained to be unsafe, and there was no time to warn him of the danger, they might seize him and turn him back, without any real infringement of his liberty; for liberty consists in doing what one desires, and he does not desire to fall into the river.[6]

The inference here is only justified on the assumption that the traveller's information about the bridge is defective. Once he has been apprised of its true state, and he still wishes to cross, the justification of seizing him and turning him back is at an end.

Irremediable defects

Some defects, particularly defects of control, may either be irremediable, or irremediable in time to make a difference to the
decision in question. There are two different sorts of cases. The
first is the case we have already briefly considered of the person
whose behaviour is controlled by desires which he wants not to
have. This is fairly straightforward, for the agent can say whether
or not he wants help in conquering the desire which he finds it
impossible to overcome. And again, if he does not, then it would
show him scant respect to force him to diet or whatever.

Where the loss of control is more comprehensive, as with some
forms of mental illness or specific delusions; if there is genuinely
no question of respecting the agent's autonomous wishes because
the agent cannot sensibly be thought of as having autonomous
wishes, then the only issue left for those who respect the individual as a person is how best to serve their welfare. If someone
believes themselves to be God, or God's chosen representative,
however deluded they might appear to be, such a belief offers no
grounds of itself for paternalist intervention. For one thing such
a belief may display no defects of reason at all. This is because
religious beliefs may not be founded on evidence or any rational
considerations, and may be treated entirely as matters of faith.
Where they are so treated, they will display no defects of reason—
reason quite literally does not come into it. Indeed many people
have had delusions of this sort and have been, and still are,
revered for having them. Where such beliefs, whether involving
defective reason or not, are harmless, it will neither serve the
welfare, nor respect the wishes, of such people to interfere in any
way.

Where they are not harmless matters may be different. If the
likelihood is that the actions of such individuals will harm others,
then they will rightfully be prevented, in the same way as would
anyone at all who, for whatever reason, planned to harm others.
Where, however, the harm is purely self-regarding, it might seem
that we should still intervene to prevent it. Suppose the deluded
individual we have imagined thinks that because he is God's
chosen representative he is impervious to harm and to prove it lies
down on the railway line in the path of an approaching express.
If divine assistance seems unlikely, some human help may appear
to be indicated. But is it? This is of course effectively the much-
discussed type of case that arises when Jehovah's Witnesses require but refuse a life-saving blood transfusion. Most human

beings tend to be highly selective about the defects in reasoning that they class as delusions and those that they respect as religious conviction. And as we have seen, where religious belief is entirely a matter of faith there may be no defects at all. So, what should we do faced with the self-destructive chosen representative of God, or with the Jehovah's Witness?

Hard cases: suicide

There are very many decisions in life where nothing much turns on the outcome, either for the agent or for others. Some decisions are, however, of major importance and suicide is one of these. We saw in Chapter 2 that refusal of life-saving measures is, as sure as shooting, a way of killing oneself. So whether we come upon someone with their head in a gas oven, or someone who has taken a massive and lethal overdose of drugs, or on someone who is refusing treatment necessary for the preservation of life, we will be faced with attempted suicide. Where a decision is of such major importance for an individual, it is certainly in their interests to make it as autonomously as possible. Anyone will therefore be perfectly justified in doing their best to discover whether the decision is autonomous and in aiding the individual to make it as autonomous as possible. So that where we come upon an attempted suicide or a would-be suicide, it is the act of someone with respect for others to try to stop the suicide for the purposes of ascertaining the cause of any distress that has prompted the action and attempting to remedy it if possible. And of ensuring that the decision was maximally autonomous.

However, if the distress is irremediable or the suicide does not want it remedied, and if the decision was maximally autonomous, then the bystander must allow the agent to control his own destiny, if that is what he wants, and no longer obstruct the attempt.[7]

If the decision was not maximally autonomous, then the bystander will be justified in helping to make it so, by providing information or helping to remedy defects in reasoning or in control if that is possible. However, once this has been done, the justification for the bystander's interference ceases. And this will be so even where there appear to be remaining irremediable defects of reasoning or of information, as may be the case with Jehovah's Witnesses. For ultimately, part of what it is to be autonomous is to have the freedom to make irrational or capricious choices, if that is what one wishes to do. The only exception is where the defects in control are so great that the individual cannot be regarded as an agent at all and so is completely incapable of making genuine choices—even irrational ones. But this will be a rare thing indeed, and will be true of only a very small sub-class even of mental patients.

Two arguments have been advanced recently against the advisability of such an approach. Tom Beauchamp and James Childress suggest that

> failure to intervene (in suicide) indicates a lack of concern about others and a diminished sense of moral responsibility in a community.... Second, many believe that most suicides are mentally ill or at least seriously disturbed and therefore are not really capable of autonomous action.[8]

The present argument has been that concern for the welfare of others has to be part of respect for persons which must give ultimate priority to respect for their wishes. So that so far from showing a 'diminished sense of moral responsibility', failure to intervene in maximally autonomous suicide attempts *will* demonstrate concern and respect for those who wish to die. Where there is some doubt as to whether the suicide wishes autonomously to die, then moral responsibility will dictate intervention, but only for the purposes, described above, of removing the doubt. Many believe erroneously that the suicide is incapable of autonomous choice simply because he wishes to die. This objection will only be well taken if it is clear that the suicide is genuinely incapable of autonomous action, but this will only be true if the defects of control are such that the agent has lost the power of choice, and not simply that his choices exhibit defects in stability or seem eccentric or bizarre.

We must bear in mind that repeated frustrations of genuinely autonomous suicide attempts exhibit a fundamental contempt for the wishes of the agent. In a social context in which it is extremely difficult for someone who wishes to end his life to obtain the means and the privacy with which to do so, any frustration of his attempt is a severe blow. This will be particularly true of suicides who are in an institution, a hospital, nursing or old people's home, or who are bedridden or otherwise very dependent on others and closely supervised. Such a person may well find it impossible to obtain the means of suicide without help. A society which recognises that autonomous suicide is justified would effectively be denying the option of suicide to such people unless aided suicide or voluntary euthanasia were permitted. It is such people, who may be nearing the end of their lives, in severe pain and with little to hope for, who are most likely to choose death autonomously.

IV Consent

It will be obvious from the argument so far that respect for the person requires a patient's autonomous consent be obtained before any treatment or procedure involving the patient can be carried out, and that no consent will be autonomous unless it is fully informed. So that any health care professional who failed to make a full and frank disclosure of all the facts, or prognoses, or suppositions about a patient's condition before obtaining her consent to proceed would not have obtained a valid consent.[9] Similarly, before a patient is entered into a clinical trial she must be informed that she is to be part of a trial and of the nature and purpose of the trial in question.

Consent to clinical trials

It is sometimes claimed that consent to participation in a trial cannot be valid because patients are not usually told that they may be part of a control group from which therapeutically effective treatment is withheld or which will be given a placebo. It is clear that it is both wrong and unnecessary to operate controls in which treatment known to be ineffective, or known to be less effective than other available treatment, is used. Trials are only justified where there is genuine uncertainty about which of two or more therapies is the more effective. Until the trial has been carried out 'the best treatment for every individual is *either* of the therapies under test, chosen at random, for no one then knows which is better. Were that uncertainty not present it would surely be unethical to make a trial.'[10] D.W. Vere, whose remarks these are, is surely correct here, and his statement of the wrongness of withholding effective treatment concisely summarises the position. Vere argues that withholding effective treatment 'need not happen and is in no sense a necessary entailment of clinical trials':

> In properly conducted trials the comparator for a new therapy must always be the best available alternative. Placebos should only be used if there is reason to think there is no more effective remedy (and they, of course, are not devoid of effect), or if the patient's complaints are minor, not dangerous to life or limb, and the patient

knows that placebo usage will be part of the trial to which he or she freely assents. In other words there is surely a place for trials where placebos are given or active therapy is withheld or washout periods are included.[11]

So, if the health care professional is to obtain a valid consent, and incidentally avoid the possibility of legal liability for negligence or for trespass to the person, she must fully inform her patients or the proposed subjects of clinical trials.

Adequate disclosure and real consent

Disclosure of information will be inadequate for the purposes of gaining a valid consent from the patient where the information supplied, or the method or circumstances of supplying it, are such that the patient could not on the basis of it make a maximally autonomous choice. The following set of criteria adapted from those originally suggested by the Law Reform Commission of Canada seem to me to be an excellent basis for achieving adequate disclosure:[12]

(1) All material or relevant facts must be disclosed as well as other factors related to the treatment which could influence the patient's decision to participate, that is the disclosure must be complete, accurate and not too complicated. Disclosure will not be complete for these purposes unless it includes a description of the proposed treatment, an indication of the alternatives, an outline of the inherent risks of death or serious bodily injury and of any problems of recuperation that may be anticipated, a clear description of any likely side-effects and a statement of the long-term prognosis.

(2) The test of materiality of information should be objective *vis à vis* a 'reasonable patient', with the proviso that this test becomes subjective to the extent that the physician knew, or ought to have known, that additional information which would not have been relevant to the 'reasonable patient' was in fact material to this particular patient. ...

(3) The test of required comprehension of the disclosure should be 'apparent subjective', that is the doctor must take reasonable steps in relation to the particular patient to ensure that he has understood and that objectively, or apparently, he did.

(4) Care should be taken that the informing process is not

coercive; and possibly in some circumstances an estimation should be made by a 'disinterested' outside party in this respect. . . .

(5) In neither therapeutic nor non-therapeutic experimentation or trial can there be any mitigation of these standards and no consent to either treatment, trial or experiment will be valid if the subject has not been fully informed in accordance with the above guidelines.[13]

In the stimulating paper by M.D. Kirby from which I have borrowed and adapted these guidelines, Kirby lists a sixth point which would allow patients or experimental subjects to waive the obligation to disclose information in some cases. While, for reasons that will appear when we discuss the right to remain in ignorance, health care professionals might be justified in withholding some information from patients, they could not do so *and* receive from those patients a valid consent. This is because patients would not know to what they were consenting, and so the whole business would be a charade.

Before discussing the question of whether there could be a right to remain in ignorance, we should note that it may well not be enough, even after a complete disclosure of information, to get the patient simply to sign a consent form. Health care professionals should satisfy themselves that the written consent is genuine by discussion with the patient, to confirm that he knows what he has done by signing the form. And in a long process of treatment the consent may well have to be regularly obtained for continuing with the treatment in the light of how the patient feels about it once she has actually experienced what is involved. Consent should not be regarded as a once and for all thing.

We have so far looked at those sorts of case in which health care professionals disclose information in order to obtain a valid consent to treatment. We must now examine the ethics of disclosure in those very many cases in which the question of disclosure might arise independently of any question of treatment. Is there then a general obligation to give complete information?

I have heard it very often said by doctors that so far from there being any duty to tell patients the truth or give them a full account of the doctor's view of their condition, that the patients have a right to remain in ignorance if they so wish, or if, in the judgment of the doctor, full disclosure would somehow harm the patient.

The right to remain in ignorance

However desirable it might be, either from the point of view of
the doctor's interests or from that of the patient's, for the patient
to remain in ignorance of his condition, it is doubtful whether
there could be any *right* to remain in ignorance. I cannot imagine
upon what such a right might be founded unless it was somehow
parasitic upon the concept of respect for persons, and was seen to
derive from the obligation to respect the individual's wishes about
himself. So that if the patient wished not to be told anything
about his condition or wished not to be told anything 'bad' about
himself, then doctors might respect that wish and refrain from
unwelcome disclosure. Even in this, perhaps the clearest of circumstances in which it might seem right to withhold disclosure,
it is doubtful if the patient possesses anything approaching a right
not to be told. There are all sorts of unpleasant things in life that
we might prefer not to know about, but it does not follow that
anyone infringes our rights if they inform us. I might well wish
to remain blissfully ignorant of the plight of the poor, or of the
starving, or of victims of disease or of accidents, and to hear about
such things might well distress me greatly, but it does not follow
from this that I possess a right that no one tells me about them.

It seems to me that here, as in all other areas of morality, talk
of rights does not help much. What we want to know in each case
is not so much what the rights of the various parties are, but what
we ought to do.

The converse view, that so far from people having a right to
remain in ignorance there is always a positive duty on people to
disclose anything they know about others that might be relevant
to any autonomous decisions they might wish to make, seems
equally implausible. This would amount to a charter for vicious
busybodies to go about telling 'home truths' and for a rash of
hate mail of the 'Dear John' variety.

It seems tempting to say that we should refrain from full disclosure of information we possess about others when such information might harm them, make them unhappy or distressed, or
when they simply don't want to know, whether or not they claim
any right not to be told. But this too seems a doubtful principle
to accept. If we compare the situation of individual patients with
that of, say, citizens of a society, the dubiousness of the principle
is more evident. A government (not unlike a doctor?) might well

argue that it would only distress the citizens if they were told all sorts of worrying things about their society, for example about the risks from nuclear power stations, or the dangers of asbestos in their homes, or of their complete vulnerability in the case of nuclear war. It might well be true that citizens would be distressed or made unhappy or anxious and so on by such information, but it is far from clear that these constitute good reasons for keeping them in ignorance. Of course governments have a much quieter time of it the less the citizens know, but that is not usually thought to be a sufficient justification for secrecy.

While it seems doubtful that there could be such a thing as a positive right to remain in ignorance, and equally doubtful that there is either a clear obligation to refrain from telling people things that might distress or make them anxious, or things they would prefer not to know, it seems equally clear that there is no general obligation to tell all, in all circumstances. However, if one clear principle emerges from this discussion of autonomy it is that there is an obligation to tell all to those who wish to be told.

The obligation to tell those who wish to know

This obligation derives from the close connexion between autonomy and the pursuit of those things, whatever they are, that make life valuable. Since autonomy is necessary in order that every individual can pursue freely and in their own way the things that for them make life valuable or meaningful, they have the strongest of entitlements to whatever information about themselves will, in their own judgment, best help them to do this. No one who either acknowledged that the lives of all people were of equal value, or who claimed to have respect for persons, could withhold such information. Yet many principled people claim that it is right to do so.

Consider the following case presented by Beauchamp and Childress and which they believe supports such a claim:

> a doctor knows that a terminally ill person, who has been his patient for many years, suffers severe and prolonged depression when given distressing news about his health. So deep is the depression when it occurs that the person is effectively incapacitated from making autonomous judgements. While he has shown tendencies in the past to suicide, he is opposed on religious grounds to the taking of his own life and always suffers both a failure of nerve and powerful guilt when he starts to devise ways of ending

his life. Though utterly unaware of his terminal condition, he asks
his doctor point blank for a complete explanation of a recent physical examination during which the doctor discovered his fatal illness. The doctor tells him that he has never been in better health.
Few would say that the doctor made a wrong choice, yet this
decision is both paternalistic and a clear cut case of lying.[14]

Beauchamp and Childress clearly accept this as an example of
justified paternalism, and are not themselves among the few who
would say that the doctor made a wrong choice.[15] One would want
to know more about the evidence accepted as demonstrating that
the patient in question suffered such debilitating depression as to
rob him of autonomy. I suspect a tendency to exaggerate the
effects of such a depression, but we must take the example as
presented. Even accepting all the claims made in the example at
face value, the facts are far from supporting the correctness of the
doctor's judgments, let alone their moral respectability. First,
the doctor's assessment of the psychological state and probable
reactions of the patient seem highly problematic. The patient has,
we are told, repeatedly contemplated suicide and has on each
occasion refrained because he lacks the courage, and in any event
opposes suicide on religious grounds. This means that the patient
has faced the imminent prospect of his own death repeatedly and
has not found the idea of it repellent or fearful, but rather has
simply lacked the courage to carry through his desires and has
principled objections to suicide. This is not the history of a man
rendered non-autonomous by the idea of his own death. Indeed
since the only things that prevented his suicide were not fear of
death, but fear of God and lack of courage, we might well judge
that he would welcome news of a death which had clearly been
arranged by God and could not be prevented by his own failure
of nerve.

Moreover, his deep preoccupation with his own health shows
how important knowledge of its state is to him, and any doctor
who respected his patient would regard this as a very good reason
to keep the patient fully informed, even though this might well
depress him. It is difficult to forecast precisely what effect the
news of the certainty of a person's death will have on them,
whatever their past reaction to information about their state of
health has been. Such news is of so different an order of magnitude to any other information, as to put such a piece of news in
a class of its own. Many people who can be agitated at the prospect of quite mild illness become calm and accepting when they

know that their own death is near. This makes prediction a hazardous business and so the doctor has no right to be as certain as he is about the effects of his news on this patient.

But let's assume that the doctor is as reasonably certain as he can be in this case that the effects of telling the truth to this patient will be as described. Still the news can only be temporarily delayed. The patient must discover the truth about his condition eventually. But it may then be too late for him to act on it in the way that he would have wished; to make his farewells, settle his affairs and so on. He might also wish to make choices about how to spend his last few weeks of reasonable health. The example will have us accept that this is just what he will be prevented from doing by the state into which the news will cast him. But he must surely be given the chance to do these important last things, however remote the chance of his achieving them might be. If he is not given the chance, all the doctor has achieved is the purchase of a few weeks of 'false consciousness' at the terrible cost of making a mockery of the last days of his life and giving him no chance, when he eventually discovers the truth, of redeeming that lost and precious time and using it in the way he would have wished to do.

If he is inevitably to fall into a permanent state of depressed incapacity, then all the doctor has achieved is the delay of that event by a few weeks. The price of that negligible gain is the loss of all chance of the patient being able to do what we all wish to do, namely give direction to the rest of our lives, however long or short they may be.[16]

We must also remember that the doctor himself only comes to be in possession of the vital information because the patient has voluntarily submitted to the examination, presumably on the implied condition that he will be told of its findings. Even if the doctor's worst fears were to be realised, he would have been right to give the information and wrong to withhold it. Unless this principle is accepted, we will none of us be in control of our own destinies.

Of course if the patient has said at the examination that he did not want to know if it was bad news, or did not want to know if nothing could be done to help him, then things would have been different. Similarly if the patient had expressed complete indifference to the issue of whether or not he was to be kept informed about his state of health. In such circumstances it would be open to the health care professional as to whether or not to give the information, or about what information to give. But even here the presumption should be in favour of telling the truth unless there are powerful reasons not to do so. For even those who don't wish to know have no *right* to remain in ignorance.

But while it might be justifiable to withhold damaging information from a patient in these circumstances, when there was no question of any further treatment; no consent to further treatment if this were required, would be valid without full disclosure, for the patient would not know to what he was consenting.

In any event no health care professional should be required to shoulder the responsibility for all the decisions about the patient's state of health that are properly the patient's own. Certainly patients should not expect that various professionals will take on this responsibility, and it may be both in the patient's particular interests, and in the interests of patients generally, if health care professionals are discouraged rather than encouraged to play God.

Moreover, the community as a whole may have a general interest in the autonomy of its members which would be served by their being encouraged to take autonomous decisions for themselves.

An autonomous community

It would be encouraging to think that the development of autonomy, of that critical self-determination in which the agent strives to make decisions which are as little marred by defects in reason, information or control as she can make them, would always be in the agent's best interests. One reason for thinking so would be that the agent stands the best chance of achieving what she wants in life the more autonomous she is. This is because autonomy is good for matching means to ends, for choosing the means best calculated to achieve one's objects. The problem, however, is that autonomy is also good for devising more complex, sophisticated and ambitious ends which are more difficult to achieve, thereby creating more room for frustration and disappointment. Autonomy also takes both practice and time which might be more agreeably or realistically spent, practice simply in making one's own decisions and time spent on information-gathering and the like. In a harsh world of limited opportunities, time spent on the development of autonomy might seem wasted and might lead to more frustration and unhappiness than if otherwise spent. Even in a less harsh world it might be more productive of happiness if individuals spent their time on simple and easily achievable pleasures rather than on developing autonomy with its enhanced risk of frustration. While it may seem doubtful to suppose that it would always be in our interests to maximise autonomy, most people would regard as a calamity the prospect of an accident which would leave them incapable of autonomous choice but after which they would live a simple-minded but happy life.

However, on the political level, a society will always have a strong interest in developing the autonomy of its citizens. For only autonomous citizens will have the ability to participate meaningfully in government and in political and social decision-making. Moreover, only self-determined critically aware citizens will have the ability to detect and combat the abuses of power which are endemic in complex societies.

For these reasons, while it may not be justifiable to impose constraints even on the non-autonomously chosen self-regarding actions of others, it may well be both justifiable and wise to remedy where possible, both the defects of reasoning and of information which militate against the individual's capacity for autonomy. The reasons for so doing would not be that such action was in the individual's own interests but rather that it was in the interests of us all.

Whether or not such interference would count as paternalistic is unclear. It certainly contravenes the wishes of the agent but it does so only temporarily and without limiting the agent's scope of action. Moreover, its purpose is to promote rather than limit autonomy and to increase rather than reduce the options available or perceived as available to the agent. It is also self-limiting in an important way in which straightforward paternalism is not. Once the information has been provided and the defect in reasoning pointed out and explained, the justification for the interference ceases. Straightforward paternalism (or moralism), on the other hand, is limitless and self-perpetuating. For wherever someone is seen to be doing something against their interests (or against morality) interference is both licensed and required, and so long as the agent wants to go on doing apparently self-damaging or immoral things they must be prevented.

The interference required to promote autonomy in the interests of us all is minimal and self-limiting. Once we have done our best to help others to autonomous decision-making that's that. There can be no further interference even where the agent wishes to ignore the information or the non-defective reasoning.

11 Respect for persons II

In this chapter we must consider some of the loose ends left by our discussion so far. There are four groups of cases which all involve the issue of respect in one form or another, and, while they are only loosely linked, it is convenient to take them all together. The first group involves discussion of how the principle of respect for persons applies to young persons—children—and to mental patients. We will also consider briefly whether some form of related respect is also owed to animals. We will then move on to consider the idea of respect for the dead, and ask whether this deep-rooted notion commits us to a particular view about using the dead as repositories for spare parts. The third sort of question we must consider is that of whether or not some diminished level of respect, and hence perhaps of care, is owed to those who knowingly bring the misfortune of disease or injury upon themselves. Finally we will turn to the vexed and traditional question of how far health professionals are obliged to keep the confidences of their patients.

I Children, lunatics, barbarians and animals

When setting out his principle of liberty which was designed to defend and promote the freedom of people to determine their own lives, John Stuart Mill specifically excluded from its protection three classes of persons. They were, children, lunatics and barbarians. While the number of barbarians, at least in Mill's sense of that term,[1] has much reduced since Mill's time, the same cannot be said of those in the other two categories.

The grounds for the exclusion of all three groups from the protection of Mill's principle were simply that they are all supposed to lack the ability to make autonomous decisions. I shall not further consider barbarians, since I will take it that in Mill's sense of this term barbarians have either ceased to exist or we have learnt enough to realise that some people were incorrectly so described.

Children

From the start of this discussion it has been clear that most children are also persons properly so called and I have suggested that persons are all equally entitled to the same concern, respect and protections. Whether or not particular children lack the ability to make autonomous decisions and therefore may or must be protected will be a question of judgment in each case, exactly in the same way as it is for adults. If with respect to the particular preferences in question, the decisions of children are not defective in any of the ways we have considered or in other words are maximally autonomous, then there is no more reason to interfere with them than there would be if they were adults deciding in the same circumstances. I have argued this point at greater length elsewhere[2] but we have said enough here to conclude that children should be in control of their destiny, including their health care, in the same way as are any other people.

We must remember that defects in stability are insufficient to warrant paternalistic interference, so that, although we know that children will change their preferences over time, this is of itself an insufficient ground on which to base a judgment that their, albeit unstable preferences, are not fully autonomous. To respect autonomy is to respect a person's decisions made in the light of their present character and priorities.

Of course, where a child is so young and immature that she is unable to make decisions that could be considered in any way autonomous and for the same reasons the defects that undermine her autonomy cannot be remedied, then clearly paternalistic intervention will be justified to prevent her from coming to grief. But where she is capable of maximally autonomous decisions, or would be, were the help necessary to remedy any defects to be supplied, then she must be allowed to decide for herself.

If, for example, a child were to be so frightened of injections that she refused an injection, say of an antibiotic or of an antidote to rabies or to snakebite, that would save her life, then she might well be properly regarded as incapable of autonomous choice.

Either because, like Mill's traveller, she clearly did not want to
die and failed to appreciate that the injection was, like avoiding
the bridge, the only way to stay alive, or, because her fear of
injections was so great as to deprive her of control and that, like
the addict who wishes to kick the habit, her second-order desire
to avoid death more truly represents her desires than does her
refusal of the injection. And this can be discovered without difficulty by asking the child about her attitude to death when the
threat of the injection is not present to her mind.

Just as we should let children decide for themselves in all cases
where they are capable of making autonomous decisions, so we
should not assume that parents are entitled to make decisions on
their behalf. Where the child can make up her own mind, the
preferences of parents for her will be like any other third-party
preference and the reasons given here for rejecting them will add
force to those given in Chapter 5. If we consider the case of the
children of the Jehovah's Witnesses we discussed earlier, three
different circumstances may each create its own dilemma.

If their child is capable of autonomously wishing either to
accept or reject a blood transfusion, then this decision should be
respected whatever the parents' wishes are. If, on the other hand,
the child is capable of expressing a preference but we doubt that
it is autonomous (either because the child is so young that it is
doubtful whether its decisions could fail to be defective in the
ways described earlier, or because the influence of the parents is
so great that the child is not really in control) then its life, like
that of any other person, should be preserved whatever the parents' wishes until such time as the child can decide for herself.

Finally, if the child is so young that she is not yet a person and
so no question of her having any preferences at all arises, then
our answer will depend on what we think about the parents' right
to determine the fate of their offspring who are not yet persons.
This, as we argued with some trepidation in Chapter 8, should
be a decision for the parents to make, preferably together, but if
either parent thought the child should be given the transfusion
then this should be done.[3]

Lunatics

There is much to be said for reviving the term 'lunatic' as a way
of reminding ourselves of the shaky theoretical basis and indeed
of the essentially normative character of the diagnosis of mental

illness. Much has been written on this subject recently, and while I share the scepticism about the theoretical base of much of the contemporary thinking about the nature of mental illness, we need not for our present purposes take that debate any further.[4] What is important is that we remind ourselves that whatever justifies a diagnosis of mental illness its effect is to classify the individual so diagnosed as to some extent neither responsible for his actions nor capable of managing his affairs.

While not denying that there are people who genuinely need both help and relief from their responsibilities, Mill noticed and deplored the tendency to enlarge the class of lunatics by including those who suffered from a 'defect' which, while it did nothing to impair their autonomy, was none the less both easily recognisable and much feared. This was a defect in orthodoxy:

> There is something both contemptible and frightful in the sort of evidence on which, of late years any person can be declared judicially unfit for the management of his affairs; ... All the minute details of his daily life are pried into, and whatever is found which, seen through the medium of the perceiving and describing faculties of the lowest of the low, bears an appearance unlike absolute commonplace, is laid before the jury as evidence of insanity and often with success; the jurors being little if at all less vulgar and ignorant than the witnesses; while the judges, with that extraordinary want of knowledge of human nature and life which continually astonishes us in English lawyers, often help to mislead them.[5]

If our respect for persons leads us to offer help in the form of care and relief from responsibilities to people who seem to be suffering from a 'mind diseased' and who either want our help or are helpless, we should remember that our concern does not entitle us to withdraw respect. So long as an individual is capable of autonomous choice, however bizarre, unorthodox or distasteful to us that choice may be, then we must respect it, as we would any other choice that does not involve harm to others.

With mental patients, as with children, there is no ground at all for paternalistic interference with their decisions unless it is clear in their individual case, and in the case of the particular decision in question, that they are not maximally autonomous with respect to their decision.

The case of mental patients is not significantly different from that of any other sector of health care. The obligation, which falls on all members of society, is to help to prevent and alleviate pain, suffering and harm to anyone who needs and wants this help. Where they cannot be consulted we may safely presume that they desire this help until they are able to and do disabuse us. However much we feel that they ought to want help or that their desire to be without it is unsoundly based or will lapse over time, we must none-the-less respect it. The best we can do is attempt to remedy the unsoundness by giving new information, showing up defects in reasoning and so on. But once we have done this and our help is still declined—there is an end of the matter.

For the protection of others

It is sometimes claimed that lunatics are a danger to others. Where this is claimed and the claim is used to justify compulsory preventive detention, there must clearly be some firm evidence that the person in question has taken some real and palpable steps to the danger of others. Moreover, these steps must be of a kind that would satisfy a court of law that the individual in question is a danger even if it were not the case that some claim he is mentally ill. Here the principle is precisely the same as that which justifies self-defence and which we examined in Chapter 4. We cannot be justified in taking a step so drastic as to deprive an individual of liberty unless we are sure that this is the only way we can prevent their inflicting harm on others. In the area of health care there will be relatively few such cases. Mental patients who have demonstrated that they can and will do harm to others will be one example and perhaps those with dangerous and communicable diseases will be another. But here the evidence that someone who is thought to be mentally ill constitutes a danger to others must be clear. He must at the very least have made some attempt to damage others or have taken palpable steps towards such an attempt. The opinion of experts, however experienced, should no more be enough to deprive a mental patient of his freedom than should the opinion of police officers be a sufficient ground for the preventive detention of 'criminals'.

Animals

Having looked at the way in which both children and lunatics may be victims of unwarranted assumptions about them made by health care professionals and indeed by society generally, we must consider briefly the plight of animals. The consideration will be brief, because the case for animals has been made eloquently and repeatedly elsewhere.[6] However, since animals are widely used in the health service and in institutions undertaking medical research, it is as well to reaffirm one important point. It is simply that although, like embryos, animals do not have the status and protection that must be accorded to persons, it does not follow that they are fair game. As in the case of the treatment of the embryo, only the most urgent and overwhelming of reasons could justify the infliction of pain and other distress. Only if it were absolutely and unequivocally necessary in order to save a person's life or to prevent *serious* injury or suffering to persons could the infliction of other than trivial pain or distress on animals be justified.[7] We must remember that the very same reasons that make it wrong to inflict pain on persons make it wrong to inflict pain on any other sentient creatures. But that persons, unlike other sentient creatures, are able to understand and consent to experiencing some necessary pain, whereas animals are not. Since animals cannot consent to pain or distress, the infliction of these upon them is always a case of torture and as such is justifiable only for the strongest of reasons.

II Respect for the dead

There is a tension between the ideas of respect for the living and respect for the dead where giving priority to respect for the dead means that we will be showing rather more of this respect than is strictly necessary. We noted this problem in Chapter 6, where we discussed the desirability of 'transplantation orders'. In the context of a discussion of respect for persons, it is important to emphasise that it is to persons, to beings that have the capacity to value their own existence, that respect is owed. The most important dimension of respect for persons is, as we have seen, respect for their wish to live, for all other wishes and their continued welfare are dependent upon this wish being respected. People also wish to respect and to have others respect their dead friends and relations. These two wishes come into conflict where by using organs and tissue from the dead we might save the living, or where by experimenting on the dead we might find ways to save the lives of the people in the future.

In addition to their traditional respect for the dead, people also wish to respect and to have others respect their friends and relations who, while still alive, have ceased to be persons.[8] I have

suggested that any insistence on a conception of respect for the
dead or for living non-persons which has as its consequence
injury to or even the death of other people must be both self-
defeating and morally indefensible. However, a prominent contemporary philosopher has suggested a defence of such a conception of respect and it is worth considering what he says.

Stuart Hampshire, in a much reprinted lecture given in 1972,[9]
argued firmly for the preservation of customs and taboos:

> the customs and rituals that govern, in different societies, relations
> between the sexes, marriage, property rights, family relationships,
> and the celebration of the dead, are primary moral customs; they
> always disclose the peculiar kind of respect for human life, and
> occasions for disrespect which a particular people or society recog-
> nises, and therefore their more fundamental moral beliefs and at-
> titudes.... If these prohibitions, whatever they are, were no longer
> observed, and the particular way of life, which depends on them,
> was lost, and not just amended or replaced, no particular reason
> would be left to protect human life more than any other natural
> phenomenon.[10]

Hampshire sees the idea of respect for persons as somehow embodied in the rituals and customs which in particular societies
govern certain key practices. He argues that we may 'respect and
reaffirm the prohibitions and the way of life that they protect, for
reasons unconnected with their known or presumed functions'.[11]
Hampshire's own reason for respecting such customs and rituals
is simply:

> because this specifically conceived way of life, with its accompany-
> ing prohibitions, has in history appeared natural and on the whole
> still feels natural, both to oneself and others. If there are no over-
> riding reasons for rejecting this way of life, or for rejecting some
> distinguishing features of it, its felt and proven naturalness is one
> reason among others for accepting it.[12]

Hampshire's other, and it seems chief, reason for accepting it is
the belief that 'the natural order as a whole is the fitting object of
that kind of unconditional interest and respect that is called
moral'.[13]

It is hard to find anything particularly persuasive in Hampshire's account. The customs and rituals that seem natural in
some epochs seem merely ridiculous in others. Moreover, things
may feel natural because we have always done them that way, but
the question of why we should continue to do so at some cost to

human happiness, or liberty or even life is more problematic. Here, instead of finding reasons to support ritual and taboo 'quite unconnected with their known or presumed functions', we might want to look closely at their known or presumed functions to see whether they served any interest of an importance comparable with the costs of continuing to observe them. If they proved costly in terms of human life or liberty or happiness,[14] an additional and overriding reason for respecting them, defended in terms of their 'feeling natural', seems pathetically weak.

And as for respecting the natural order as a whole, well, it depends what description of the natural order one takes or of what the natural order happens to be doing. If it is wreaking its usual toll of disaster and mayhem in terms of disease, famine, violence, and so on, we might well wish to reserve some portion of our respect. We might also think that the natural order as a whole could stand some improvement, which, as we have repeatedly emphasised in this work, is one reasonable account of the aims and hopes of the practice of medicine. How far one feels compelled to object to Hampshire may well turn on how much is permitted by his escape clause, allowing overriding reasons for rejecting the customs and rituals of the natural way of life. It is clear from Hampshire's whole argument that he would allow very few, for that would undermine the whole point of respect for rituals and customs *regardless* of their functions.

However, what I wish now to propose could conceivably be allowed by Hampshire's escape clause. What we need to do, I suggest, is not so much abandon our notions of respect for the dead as to modify our conception of what such respect involves.

The gift relationship

We need to ask not so much what we can do for the dead, but what they can do for humankind. Or rather, we, the living, should come to regard death or the extinction of personhood as providing us with a unique opportunity to help others. An opportunity, moreover, which lets us bestow an immense, almost incalculable, benefit on others at absolutely no personal cost! This factor alone is enough to recommend it to all but the most mean or the most maniacally self-denying.

In short, our conception of respect for the dead should be modified to a convention in which we respect the best aspects of their former selves, and make it a rule that all persons on departing from that state, whether to death or to non-personhood, will

celebrate their passing by a bequest to people generally of anything of value that can be salvaged from their bodies. On this
conception of respect for the dead, it would be a mark of supreme
disrespect to assume that anyone would be so mean as to wish to
deny their former fellows the chance of life or of a better life that
their demise could bestow. Anyone who wished to exempt themselves would be regarded as mean and base in the extreme, and
wise friends and relations, wishing the best to be thought of their
dear dead departed, would suppress the dying wish and make
sure that everyone believed that the deceased had not shamed
himself and his family by such a mean final act.

We would then move from an opting in to an opting out scheme
for tissue and organ donation. This would preserve the idea of a
'gift' and we could hope that social pressure would make the
practice almost universal. An added attraction of avoiding a compulsory scheme might be that under such a scheme organ donation might be regarded as a tax, and resented, rather than as a gift
and a last chance for the exercise of virtue.

However, we should bear in mind what's at stake for those at
risk if sufficient cadaver donors are not forthcoming under a voluntary opting out scheme. As a last resort we should have in
reserve a power for the transplantation orders (envisaged in Chapter 6) to be made, where this is the only way to provide the
necessary donor organs for those at risk.

III Self-inflicted illness

In Chapter 5 we looked at the question of whether the moral
character of a person should count against them, or indeed for
them, in the allocation of health care. We concluded that it would
be difficult in the extreme to come to any reliable conclusions
about the moral character of most people, and that even where
we could, as in the case, say, of convicted murderers, there was
something unjust about adding to the penalties already deemed
sufficient. One problem that remains, and which is frequently
mentioned as a possible reason for refusing people health care, or
at least for refusing them priority in health care, is that of self-
inflicted illness.

Should those who have brought their illness upon themselves
rank equally in the competition for scarce health resources with
those for whom illness or injury has come literally as a bolt from
the blue?

Justice

At first sight there seems to be something unjust about the possibility of preferring to rescue someone who has knowingly put themselves in need of rescue rather than their innocent neighbour who, through no fault of her own, has been struck down by disaster. If, for example, lung transplants became as easy and as effective as are kidney transplants today, but donor organs were in very short supply, we might think that there was something wrong in giving the only available lung to the person who has destroyed his own lung through smoking, and showed every sign and intention of doing the same to his new lung, rather than, say, giving it to the woman next door whose need for a new lung has been in no way self-inflicted. Do we, however, feel the same sense of injustice when contemplating the competition for the necessary intensive care between someone who has broken her neck hang-gliding and the man whose neck has been broken by a motor accident in which he was the innocent victim?

One problem is that we seem to operate with a preference for some rather than other sources of risk. We seem to prefer that people risk their lives mountaineering rather than smoking, for example. Now there may be a rational basis for this. Mountaineering is 'healthy' in the sense of providing exercise and, where accident-free, each climb is a contribution to the fitness of the mountaineer. Each cigarette, on the other hand, is another 'nail in the coffin' of the smoker. However, we also have other less easily justifiable preferences between different practices which attack health or increase risk of illness. We condemn sloth less than gluttony, and both less than smoking, although each is a significant risk factor in various serious illnesses.

One problem is that there are so many factors that influence health and so many things that we can manipulate that affect the risk of falling prey to particular ailments. It might be possible to put some percentage figure of each risky practice or failure to practise and tot up all the risk factors for each individual. This might yield a total figure for self-inflicted risk which could be used to rank-order candidates for therapy, priority being given to those with the lowest percentile of self-inflicted risk.

The idea that bad habits not only increased the risk of illness, but decreased the chance of obtaining cure or therapy, might be helpful in both bringing home to people the risks that they run, and also in persuading them to reduce their level of self-inflicted risk.

Liberty or justice?

There is a dilemma here, however. Whereas it might well be unjust to save the life of someone who has wantonly risked her life rather than that of her rival for rescue, who had taken every care throughout her life to avoid risk, to some, perhaps to many, life is only worth living if it can be lived as they choose. And this choice might involve the risk to health of living life 'to the full' with drunkenness, debauchery and every other kind of dangerous vice. Others might choose a less reprehensible (?) but equally risky way of life—bearing children, or hang-gliding, or taking any other sort of risk. Some will even choose to take risks for their own sake, for the love of risk itself.

Much earlier in our discussion we carefully avoided the invidiousness of examining the different choices of life-style or of anything else with a view to deciding which sort of life or which decisions might be more worthwhile. We argued that, short of inflicting harm on others, it was better to concentrate simply on the fact that people did value different things and valued life so that they could pursue whatever it was they found of value. All things being equal, we should continue to refrain from judging between preferences or life-styles, and not judge the risk-free life better, or more worthy of being lived, than one filled with risk of various sorts.

The problem is, of course, that all is not equal. The life of risk, when that risk includes risk to life and health, is damaging to others—for by risking my own life I increase the competition for scarce medical resources and so increase the risk that others who do not choose to run risks at all,[15] or to the same extent or in the same way that I do, will lose out in the competition for rescue and health care generally.

However this may be, it seems to me better to attempt, as far as is possible, to provide health care and rescue for all, irrespective of the extent to which they may have contributed to their own need for help, and even though this fact adversely affects others to some extent. I don't think there are any totally convincing reasons why everyone should agree with me about this. It seems to me, however, that the invidiousness of respecting less those who choose to run risks is worse than the alternative. For we can reduce the risk to innocent third parties almost to vanishing point by increasing the social priority that we give to health care. Those who attempt to avoid risk altogether will then have no prudential reason for objecting.

Moreover, since most people are likely voluntarily to choose to undergo some degree of risk to health, either in the sport they prefer, or in their diet, or in their occupation, or in their choice of lovers (indeed for women the choice to have a lover at all is risky since cervical cancer is unknown among virgins) or in their choice not to indulge in exercise or ... The list is endless, and small indeed are the chances of being able to be confident in any actual competition for scarce medical resources that one of the competitors was clearly a non-contributor. Moreover, would they have to be innocent of all contribution to the risk of ill-health or injury, or merely of contribution to the risk that has actually laid them low?

However, convincing arguments one way or the other are here in short supply, and it would be rash to rule out the possibility of wishing to use the fact that someone in particular had inflicted harm on herself as a reason for preferring to help someone else, where both cannot be saved and some reason for selection is needed.

There are, however, convincing arguments against doing this arbitrarily. In particular we should guard against allowing mere prejudice to influence which risks we judge to be unacceptable and which would therefore bar those who run them from health care or rescue. In particular we should be able and willing to justify our selection. For example, it is far from clear that risks to health resulting from too much exercise are more acceptable than are risks to health consequent upon too little exercise.

We must now turn to the final issue that remains to be discussed under the heading of respect for persons, and ask how and to what extent confidentiality is a requirement of the health care professional's respect for her patients and clients.

IV Confidentiality

The idea that health care professionals have a binding obligation to keep the secrets of their patients and regard as confidential any information about the patient, including that which arises from casual observation, which comes their way while the professional-patient relationship subsists, has long been regarded as one of the most important principles of medical ethics. It is prominent in the Hippocratic Oath,[16] which may go some way to accounting for its tenacity. The Hippocratic Oath has probably done more harm than good in contemporary medical ethics. It's an odd mixture. It starts, as one might expect from the oath of an exclusive guild, with principles to ensure the perpetuation and success of the guild. Members first swear to honour their teachers and help them financially where necessary. The second most important principle seems to involve the obligation to provide free medical education to the sons (but not the daughters) of other doctors. Thereafter, follows a limited set of more universal ethical principles including the commitment to confidentiality.

Medical practitioners seem to have very readily abandoned the commitment to provide medical education without fee, and to help out their teachers financially. A similar selectivity has been much in evidence with regard to the commitment to refrain from procuring abortions which is also part of the Oath. However, despite this selectivity among the Hippocratic principles, respect for the principle of confidentiality has survived relatively unimpaired. The problem of how to interpret and apply the principle has remained one of the chief sources of difficulty and has generated some of the most interesting and intractable cases in medical ethics.

The arguments that we have been developing so far in this book will enable us to, if not resolve, at least see how to try to resolve these dilemmas. But before making that attempt to resolve the difficulties surrounding confidentiality, we must trace the various sources of our respect for confidentiality and then look at some leading and difficult cases in which confidentiality and its limits are the central issue.

Why keep confidences?

1 Hippocracy. The first reason for health professionals keeping the confidences of their patients is simply that they believe they ought to. The Hippocratic Oath is very often cited as the source or authority for this belief. However, those who believe themselves bound to keep this part of the oath while discarding others of its injunctions, clearly have other reasons for so doing. The oath, after all, is taken by very few doctors these days, and even someone who both took the oath and felt bound by all its clauses might be curious as to why this was the right oath for a health professional to take. Such curiosity might be satisfied by reflection on the following three reasons.

2 Utility There is a strong utilitarian argument as to why health care professionals should keep the secrets of their patients. Firstly, belief that professionals will keep their confidences enables patients to seek help without fear of any stigma, or other repercussions, that might result from public knowledge of their problem. This both keeps doctors in work, encourages patients to seek early help, and so aids in the preservation of a healthy society. Once they have sought help, patients will have the further confidence to make very full disclosure of any material facts, and the mutual trust that will develop—trust on the part of the doctor that the patient will tell all, and on the part of the patient that the doctor will keep all to himself (or to other equally discreet professionals)—will of itself be material to the success of any treatment.

3 Contract A further suggestion is that there is either an express or an implied contract between the professional and the patient, that the professional only acquires the information she receives from or about her patient on the understanding that she will keep it secret. Part of the evidence for this implied contract is often said to be the fact that patients almost universally expect that doctors are obliged to keep their secrets, and act on this assumption.

4 Right to privacy It is sometimes claimed that there is a right to privacy, and that this must include 'personal control over information about oneself and over access to that information. Without such personal control, important human relationships such as love, friendship and trust would be diminished.'[17] It can be seen that this supposed right rests on an unashamedly utilitarian justification. Certainly privacy is useful, and would be badly undermined without some reasonable expectation that health care professionals should keep our confidences.

A combination of at least the last three of these four reasons would seem to establish that we all have a strong interest in encouraging, and perhaps even enforcing, some principle of professional confidentiality. The problems of course arise when other strong principles pull in the direction of disclosure. If we examine some clear cases where this is so it may be possible to outline a general approach which will reconcile these apparently opposed principles.

Four cases

I will begin by outlining the facts of each case as briefly as possible and then move to a discussion of how the dilemmas they
present are to be resolved. The first two cases are real and were
the subject of judicial, or quasi-judicial proceedings. The third
was also 'real', but is more heavily disguised, while the fourth I
have constructed from current medical practice supplemented
with an assumption that procedures which will certainly be available in the very near future are already with us.

1 The Tarasoff Case[18] This real and much-discussed case occurred
in 1969 and concerned a student, Prosenjit Poddar, who fell in
love with Tatiana Tarasoff. When she rejected him he became
depressed and consulted a psychologist, Dr Lawrence Moore, to
whom he confided his intention to kill Ms Tarasoff. Although the
police were informed and detained Mr Poddar, they released him
again when he promised to stay away from Ms Tarasoff. No one
warned either Ms Tarasoff or her parents of the danger, and Mr
Poddar killed her two months from the date on which he first
confided in Dr Moore his intention so to do. Her parents brought
an action against the Regents of the University of California, who
employed Dr Moore, alleging negligence in not informing them
of the danger to their daughter.

2 Miss X and Dr Browne[19] Miss X, an intelligent and mature 16-
year-old, decided not to seek contraceptive advice from her family
physician, Dr Browne, but went instead to a clinic specialising in
providing such advice for young people. The clinic, with Miss
X's consent, informed Dr Browne that she had been prescribed
an oral contraceptive, so that he should be fully aware of her
medical history. Dr Browne was worried about Miss X on two
grounds: he was concerned about physical dangers from oral con-
traceptives, but he was also concerned for the moral and psychological dangers that might face his young patient. He decided that
Miss X's parents should be informed and that this course of
action was in her best interests. Dr Browne did this without first
informing Miss X of his intention so to do and without asking for
her consent to disclose the information. The clinic then brought
a complaint against Dr Browne to the General Medical Council
alleging serious professional misconduct.

3 The O'Reilly case[20] Mr O'Reilly, a married man, consulted his
doctor and confessed to what eventually transpired as a casual
homosexual encounter. As a result of this Mr O'Reilly had contracted non-specific urethritis and was terrified lest his wife

should find out—this he believed would surely result in her taking the children and leaving him. Mr O'Reilly believed that his wife may well have contracted the infection from him and wanted his doctor to treat his wife without revealing to her the reason. The doctor tried to persuade Mr O'Reilly that he should be honest with his wife but when this attempt proved unsuccessful he agreed to tell Mrs O'Reilly that she needed some pills for 'a little infection of the cervix' when she came to him for a routine cervical smear test.

4 Huntington's Chorea As a result of the development of a genetic marker for Huntington's Chorea, a predictive test with a very high degree of accuracy is imminent.[21] When this is available the 20,000 or so people in Britain who have a high risk of developing this inherited genetic disorder will be able to know for sure whether or not they have a disease which will bring their life disastrously and prematurely to an end, and whether or not they will be able to have children who will be free of the disorder.

> Those with an affected parent and other relatives at high risk have faced a dilemma: either they may choose to have children, only to find that they later develop the disease and have passed the risk on to their offspring, each of whom will have a 50% chance of being affected; or they may decide against childbearing when in reality they do not carry the harmful gene.[22]

When the test is available such people will be able to find out for sure whether or not they are affected. This will bring with it new and more radical dilemmas. While many of those who have hitherto had to live with the knowledge that they have a high risk of developing the disease will be reassured and can have their fear removed, others, though fewer, will have their fears confirmed. As Peter Harper, a leading British expert on Huntington's Chorea has observed:

> Living under the shadow of the disorder with a 50% risk is itself traumatic, but the removal of most or all of the uncertainty, may radically alter the person's reaction. Some relatives may choose not to be tested (between 10% and 40%, according to previous studies), others who request testing may not be able to cope with the burden that the new knowledge places on them. ... Confidentiality of results will be essential, yet in some circumstances the result for one person will directly affect the risks for other family members. What will happen if there is disagreement within a family about testing? Will pressure be brought to bear on indi-

viduals at risk to be tested when faced with problems of insurance
or employment?[23]

Respect for persons revisited

If patients wish, as most do, that health professionals respect as
confidential information they acquire in the course of their professional relationship with the patient, then this gives health professionals a good reason to respect the confidences of their patients.
If we add to this the actual or implied contract to this effect and
the utilitarian reasons for preserving the convention of confidentiality, the case becomes very strong indeed. However, good
reasons must perforce give way to better; and the only remaining
question is what sorts of reason for breaking confidences are
strong enough to outweigh this accumulation of good reasons for
keeping them?

One of the arguments of this book has been that the obligation
to minimise suffering and injury to others which falls on us all
also falls on health professionals. Such professionals are, however,
hit no harder by this obligation than is anyone else who could
discharge it. Anyone at all who has received a confidence, even if
they have received it in a context in which an express or implied
contract to keep that confidence exists, must ask herself the following question. If I keep this confidence, will that result in the
occurrence of the sort of harm or suffering that I should not
inflict on others, and is the importance of keeping the confidence
so great as to justify the infliction of that harm or suffering?

Sometimes, of course, the answer will be 'yes' and sometimes
not. Neither the obligation to refrain from decisions which harm
others, nor the obligation to keep faith, is sacrosanct. The individual must always decide what it is more important to do. Of
course the professional must also bear in mind the good that
public confidence in the ethic of professional confidence-keeping
does, in encouraging people to come forward for treatment who
might otherwise hesitate. But not all breaches of confidence will
undermine this confidence and some will do some countervailing
good.

One constraint upon the universal, and perhaps blind, application of the above principle is the one we have most recently been
considering, that of respecting persons by respecting their autonomy. So that where the greater good to be done by the breach of
a confidence (or by the keeping of one) is paternalistic and the

justifications for paternalism we have been considering are not present, where there is no defect, or no relevant defect, in the autonomy of the individual concerned, then again, even if it will do more good than harm, our respect for persons gives us a strong reason to avoid the paternalistic interference. If we look again at the four cases we can see how these considerations might guide our judgments.

In the Tarasoff case, it may or may not be a matter for fine judgment, but the balance that has to be struck is that between the risk of death to Ms Tarasoff, on the one hand, and the obligation to keep Mr Poddar's secrets coupled with the overall utility of a convention of secret-keeping between professional and client, on the other. Where the danger to a possible victim is both real, present and serious, there must surely be a good case for a breach of confidence. Particularly where, as in this case, the confidence is owed to an intending, albeit 'disturbed', murderer. True, the likelihood of the murderer's carrying out his threat is hard to gauge, and for this reason legal grounds for detention would be hard to find. However, when we compare what Ms Tarasoff stands to lose with what Mr Poddar stands to lose, it is difficult to feel confident that there are any grounds for not alerting Ms Tarasoff to the possible dangers. The fact that a warning had been issued might of course be kept relatively secret, and so not undermine too much public confidence in professional confidence-keeping.

We must also remember that the psychologist Dr Moore had already broken confidence to a number of people. He may not have mentioned very specific details, but he had written to the police a 'letter of diagnosis' requesting them to detain Mr Poddar for emergency psychiatric evaluation. This 'betrayal' is likely to be regarded by Mr Poddar as significant, and beyond the bounds of professional ethics, and yet the idea that this might be a breach of professional ethics was not, so far as I am aware, ever canvassed.

The good that Dr Browne contemplated, on the other hand, was purely paternalistic. All his duty was to Miss X. There was no evidence at all that her decision was other than autonomous, and it was one, moreover, that she was both legally and morally entitled to make for herself. At the most Dr Browne could act like any other caring friend of Miss X and reason with her. That he made no attempt to do so is some evidence of his lack of good faith. In the real case from which this example is taken, Dr

Browne's view was upheld by the General Medical Council, because he was judged to have acted in his patient's best interests. After this case was resolved in Dr Browne's favour the British Medical Association recommended that the physician should always try to get the permission of the patient to break the confidence, but if this were not forthcoming should accept the patient's decision. While this instruction yields the right decision in this case, it cannot, as we have seen, be a principle well calculated to give the right answer in all cases. There can be no simple rubric in these matters. Health professionals must, like anyone else, weigh up what is at stake and see how that affects their interpretation of other principles that they accept, like that of respect for persons.

The case of the O'Reillys is more complex. The doctor clearly felt that his duty to keep Mr O'Reilly's confidences was greater than his duty to tell Mrs O'Reilly the truth about what was wrong with her. It is not clear why he might have thought this or what would justify it. Moreover, Mrs O'Reilly might, like her husband, have lovers of her own who might be endangered by the doctor's secrecy.[24] The doctor clearly thought that preserving their marriage was both in the best interests of both his patients and of overriding importance. However, it is the grossest paternalism to attempt to preserve this marriage when the parties to it, or at least one of them, might not want it artificially preserved at such a cost. The doctor, after all, was given due notice by Mr O'Reilly that his wife would leave him if she found out. Clear evidence that she would want to know what was wrong with her so that she could make her own decisions about it. Clear evidence also that she probably did not value her marriage if it involved her husband's infidelity. Here again, it is not up to the doctor to decide what should be an acceptable basis for other people's marriages. Nor should he decide without a very good reason for so doing, that his obligation to keep the husband's secrets was so much more important than his obligation to give a proper and full diagnosis to the wife, so that she could make her own decisions, particularly when he had been given notice by the husband that she would want to know.

The imminence of an accurate predictive test for Huntington's Chorea, using recombinant DNA techniques, signals the use of such techniques to provide predictive tests for other disorders. The ethical dilemmas that these tests will bring with them will be both varied and very difficult to resolve. While it will always be open to individuals to refuse such tests for themselves, they may not be able to so effectively shield themselves from the increased knowledge of their own chances, which will come from relatives who do opt for the test. They will also have to consider whether they are justified in having children who will certainly, or probably, have the disease.

This is a particularly poignant problem since the possibility of an accurate predictive test makes possible the complete eradication of Huntington's Chorea. If all at risk took the test and refrained from reproduction if the test proved positive the condition could be wiped out in a generation or so. The issue of confidentiality, however, concerns principally the question of whether or not health professionals must keep their knowledge of the results of such tests confidential, where, for example, employers or insurance companies are affected. Here, unless there is some danger to third parties as in the Tarasoff case, health professionals have no reason to break the confidences of their patients. What the patients do or do not say to others is for them to decide.

Confidentiality, as we have seen, should be respected when the good reasons for so doing are not outweighed by better reasons for breaking the confidence. No one can complain that an obligation of confidentiality owed to them has been flouted, where, for example, such an obligation can be respected only at the cost of the life or of other serious injury to third parties. In each case the considerations on either side must be carefully weighed. One thing, however, is clear. It is that anyone who accepts the requirement to keep confidential the transactions between themselves and a patient and the knowledge they acquire of the patient's affairs, must be prepared to defend in detail both adherence to and breaches of the principle in particular cases.

V Ultimate principles and moral values

While confidentiality has almost universally been acknowledged as a binding obligation and a fundamental principle of medical ethics, respect for confidentiality has been in practice governed by a sort of schizophrenia. On the one hand, health professionals have been prepared rigidly to respect the confidences between doctor and patient, sometimes at substantial personal cost. On the other hand, the same professionals who have so carefully preserved and respected the ethic of confidentiality, have seen no

inconsistency at all in telling all the relatives and many of the
friends of terminally ill patients the full details of their condition
before, and often instead of, telling the patients themselves! This
schizophrenia shows that even those who believe fairly implicitly
in the principle of confidentiality are prepared to waive it when
they judge that more important things are at stake.

Our attitude to confidentiality demonstrate something very
important about the ways in which moral principles operate
within a broad system of morality. Blind adherence to the principle of confidentiality, like blind adherence to any principle, is
indefensible. We must always be aware of the possibility that our
principles may be defective, or that there may be a more important principle which requires us in these circumstances to abandon or modify our rules of conduct. Or it may be that if we reflect
upon our reasons for adopting and approving of the principle in
question, we will find that to follow it in these particular circumstances will be self-defeating. This might happen in a number of
ways. It might be that the operation of this principle in these
circumstances will subvert the very interests that we adopted the
principle to protect. Or it might be that the principle is a sort of
shorthand for the expression of more complex values which will
be undermined or negated if we act on the principle in the present
circumstances.

We saw in Chapter 4, for example, that we might accept a
principle that required us to refrain from killing other people but
see that the principle was not an end in itself but was rather a
part of what is involved in accepting that other people's lives are
valuable. Seeing the principle in the context of a more general
view about which lives are valuable and of what it is to respect
the value of the lives of others in turn enables us to see that
exceptions can be made to this principle without inconsistency.
Where in extreme circumstances the other person's life is so terrible that death is preferable, we can see that the same considerations which explain and justify our acceptance of the principle in
the first place, also explain and justify our making an exception
to it in such a case.

Similarly in the present case. It is only by having a lively sense
of the point of, and the justifications for, any principle that we
are inclined to accept, that we can judge just how important that
principle is and what sacrifices may defensibly be made to preserve it. By seeing what interests and indeed what other values are
subserved by accepting a general obligation to keep confidential

a patient's or a client's 'secrets', we can begin to acquire a sense of when respect for confidentiality must give way so that other more important values or interests may be protected.

When we treat any principle as inviolable we turn our backs on morality; we say in effect 'I will not ask myself why following this principle in these circumstances is right, for fear of discovering that it is not.' But where we accept nothing on trust and no principle as inviolable, where moreover we have thought about and questioned the point of the principles we accept, and the justifications that can be given for adhering to them, we can begin to see whether those things we regard as morally important are better served by adherence to this principle in this case or not.

Some principles, however, do not seem to have some further point, nor are they apparently justified by reference to more basic values. Indeed, it is common to regard such principles just as the expression of the most basic values, and therefore as standing in need of no further justification in terms of still further values that they are supposed to protect or subserve. It is sometimes thought that there is no way these most basic principles can be questioned or criticised—they just are, for a particular individual, the values he or she accepts; they are simply ultimate values.

The idea here is that you can go on asking an individual to justify her position and that in doing so the moral agent is likely to produce more and more abstract principles in justification of their moral views until at last bedrock is reached in the shape of something that is for that person a basic value. It is at this point that moral argument runs out. Either these basic values are acceptable or they are not—there is nothing left on which moral argument can get a grip.

Now this picture of the structure of moral positions and of the way in which moral argument functions is unnecessarily pessimistic. There are at least two strategies that can be used to test principles that for particular individuals constitute the expression of basic or ultimate values, and we have used both of them already in this book.

The first strategy involves the invention of hypothetical counter-examples. These can be effective because an ultimate value depends on nothing further, and in particular, it cannot depend on any facts about the world as it happens to be at a particular time. Ultimate values should hold good not only in the world as it is but also in any imaginable or possible world. If one can invent imaginable circumstances, however remote or unlikely, in which the basic principles would not hold good or in which people would wish to revise or abandon those principles, then this shows at the very least that there is something wrong with those values. This both explains, and I hope justifies, the periodic resort to extreme and fanciful examples in the course of our discussion. It also and incidentally helps to explain why medical science is so important a subject of study for those interested in ethics. For it is medical science that has generated some of the most dramatic new possibilities which have challenged the basic values of many people. The new situations with which it presents us are at the same time increasingly strange and decreasingly fanciful.

The second strategy that can lead to the revision even of ultimate values involves setting the principles which are the expression of those values in the context of the network of values that hold good for an individual, and of asking whether those values taken as a whole are well calculated to make the world a better place. We tend to operate with a picture of morality as a house built on unshakeable foundations which an individual can redecorate from time to time, and modify occasionally, but of which the foundations must remain constant. The foundations must remain simply because if they shift the house falls. However, a better picture of morality might be provided by thinking of it not as a house but as a houseboat, 'afloat on the sea of life and heading for a better world'. Despite the rather pretentious hyperbole of this example, it has its uses, as will I hope appear.

No plank of the houseboat is basic in the sense of being irreplaceable, although some planks do support others. Each and every plank may be examined during the voyage and found wanting and replaced (using the large supply of spare timber that is always carried). The only constraints upon examination and replacement of planks are the obvious ones, that while afloat the whole structure cannot be junked and re-built from scratch. Enough of the ship must always be left intact so that it stays afloat while repairs are carried out. But any particular plank can, with ingenuity, be replaced *en route* without sinking the whole enterprise.

The inhabitants of the moral houseboat may have all sorts of good reasons for wanting to replace even very basic planks. They might simply be carrying out routine examination and discover that a plank, that once seemed sound, has become rotten or is riddled with death watch beetle. They might change so much of the rest of the boat that a particular plank, while sound in itself, no longer fits with the others. One reason that the moral mariner might have for changing much of the boat in mid-stream might be the discovery that the boat, while sound, is not best constructed to reach the chosen destination, or that a new and better destination has appeared on the horizon and a rather different boat is required in order to reach it.

To return from our nautical metaphor to the *terra firma* of ordinary philosophising, the elements of a morality must fit together to form a coherent whole. The principles must not be inconsistent one with another and the whole system must form a coherent basis for the decisions of life. Moreover anything which can be called a morality must be well calculated to promote the moral objectives of the individual in question. So that even very basic or ultimate principles may be tested by reference to the other principles a particular individual also holds, and if they are inconsistent with those other principles, one or the other will have to be modified or replaced. The whole set of principles can be tested by the invention of examples or situations which show that this moral system leads in a direction that the particular moral agent would prefer, for moral reasons, not to go. Or, that the individual develops a new moral objective and finds that his existing moral system has elements that are ill equipped to achieve that objective. In either case we have a way of questioning and criticising even basic principles and perhaps equally importantly, the individual has a way of reviewing and assessing his own principles.

12 Death is abolished

It is appropriate at the end to talk of death. Human beings have always been obsessed by death, and not only because they usually wish to avoid it for as long as possible. In medical practice the fascination is no less evident, and the controversy surrounding death as an issue in its own right has centred on three main questions: What is death? When is it right to say that death has occurred? And, how do we know when it's right to say that death has occurred? Put another way these three questions concern the definition of death, the criterion for determining the occurrence of death and the tests that might show that the criterion has been met.

These questions have assumed a new interest and importance with the advent of our ability to use organs and other tissue for transplantation from one human being to another. Most live human beings both want to keep, and are justified in wanting to keep, all their organs and tissue in place. The dead, however, can make no such claims and are owed no duties.[1] Since most organs and other tissue must be taken from either a living, or a very recently dead, body the determination of the moment of death assumes a special significance.

I What is death?

There are two main sorts of answer given to the question of what is death. The first style of answer, exemplified by Robert Veatch, takes death to be a moral not a biological question. Veatch argues that what we want to know is 'when it is appropriate to treat someone as dead'.[2] And the answer Veatch gives to this question is, that this is when 'the moral standing of the individual change[s] so radically that the same rights claims attributed to living persons are no longer attributed'.[3] Veatch thinks that moral standing disappears when a person comes irreversibly to lack 'an embodied capacity for consciousness or social interaction'.[4] The oddity of Veatch's definition as a definition of *death* is brought out when he has to remind us that 'when a person is dead, by definition, that person loses the right not to be killed'.[5] The necessity of reminding us that the *dead* have no right not to be *killed*, arises from Veatch not sufficiently clearly emphasising that he is distinguishing the death of the person from the death of the human being, and allowing that the person might die while his human body still lives on.

The merit of Veatch's style of answer is that it draws attention to the important fact that what we are interested in and care about are persons, and that when an individual permanently loses the characteristics of personhood there is nothing left for us to care for, and nothing left that has wishes we must respect. Its drawback is of course that it is not really a definition of *death*, since he himself has still to remind us that we can, when personality is absent, go ahead and kill the dead.

Death of the human organism

Ian Kennedy, on the other hand, talks as if he also is concerned with the death of the person, but he is confused in a way that Veatch is not. He begins in fine style, noting that:

> we are equally interested in the meaning of life. We are asking, when does life leave someone? Put another way, when does someone cease to be a person? A person is someone whom the law protects, to whom duties are owed both legal and ethical, and who may make claims on others. What we are concerned with is the identification of that which is crucial to being a person.[6]

The identification of these features Kennedy notes is 'clearly a philosophical and spiritual issue ... [which] calls for the selection of a point beyond which we are prepared to say someone is no longer a person'.[7] However, Kennedy has absolutely nothing to say about the meaning of life or about what it is that makes someone a person. The definition of death he chooses is essentially 'that point at which the vital functions of breathing, heartbeat and the capacity for consciousness have ceased for ever'.[8] In arguing for the importance of all three elements Kennedy notes that 'if we were to regard permanent loss of consciousness as

death, it would mean that someone would be dead who was breathing of his own accord. Clearly this is unacceptable . . .'[9]

Kennedy does not say why this is unacceptable, nor does he
argue for any of the three essential elements of personhood. This
is because he has conflated life with personhood. What he is really
interested in is the definition of death. And the unacceptability he
points to is the unacceptability of regarding someone as dead who
is spontaneously breathing. This is unacceptable in a way that
regarding an individual (a dog) as not a person despite spontaneous breathing is not.

Although he claims to be developing a philosophical and spiritual account of life and death, Kennedy is really only interested
in a scientific or biological account. He eventually argues for
brain-stem death as the criterion for death. If the brain-stem 'is
destroyed nothing can function. There can be no breathing, no
heartbeat, no thought. Thus, what is crucial to personality is the
brain-stem, not the total brain ... Death on this basis therefore
is the total and irreversible loss of all brain-stem function.'[10] But
this is because the brain-stem is necessary because nothing can
function without it, not because it is necessary for personality
rather than say for life without personality.

Biological death

If we are interested in the definition of death, it seems better to
adopt an account which concentrates on the biology rather than
on the personality. There is something irredeemably odd about
saying that a person is dead and then going on to argue that this
justifies their being killed. There is fairly wide agreement about
the very commonsense definition of death as 'the permanent cessation of the functioning of the organism as a whole'.[11] The problem arises when it is asked what is the criterion that this has
occurred? Here there are two main accounts: one argues that
death has occurred when the entire brain has ceased to function.
This is the view which predominates in the United States as a
partial consequence of the view taken by the President's Commission for the Study of Ethical Problems in Medicine and
Biomedical and Behavioural Research in its report on *Defining
Death* published in July 1981. The other main view is that death
occurs when the brain-stem has ceased to function. This is the
view taken by Kennedy and many others and which predominates
in the United Kingdom.[12]

I shall not be concerned here to adjudicate between these two criteria of death. Both concentrate on the role that the brain plays in the functioning of the organism as a whole; both rely on the fact that when the whole brain or the brain-stem is dead, the so-called *vital* functions, the parts of the organism whose functioning is necessary for the continued functioning of the organism as a whole, can no longer be maintained. Advocates of brain-stem death argue that any remaining electrical activity in the upper brain that persists after brain-stem death is not evidence of consciousness, but is rather like the continued growth of fingernails or hair—the spontaneous turning of a few remaining cogs that are no longer connected to the machinery, and though they turn, nothing turns with them. Advocates of whole-brain death are not so sure about this and would prefer to wait until the cog of electrical activity in the upper brain also ceases to turn just in case something important turns with it.

I am not here concerned to adjudicate between these criteria for the death of the organism because it seems to me relatively unimportant. What matters is whether or not the organism is still a person, not whether or not it is dead.

II Live persons and dead bodies

It is persons that matter morally. On the account of the person developed in Chapter 1, any being that has possessed the capacity to want to exist will be a person and will continue to be one until he or she loses that capacity. It is not, then, life that is important, but 'personality' thus defined. For most of us the two go together, but, as we have seen, they can come apart and when they do it is personality that matters. For example, it would be theoretically possible[13] for complex machines, perhaps very sophisticated computers, to count as persons if they were capable of valuing their own existence and of wishing not to cease to exist.[14] Whether we would call their existence 'life' or not is not important—it may be that life is only possessed by biological organisms which are also the only sorts of thing that can die. If personality is the name we give to something like a state of consciousness possessed by organisms and possibly by machines, then what matters is whether or not a particular organism or machine's capacity for the sort of consciousness characteristic of personhood or personality has or has not ceased. If it has, then all that matters morally is absent as well, whether or not the organism still lives or the machine is still intact in other respects.

Loss of personhood

What we need, then, is not a definition of death but an account
of when it is right to say that personhood is lost. All definitions
of death are united by their agreement that death, whatever else
it is and whatever the criteria of death may be, involves the *permanent* and *irreversible* loss of life. Personhood, as we have seen,
involves the capacity to want to exist and the sort of self-consciousness that makes the possession of such a want possible.
When these are present it is clear that the being in whom they
are present is a person. Once they are lost, the being has ceased
to be a person and then, even if their body is still technically
alive, it has lost its moral significance and can either be killed or
allowed to die or preserved alive as we choose. Where its organs
or tissue can be used to save the lives of other people who have
not lost personhood but who may be in danger of losing their
personhood through death or some other cause, then we have a
motive for keeping alive the body of the former person so that the
tissue and organs remain alive and usable.

An acute problem is whether or not the loss of personhood will
only be judged to have occurred when the loss is clearly permanent or whether we might judge a being to have lost personality
in circumstances in which the personality might return? This
problem may be very important indeed, but we will not return to
it until we have seen just why it is so important. To do so we
must examine the idea of permanence at some length, and consider in particular a problem that has hitherto been thought of as
unproblematic—that of when life in particular may be said permanently and irreversibly to have ended.

III Machine people

Suppose that we do eventually build computers that are capable
of the sort of self-consciousness that makes for personhood. Suppose that so long as they are connected to the electrical current
they are fully self-conscious and capable of wishing to continue
to exist. Suppose there are two different models of such a
machine-person. The model 2001 and the model $2001\frac{1}{2}$. Suppose
when the model $2001\frac{1}{2}$ was disconnected from the electric supply
all its memories were wiped clean and it became like a brand new
machine, requiring complete re-programming. Here switching off

the 2001½ would effectively end its existence as a person permanently. Its state of being after disconnection (so long as it remained in a state where it could be re-connected) would be like that of a new-born infant 'frozen' permanently in infancy and needing 'education' to become again a person. The 2001½ would become a person once it had been programmed sufficiently to have acquired self-consciousness but would cease to be a person when its memories were wiped by disconnection. 2001½ persons would have a good moral claim on the bodies of 2001½ non-persons for spare parts should they need them to continue to exist as persons, and would have very strong claims on the electrical supply industry.

The 2001 is rather different. Like its sister, the 2001, once built, requires to be educated by sophisticated programming until it reaches a stage where it is fully self-conscious. It shares its sisters' rapid rate of maturation and can move from construction or 'birth' to full self-conscious personhood in thirty-five minutes flat. However, unlike the 2001½, the 2001 has the capacity to retain all its memory and hence all its personhood functions while disconnected. So that so long as the 2001 is connected to the electric supply it is, once programmed or educated, fully self-conscious. If it is disconnected it becomes unconscious and will remain so until revived by an infusion of electricity. However, once revived it will immediately recover full self-consciousness and hence will also immediately recover personality. While unconscious or switched off it will be rather like a human person who is asleep or in a coma from which he or she can recover. Both the human person and the machine person would presumably be *regarded* as still a person while unconscious so long as they each retained the capacity for self-consciousness. But, would it be reasonable to say of both the human person and the machine person (of the 2001 variety anyway) that they each retained the capacity to wish to continue to exist even while incapable of exercising that capacity?[15]

The frozen un-dead

If the problem were confined to machines, we might be able to forget about it until machines have become persons. However, it is not only machines who might in theory, and perhaps in practice, remain switched off for very long, and even for indefinite, periods, without permanent loss of their personhood. The problem is likely to be acute because almost all definitions of death are agreed on one point at least, that death is permanent. As David Lamb puts it:[16]

> Essential to any valid concept of death is the prediction of irreversibility. Criteria and tests must be so devised that once the requirements of the definition have been satisfied, there can be no return with or without mechanical assistance, to the organism's previous state.

We have already noted that some countries have adopted the practice of freezing the spare embryos produced by *in vitro* embryology as an effective way of postponing any moral decisions about their ultimate fate.[17] The frozen embryo is not dead, for it might well be thawed out and implanted; its suspension of animation is not permanent. We know also that a number of rich and optimistic people have had their own 'dead' bodies frozen against the day when means might be found to cure whatever it is that they died of and restore them to life. Their optimism may well be ill-founded by present standards of knowledge, since if they were 'dead' by our present criteria before being frozen too much damage is likely to have been done to the brain to make it worthwhile to attempt resuscitation in the future.

But suppose, taking the lessons of these two cases to heart, people began to have themselves frozen at a time when they were declared moribund but were by no means dead.[18] It might be very sensible for them to trade off the few extra weeks or even months that they were likely to have now for some much greater period of remission in a thawed and technologically more competent future. Indeed the optimism with which they might enter the fridge could well prove so seductive that the practice might well catch on to an alarming extent.

IV Death is abolished

Suppose this practice became very widespread indeed, as well it might. The insurance market could be relied upon to introduce schemes in which all people could, by paying an annual premium from an early age, ensure for themselves a small fridge in a large frozen haven. These would spring up like supermarkets; for death would have been abolished. The reason for such optimism is easy to see once the practical details are clear.

This is how it would work: each fridge door would contain a computer record of the medical history of each occupant and the reason why they were considered technically moribund would be highlighted. When a cure or therapy for this condition became reasonably well established, this fact would be entered into the computer by the non-frozen members of society and all those who could benefit from the procedure would be automatically noted for thawing and curing. It wouldn't matter that the therapy was not one hundred per cent effective for the person could always be re-frozen if it looked as though things weren't going too well. We might expect that in only a few cases would this not be noticed before the fast-freeze team could reach the patient.[19]

This process could be repeated endlessly. It's likely that the periods of remission that could thereby be gained would get shorter and shorter and so less and less attractive and people might eventually be content to call it a day, or a death. But this need never happen, although in practice we may assume that it almost always would. For like Zeno's paradox so well summarised by Tom Stoppard, though the periods of remission would get shorter and shorter there is no reason why they should not be infinitely extended and death ultimately cheated.

> But it was precisely this notion of infinite series which in the sixth century BC led the Greek philosopher Zeno to conclude that since an arrow shot towards a target first had to cover half the distance, and then half the remainder, and then half the remainder after that, and so on *ad infinitum*, the result was ... that though an arrow, is always approaching its target, it never quite gets there, and Saint Sebastian died of fright.[20]

In the present case Saint Sebastian would not die at all—not because the arrow could not reach him which of course it could and did, but because he would be instantly quick frozen pending a heart transplant and would not venture forth from his fridge until one was available. Those frozen un-dead who are very old, and for whom the prognosis of remission is poor, might, as we have said, decide that enough is enough. But suppose they don't. Suppose they merely instruct us to re-freeze them until the aging process can be totally reversed. They might well have to stay frozen a long time—but then you're a long time dead.

The problem that this perhaps over-fanciful example highlights is not so much a practical one but a theoretical one. If any definition of death includes the requirement that the condition be permanent and irreversible, the possibility of freezing and thawing living people, and switching on and off any machine people

that turn up, casts a permanent shadow over the notion of permanence and leaves immense practical problems in its wake.

Would frozen people remain officially alive (for they are not
dead)? Could their families inherit their estate? Would they remain on the population roll or the voting register? These problems are perhaps easy to solve but the biggest remains.

Could we either refuse to permit freezing or refuse to countenance thawing?

Refusing freezing

We could give the provision of public resources for the purposes
of freezing citizens who, by present standards of medical technology, were moribund, a very low priority. But if people had
supplied their own fridges and cold stores, how could we prevent
them from electing to be frozen rather than simply to die? To do
so would involve the completely unsubstantiated belief that life-
time lived in the distant future was somehow much less valuable
(zero rated) than life-time lived in the near or immediate future.
That would require a highly ingenious argument of a form I am
not now able to imagine. If we are not entitled to prevent people
from saving their own lives by purchasing, say, transplant facilities, dialysis machines or any other medical technology that a
society has decided it cannot afford to provide for all, how could
we deny people the freedom to purchase their own personal
fridge, if *that* were what was required to save their life (or of
course to postpone their death which is exactly the same thing).

Refusing revival

At any given time in the future there will be a certain number of
people whose lives could be saved by an advance in medical technology or expertise. Let's suppose that in 2085 a hundred places
are available on a new programme for 'de-fyrring' coronary ar-
teries, and there are one hundred people alive—no! one hundred
non-frozen or 'fresh' people who could benefit from the procedure and one hundred frozen people whom the computer has
alerted us could be thawed, and would also gain the same degree
of benefit and expected remission from the process. On what basis
would the fresh be preferred to the frozen, or vice versa?

It could not be argued that people who fall ill in the future
have a better claim to resources than people who fell ill in the

past. The fresh may claim that their taxes have contributed to the breakthrough that can now save them. But the frozen may claim (the computer automatically makes the claim on their behalf) that not only did their taxes make possible the science that made possible the breakthrough, but also that had it not been for them and their generation there simply would not be future people to benefit from anything. It may well be that the fresh would, in 2085, have more friends, relatives and dependants to plead for them, but we saw in Chapter 5 that this was not a good enough reason to prefer some people to others. Similarly, the fresh citizens may have more presently useful skills and be better able to contribute to society as a whole if they are preserved. To counter-balance this, the frozen have also frozen assets—they have invested sums of money to accumulate at compound interest and which thus hugely magnified, can only be thawed to benefit their new world when the owners are thawed and cured. In any event it is doubtful whether ability to contribute is sufficient ground to condemn some people to death and grant others life.[21]

True also that the inhabitants of 1985 will find 2085 strange and unfamiliar, and will initially lack many friends and an obvious place in society. But they will presumably find a new lease of life well worth the problems of acclimatisation; and the people of 2085 should not regard these difficulties as a reason never to help those who fell ill in the past, rather than those who fall ill in the present. At least as no more relevant than similar difficulties are to the refusal to help those whom it is difficult to help in the present.

We must remember that all the people concerned are citizens of the society in question.[22] So long as they are alive and can be helped, the time at which they originally fell ill is hardly relevant to the obligation of others to help them.

The difficulty of justifying a refusal to allow people to suspend their animation by freezing if they so choose is likely to be matched by the difficulty of justifying a refusal to revive and cure them. This may eventually lead to very major problems indeed. As the numbers of frozen or otherwise preserved un-dead increases, the burden that any future society would face when considering their claims to revival and cure will be increasingly onerous. However, this fact cannot of itself be a reason to ignore the plight and the claims of the frozen citizens. The fact that it's hard to do what's right cannot mean that it isn't right after all.

Distribution of resources

Faced with the claims of many thousands of frozen citizens and
also with the claims of many thousands of its contemporary citizens for the life-saving resources, a future society would have to
adopt some just strategy for achieving the maximum possible
benefit. One such strategy might be to distribute such life-saving
resources as become available equally between fresh and frozen
citizens. An argument for doing this might well be that some
balance has to be struck between the claims of contemporary
citizens on the one hand and those of the potentially much larger
group of frozen citizens on the other. It is the contemporary
citizens who would have to operate any such scheme and it might
be prudent to see that their interests were at least equally well
served as those of the refrigerated citizens.

The frozen dead may, however, be less worried about prudence
than about justice. Suppose they claim, through their computer
which is programmed to make claims on their behalf, that a policy
of distributing life chances between the fresh and the frozen on
a fifty/fifty basis is unjust. They argue that the only fair policy is
one where all people who could benefit from a given therapy,
whether fresh or frozen, should be in open competition for the
therapy and the maximum number who can be accommodated
should be chosen at random from all those who need help. The
computer, who was well briefed centuries ago,[23] argues that any
other policy would amount to unfair discrimination against those
citizens who are in suspended animation and that the contemporary citizens should not be tempted to abuse their power to
revive nor argue that the relationship of dependence that exists
between the two communities gives any reason to prefer one to
the other when such vital interests are at stake.

However, the contemporary citizens have not been slow to notice other differences between the two groups that they think make
for an important moral difference. The plight of contemporary
citizens passed over in favour of their frozen fellows would be
worse because of the distress and disappointment they would feel
at being passed over, which of course their frozen fellows would
not experience. This possibility forces on us consideration of two
distinct and interesting arguments for always preferring contemporary to frozen citizens where there are insufficient resources for
both groups to be helped when new techniques are introduced.
The first argument involves our giving weight to the degree of

pain and distress involved in each of our alternatives. The second demands a more sophisticated consideration of how the wish to live of the various parties involved is to be understood. If either is successful the problems faced by future societies in deciding whether or not to unfreeze the un-dead would be considerably diminished.

Minimising distress

Since contemporary citizens would feel distress and disappointment at being passed over for life-saving therapy in favour of their frozen fellow-citizens which these latter could not feel, Classical Utility will always demand that we favour the contemporary conscious citizens over the frozen and unconscious ones. For this course will save the same number of lives as the alternative, but will have the added advantage of causing much less pain and distress.

It is doubtful if such an argument would solve the dilemma and allow the frozen to be permanently forgotten. For one thing it would be unjust; for another it would neglect the equally compelling distress that would be caused to the contemporary citizens who suffered from conditions that could not presently be cured and who consequently contemplated freezing to await a future chance. The knowledge that, once frozen, their claims would be perpetually ignored (because saving contemporary citizens would always involve less distress) would itself cause sufficient distress to counterbalance the other contemporary claims.

This possibility of freezing all who could not be immediately helped would also ease the chagrin of contemporary citizens who could technically be helped immediately, but who had been passed over in favour of their frozen fellows. They could be told that they would indeed be helped in the future and that meanwhile their animation was merely to be suspended while they waited their turn.[24] But would it ease their chagrin enough?

Satisfying the wish to live

The problem here is that most people who wish their lives to continue do not simply wish for an extra ration of years no matter when. They wish *their lives* to continue. And *their lives* are the lives they have been living. Their lives have particular plans and projects at their centre, and these are related to their contemporary circumstances and society. These lives are made worthwhile by the friends, relatives and familiar things that surround them, as well as by the skills, pastimes and occupations that they have developed. Of course, continued existence, even in the far future, may be preferable to no existence at all. But those who could be helped now are not in the position of having to accept freezing as the only alternative to death. They could be saved now if the claims of the frozen could be ignored. And since the frozen will lose none of these things if their revival is further postponed, the argument in favour of satisfying the wishes of all those contemporary people who wish to go on living their lives and whose wish could be granted is surely powerful indeed.

While this argument in favour of giving priority to the contemporary citizenry seems powerful, its power may be limited. Suppose the best guess is that if preference is always given to contemporaries they will always use up all available resources and the frozen will therefore face permanent limbo. If this is right, what started as an argument for giving contemporaries a higher place in the queue effectively turns out to be an argument for removing the frozen from the queue altogether! For if beyond a certain point it is clear that the queue will never reach the box office, then all those at the tail end will be queueing for nothing. They will not only be at the back of the queue but out of the game altogether.

If this would be the effect of giving preference to the particular character of the claim of contemporary people, it would amount to a policy of choosing to characterise some sorts of lives as more valuable than others where the consequence of this is that less valuable lives will not be further lived at all. It is important to be clear as to what is involved here.

Worthwhile lives again

It's not difficult to imagine that everyone might agree that continued uninterrupted existence is very much better and always preferable to an existence interrupted by an unspecified period of time, for the reasons we have just reviewed. And 'everyone' here might well include all those whose only chance of continued existence was an interrupted one. However, it does not follow from this that the competition for scarce resources is always to be won by those for whom those resources would mean continued uninterrupted existence rather than the restoration of an already interrupted existence.

Suppose, similarly, that everyone were to agree, as probably they do, that life without any degree of handicap at all is always preferable to life with some, even quite small, handicap. Or suppose everyone were to agree that a life with lots of friends and money is always better than life with few friends and little money. It would not follow that the lives of the more fortunate in each case were always to be given priority when set in the balance with the less fortunate. It seems neither a strong argument for putting the fortunate at the top of the list for rescue when this means that the unfortunate or less fortunate will not be rescued at all, nor does it seem a good reason simply to make sure that the fortunate are cared for first.

But this is not comparing like with like. For the plausibility of the argument for preferring to help contemporaries stemmed from the idea that the frozen would lose nothing by having their revival further postponed. They would after all be unaware that their revival had been postponed, and indeed might never come to know of it. If this were so the frozen would lose nothing by postponement whereas the fresh would lose many of the very things that made them want to go on living.

The argument that the frozen will lose nothing by postponement because they will experience no disappointment, and can always be revived later is, however, misleading as we have seen. While it is of course true that the unconscious will experience no disappointment, it is not the case that they will lose nothing. So long as new people are being added to the numbers of those in cold store, each postponement will inevitably reduce the chances of revival for any particular individual. Moreover, though, less importantly, each postponement will inevitably further distance each individual from his or her own time and make the adjustment to the new world into which they will emerge harder to make. Against this, of course, must be set the possibility that the far-distant future will be both more exciting and have other advantages that will compensate for the delay.

Two further assumptions that underlie the idea that delay costs nothing need to be mentioned, although it is difficult to know how to assess them. The first is that it is assumed that the future will exist—that people manage to avoid destroying themselves and the world or that it is not destroyed by say a chance collision with another planetary body or by the folly of nuclear war. The second assumption is that technological advance and the energy on which it depends will continue. We must assume that they both will, though the confidence with which this assumption is made is periodically shaken.

Finally and ultimately, both storage capacity and indeed the life of this particular planet will eventually run out and at some time in the future, further delay will become critical.

However, if, as seems highly probable, the employment of the idea that the frozen will lose nothing by mere postponement will in effect turn postponement into cancellation, then the frozen will lose everything. There is an obvious reason for this. It is simply that unless things change (and of course they might in which case this part of the argument will cease to be valid), it is very probable that the number of contemporary 'fresh' people who require help and whom we have the technical capacity to save will far outstrip our ability to deploy the resources necessary to save them. If this remains so and the fresh are always given priority, the frozen will in fact lose everything by postponement. They will effectively lose all chance of revival. They would be condemned to perpetual limbo—though not of course actually to death, for even in such a hopeless case the frozen would still not be dead by any of the current definitions. For while their condition might perpetually be unreversed, so long as they remained frozen and there existed people who might and could revive them their condition would not be 'irreversible'.

V Are the frozen really persons?

While all definitions of death are agreed upon and committed to the permanence and irreversibility of the condition, however else it is defined and whatever the criteria of death turn out to be, it is not clear whether or not the same must be true of personhood. I have postponed consideration of this vital issue until now so that the point and necessity of resolving the question should be clear. If, for example, it ceased to be plausible to attribute to individuals the possession of capacities that had been dormant or inactive for some time and if this proved to be the case with the capacity for wishing to continue to exist, then the status of those in suspended animation would dramatically and significantly change. It might, for example, then be clear that after reasonably long periods in suspended animation individuals moved from the class of people who possess self-consciousness but who merely cannot at the moment exercise it, to the class of potential people who do not possess self-consciousness but who might re-acquire it, who have the potential for it.

If this were a reasonable interpretation of their state then, like the foetus and the neonate, the frozen un-dead would not have to be protected in quite the same way as are persons. There are two difficulties here. The first is that of resolving whether or not it is right to say that the frozen still retain a capacity for wishing to live. The second problem is whether or not we can be sufficiently confident of our answer to the first question to allow so much to turn on it. It may after all be a matter of life or death for those involved.

One problem here is that the criteria for attributing capacities to people are so variable. Some capacities, take that of say running a mile in under four minutes or a marathon in under two and a half hours, require the individual who claims that capacity to be in good physical condition and in training before we will grant that she has that capacity, however many times she has exercised it in the past. If she became frozen we would know that she had almost certainly lost the capacity, and would, if she remained in good shape, perhaps have the potential for regaining it. Other capacities, once acquired, seem to stay with us, like say the ability to ride a bicycle or to fry an egg. Still others, like the ability to speak a foreign language, gradually fade through lack of practice.

The nearest case to the one we are considering with which we are at all familiar is that of the person who falls into a coma and remains unconscious for long periods of time, perhaps even for years. If they are not brain dead we are unsure what to say. If the individual eventually regains consciousness and is much as she was before we might well be inclined to say that she had never ceased to be a person and that her spontaneous return to full self-consciousness somehow demonstrated this. If she dies without regaining consciousness, we might be inclined to trace her loss of personhood back to the origin of the coma.

Before coming to any conclusions about frozen individuals, we might well want to experiment a little. If, after say two hundred years of 'sleep', we woke one of our frozen citizens and she had lost all capacity for speech and all memories, but proved educable, we might think that, like the model $2001\frac{1}{2}$, she had ceased to be a person during the frozen period but had retained the potential for personality. If, on the other hand, the individual retained most of her memory and abilities on waking, we would regard her more like the 2001 and judge that she was instantly a person again and had revived with more than mere potential.

But would we judge that she had retained her capacity for wishing to live and hence for self-consciousness throughout the two hundred years of sleep? Would it be correct to say of her at any moment during that period that she still wished to live? Would she in that respect have remained like you or I when asleep? If I wish to live and wish to go to Venice in April, both of these wishes remain true of me when I am asleep or not addressing my mind to the prospect of death or of Venice. But if I have myself frozen wishing that this will give me an extra lease of life, and wishing to go to Venice the April next after my awakening and cure, are these wishes still attributable to me throughout the intervening period—however long that period of suspended animation may be?

I don't know how questions like these could be resolved. It is not clear that the mere accumulation of time without consciousness could allow us to say that someone had moved from the condition of possessing self-consciousness to that of having merely the potential for self-consciousness, if after all, it's a capacity that they would regain instantly on revival. Although, of course, without the appropriate therapy it might soon be permanently extinguished. But that is true of all persons who require immediate therapy for survival whether frozen or not.

If we perfected freezing or any other technique for suspended animation and used it, say, to send astronauts on long journeys to distant galaxies which would require say several hundred years of travel, we would not regard the frozen members of the crew as merely potential people, without the rights and protections of the other members of the crew merely because the suspension of their animation lasted a very long time. This would be the case particularly if we knew that, as in other forms of sleep or unconsciousness which are of much shorter duration, the astronauts would, whenever we woke them, be instantly their former selves.

Tempting as it would be to regard the frozen as having ceased to be persons while they have not ceased to be alive, it seems to me to be genuinely unclear as to how we should regard them. Certainly, the account we have given of the concept of the person leaves it unclear as to what we should say of the frozen un-dead. This may be thought to be a weakness of the account and another account which would solve this problem might be preferable.

However, it is clear that no currently accepted definitions of death help at all.

So long as freezing or other methods of suspending animation are a possibility no definition of death or even of loss of personality in terms of the permanence or irreversibility of such a condition will be adequate. The problem of the un-dead will remain, although how long it will remain a problem of merely academic interest remains to be seen.

Notes

Introduction

1 I should strictly speaking say 'universe' here, see Chapter 1.

Chapter 1 Beings, human beings and persons

1 The embryo might well be grown for its tissue and organs; see Chapter 6.
2 We shall examine some of these considerations in Chapter 5.
3 See Ronald Dworkin, *Taking Rights Seriously* Duckworth, London, 1977, especially ch. 7.
4 H.W. Jones Jnr, 'The Ethics of In Vitro Fertilization—1981', in Edwards and Purdy (eds), London, *Human Conception In Vitro*, Academic Press, London, 1981, 353.
5 Clifford Grobstein, *From Chance to Purpose* Addison Wesley, London, 1981, p. 84.
6 Ibid.
7 Ibid., p. 89. This is the point at which 'quickening' is first evident although the time usually allotted to quickening is the point at which the mother first *feels* the movement of the foetus. The moral irrelevance of quickening will I hope be clear from the present argument. Perhaps we should also note that the other point that is sometimes accorded significance, that of 'viability', the capacity of the embryo to exist independently of the mother, is rendered even more dubious by external fertilisation, for in the laboratory dish the embryo is existing independently and we may ultimately be able to grow embryos entirely externally. Whatever moral significance the embryo has must be independent of the accident of where it happens to be growing.
8 Ibid., p. 88.
9 Ibid., see p. 101.
10 Ibid., p. 102.
11 Ibid.

12 Ibid., p. 85.
13 John Locke, *An Essay Concerning Human Understanding*, bk II, ch. 27, Oxford University Press, London, 1964.
14 Here the argument parallels that of Ludwig Wittgenstein in *On Certainty*, Blackwell, Oxford, 1969, para. 111.
15 The point here is very like that made by Wittgenstein in his famous 'beetle in the box' analogy. See *Philosophical Investigations*, Blackwell, Oxford, 1963, pt I, para. 293.
16 Of course we must be sure that if we kill people in accordance with their wishes for us to do so, then all aspects of that act are in accord with their wishes. See also Chapter 4 for further discussion of this point.
17 We shall not be exploring the problem of 'animal rights' in any detail here. It is taken up briefly in Chapter 11 and note 6 to that chapter gives further reading on this important but separate issue.
18 I am thinking of the work of Dr Gordon Gallup as reported by Keith Laidler in the *Guardian* newspaper, London, 12 November 1981 in an article entitled 'Take a Look at Yourself'. Raanan Gillon pointed this work out to me.
19 For reports of the Education of Washoe see R. Allen and Beatrice Gardner 'Teaching Sign Language to Chimpanzees', *Science*, vol. 165, 1969, pp. 664–72; and also Eugene Linden, *Apes, Men and Language*, Penguin, Harmondsworth, 1975; and Keith Laidler, *The Talking Ape*, Stein & Day, New York, 1980.
20 Of course I'm talking here of a genuine language, not mere parroting or other 'talk' or non-linguistic communication like smiles or growls.
21 See John M. Taurek, 'Should the Numbers Count?', *Philosophy & Public Affairs*, vol. 6, no. 4, 1977; and Derek Parfit's reply, 'Innumerate Ethics', *Philosophy & Public Affairs*, vol. 7, no. 4, 1978. Others who think that numbers do not count are the authors of the Linacre Centre Report 1, *Euthanasia and Clinical Practice*, Linacre Centre, London, 1982, especially pp. 34–5.
22 Mary Warnock is Chairman of the Government Inquiry into Human Fertilisation and Embryology. She was replying to my 'In Vitro Fertilisation: The Ethical Issues', *Philosophical Quarterly*, vol. 33, no. 132, 1983.
23 Ibid., p. 241.
24 Some may regard nationality as a more controversial item than the others here listed. In Chapter 3 it is suggested, building on the arguments of Chapter 2, that our responsibility for others cannot stop at the frontier. Meanwhile those who disagree can delete this term.
25 Warnock, op. cit., p. 241.
26 Ibid., p. 242.
27 Ibid., p. 246.

28 In Australia the practice is to freeze all spare embryos on the grounds that this is morally preferable because to do so cannot be regarded as killing the embryos. See Chapter 6.

29 See Chapter 12.

Chapter 2 Above all do no harm

1 See my *Violence and Responsibility*, Routledge & Kegan Paul, 1980, pp. 1–2, where this argument is elaborated but with rather different emphasis and concerns.

2 For example Jonathan Glover, *Causing Death and Saving Lives*, Pelican, Harmondsworth, 1977; Bonnie Steinbock (ed.), *Killing and Letting Die*, Prentice Hall, Englewood Cliffs, 1980, and also my *Violence and Responsibility*. See above.

3 This is of course the same for positive actions. Where I perform an action genuinely unaware of a particularly unfortunate consequence— say I persuade you to try a mushroom unaware that it is poison or shoot you while hunting reasonably and sincerely mistaking your fur coat for a bear—then in each case I am responsible for your death, you would not have died but for what I did, but I may not be to blame. Legal excuses such as insanity and diminished responsibility make use of related ideas.

4 Among such odd people are: Eric Mack, 'Bad Samaritanism and the Causation of Harm', *Philosophy and Public Affairs*, vol. 9, 1980; and Elazar Weinryb, 'Omissions and Responsibility', *Philosophical Quarterly*, vol. 30, 1980.

5 There are a number of such regimes but one will be described in more detail soon. See p. 33, below.

6 John Lorber, 'Ethical Problems in the Management of Myelomeningocele and Hydrocephalus', *Journal of the Royal College of Physicians*, vol. 10, no. 1, 1975.

7 Ibid.

8 Ibid., p. 54.

9 Ibid., p. 55.

10 Ibid., p. 54.

11 Ibid., p. 55.

12 Ibid., p. 58.

13 Ibid., p. 57.

14 Ibid.

15 Ibid.

16 Ibid., pp. 57 and 58. We will have to examine the different problems posed by slippery slope arguments at various points in the book.

17 One way to ensure this would be to legalise non-voluntary euthanasia only for those individuals who were incapable of consenting and only where (and if) death was clearly in their best interests. We could build into the legislation whatever safeguards and criteria we wished.

It has been suggested that positive euthanasia was introduced by the
Nazis as a 'privilege which was accorded to Aryans' (G. E. M. Anscombe, Commentary 2, *Journal of Medical Ethics*, vol. 7, no. 3, 1981)
and that the slide from this to genocide demonstrates the slipperyness
of this slope. However, it is not the fate of Aryans that disturbs us
about the prospect of Nazism!

18 Lorber, op. cit., p. 58.
19 Oliver Gillie, 'A Matter of Life and Death', *Sunday Times*, London,
    22 February 1981.
20 For example Hugh Jolly interviewed on Independent TV in the pro-
    gramme *Jaywalking*, on 1 March 1981.
21 We will examine this point in more detail in Chapter 11.
22 See for example Tristram H. Engelhardt Jr., 'Ethical Issues in Aiding
    the Death of Young Children' in Steinbock, 1980; and also Helga
    Kuhse, 'Extraordinary Means and the Sanctity of Life', *Journal of
    Medical Ethics*, vol. 7, 1981. Like Slippery Slopes, Extraordinary
    Treatment will be considered again.
23 This consideration will be taken up in more detail in Chapter 3.
24 D. J. Cusine, 'Commentary 3', *Journal of Medical Ethics*, vol. 7, 1981.
25 *Guardian*, London, 6 November, 1981.
26 Lorber, op. cit.
27 Nor of course does the absence of guilt indicate that no wrong has
    been done.
28 Perhaps because he wishes to die for any 3 of the reasons considered
    in Chapters 3 and 4.
29 'Euthanasia and Clinical Practice', The Linacre Centre, London,
    1982.
30 Ibid. Since two very eminent Catholic philosophers were involved in
    the publication, it is safe enough to do so.
31 Ibid., p. 34.
32 Ibid., pp. 34, 35.
33 The responsibility may of course be shared particularly where the
    patient gives informed consent. See Chapter 10.
34 Ian Kennedy, *The Unmasking of Medicine*, Granada, 1983. The same
    nervousness is shown by Jay F. Rosenberg, London, *Thinking Clearly
    About Death*, Prentice Hall, Englewood Cliffs, NJ, 1983, see chs. 6
    and 7.
35 Ibid., p. 196.
36 Ibid., p. 197.
37 Ibid.

Chapter 3 Must doctors help their patients?

1 G. E. M. Anscombe 'Commentary 2' *Journal of Medical Ethics*, vol.
   7, no. 3, September 1981.

2 For economy I will usually use the word 'doctor' to cover health-care professionals more generally in this chapter.

3 And of course our decision may equally well be one not to provide life-saving resources: 'Funds for kidney units are running seriously short. About half the 2,200 people whose kidneys fail die *because* there are no facilities to save them, Professor Cyril Chantler of Guy's Hospital said yesterday', reported in *Guardian*, 15 January 1982. Or 'It has been estimated that some 2,000 or more patients die each year because sufficient treatment is not available for them all', *Guardian*, 18 October 1983 in a leader article.

4 Our obligation is of course clear even if we don't share this belief because we ought to share it!

5 We will be discussing other aspects of this vexed question in Chapter 5, and have already looked at others in Chapter 1.

6 See p. 63 below.

7 Of course contracts may provide specific penalties for breach of contract enforceable at law, but that is another matter.

8 See Chapters 5, 8 and 12.

9 This belief supports the widespread practice whereby doctors mark some patients for resuscitation and not others in case these patients suffer 'cardiac arrest' while in hospital. The same belief supports the equally widespread practice of allowing geriatric patients to die when their lives could be further prolonged. The moral grounds for such decisions need to be much more clearly articulated than they have been. See Chapter 5.

10 Many of which we will consider in more detail in the next two chapters.

11 And of course other rescue and life-saving equipment and personnel.

Chapter 4 Killing: a caring thing to do?

1 Shakespeare, *Julius Caesar*, Act III, Scene 1.

2 Ibid., Act II, Scene II. Caesar may of course be speaking here with his 'official' voice.

3 This possibility may sound outrageous, but it is precisely the sort of calculation that is made whenever life-saving resources are 'spent' on things other than saving lives.

4 Robert Nozick, *Anarchy, State and Utopia*, Basil Blackwell, Oxford, 1974, pp. 34, 35.

5 Ibid., p. 34.

6 Ibid., p. 35.

7 From the *Observer*, London, 13 March 1983.

8 Or the preservation of some value of comparable importance.

9 Further reasons for this will be examined in Chapter 5, when we consider, among many other cases, whether convicts might be less deserving of care than others.

10 Nozick, op. cit., p. 34.

11 The word 'vicious' is used to distinguish such discrimination from benign discrimination or affirmative action.

12 See Derek Parfit, *Reasons and Persons*, OUP, London, 1984, pp. 31–40.

13 Ibid., p. 33.

14 This would of course be the situation which faced any nuclear power responding to a first strike against itself. Once it was clear that no response could avert the destruction that had been loosed against it, then any retaliation would be unjustified. The deterrent principle is thus only morally defensible on the clear understanding that the weapons will never be used.

15 See Ronald Dworkin's attempts to provide such a theory in his 'What is Equality?' *Philosophy & Public Affairs*, Vol. 10, no. 4, and no. 5, 1981.

16 Robert Young, 'What is so Wrong with Killing People?', *Philosophy*, vol. 54, 1979, p. 520.

17 Ibid., p. 519.

18 Ibid., p. 520.

19 See Chapter 5.

20 Shakespeare, *Richard III*, Act 1, Scene II.

21 'That to which a man consents cannot be considered an injury.'

22 Draft unpublished statement by the Faculty of Community Medicine of the Royal College of Physicians.

23 Ibid., p. 14. There would also of course be a shortage of pain-killing and indeed of all other drugs.

24 Ibid.

25 This was perhaps a more notorious problem in medieval times when heretics were pressed to death with stones and their motive for failing to recant and so being tortured to death was often not fidelity to God but to their heirs, for if they confessed they might be 'saved' but as heretics they would lose their estate which would be forfeit to the crown.

26 Children are a special case as perhaps are the mentally handicapped. See my 'The Political Status of Children', in Keith Graham (ed.) *Contemporary Political Philosophy*, Cambridge University Press, Cambridge, 1982.

27 As for example where madness, unconsciousness or lack of ability to understand prevents the possibility of any genuine consent.

28 Although it might be possible to alleviate rather than remedy the suffering somewhat. The cases of severe spina bifida discussed in Chapter 2 are what I have in mind here.

29 In Chapter 2.

30 See, for example, those discussed in my *Violence and Responsibility*, Routledge & Kegan Paul, London, 1980, especially ch. 6.

31 *Guardian*, 20 November 1982, p. 3.

32 Ibid.
33 *Guardian*, 18 October 1983 (second leader). The same sort of claim was made by the British Transplantation Society, 'The Shortage of Organs for Clinical Transplant', *British Medical Journal*, vol. 1, 1975, pp. 251–5.
34 *Guardian*, 6 January 1984. The report quoted Mr John Dark, the Senior Consultant in Thorasic Surgery, as saying: 'Premature deaths are occurring which could have been avoided if we could do more operations each week.'

Chapter 5 The value of life

1 Triage is a policy for coping with disasters where resources are insufficient to provide the normal standard of care for all. It involves dividing survivors into three groups: those who will die in any event, those who will live in any event, and those for whom care will make the difference between life and death. Care is then given only to this latter group. The argument is that this is the most economical use of resources where resources are insufficient to help all.
2 This may be a rash assumption because of the voluntary nature of many risks.
3 Of course if I don't value it because it is so short as to be scarcely worth having then the point does not apply in such a case.
4 I owe this objection to Tom Sorrel and am greatly in his debt here and elsewhere in this chapter for his generous and penetrating criticisms and comments.
5 No non-sexist form is available here nor is one desirable since a different formulation would lose the resonance of the phrase.
6 Jonathan Glover, *Causing Death and Saving Lives*, Penguin, Harmondsworth, 1977, p. 221.
7 I'm assuming 70 as the full measure of life expectancy of healthy people and that all candidates are healthy in the sense that there is no reason to regard their life expectancy as less than average.
8 Quoted by Jonathan Glover in Glover, *op. cit.*, p. 221. I am indebted here and elsewhere to Glover's stimulating discussion of these matters.
9 Because any figure of life expectancy will be arbitrary and one has to be taken.
10 The elixir of life example which prompted this argument about the fallacy of life-time views in stable or increasing populations I owe to Tom Sorrel whose formulation of it I largely use.
11 See Chapter 2.
12 Many people have argued of course that it is always futile to plan for the future because the inevitability of our world's ultimate destruction makes everything futile.
13 For the record we should note that small gains in life-time will only

seem to be worthless to those who gain them if it is known that they will be short. If the potential beneficiaries are kept in ignorance of the fact that they can be granted only a short remission then the extra time will not be clouded by the futility deriving from its short duration and the gain, though small, will be as worthwhile as any other segment of their lives of comparable duration. Of course the deception may not be justified. That is a point we will be examining in Chapter 10.

14 Glover, *op. cit.*, p. 224.
15 Ibid., p. 222.
16 Ibid., p. 223.
17 I use this term in its only precise sense that is, in the non-technical everyday way.
18 See for example my 'The Political Status of Children' in Keith Graham (ed.), *Contemporary Political Philosophy*, Cambridge University Press, Cambridge, 1982.
19 Glover, op. cit., p. 223.
20 Janet Radcliffe Richards reminded me that I should not forget this lady.
21 See my discussion of the Survival Lottery in *Violence and Responsibility*, Routledge & Kegan Paul, London, 1980.

Chapter 6 The beginnings of life

1 See, for example, the *Guardian*, 1 October 1982 and 8 October 1982, the *Observer*, 3 October 1982, the *Sunday Times*, 3 October 1982 and the *London Standard*, 27 September 1982.
2 That of R. G. Edwards and Patrick Steptoe. See particularly Edwards and Purdy (eds), *Human Conception In Vitro*, Academic Press, London, 1981.
3 Ibid.
4 See the *Guardian*, 25 October 1982.
5 See Report in the *Guardian*, 8 October 1982.
6 This is the practice in Australia: See Edwards and Purdy, 1981, op. cit.
7 The *Observer*, 3 October 1982.
8 She may have a condition that makes birth dangerous.
9 Edwards and Purdy, 1981, op. cit., p. 360.
10 Clifford Grobstein, 'Coming to terms with test-tube babies', *New Scientist*, 7 October 1982.
11 Edwards and Purdy, 1981, op. cit., p. 361.
12 Grobstein, 1982, op. cit., p. 16.
13 The *Guardian*, 25 October 1982. About one in ten women are infertile.
14 Edwards and Purdy, op. cit., p. 373.
15 Ibid., pp. 372 ff.

16 Ibid., p. 380.

17 Ibid.

18 Ibid.

19 Ibid., p. 381.

20 Ibid.

21 Ibid. The pancreas may also be transplanted from the foetus at 20 weeks and may be used eventually to cure diabetes.

22 Ibid., p. 382.

23 Ibid.

24 F. M. Cornford, *The Microcosmographia Academica*, Cambridge University Press, Cambridge, 1908.

25 Around 150,000 abortions are performed annually in the United Kingdom (149,746 in 1979), Office of Population Census, Abortion Statistics, 1979, AB No. 6. HMSO, London.

26 The motives of sex are not obviously less frivolous or immoral than those of science.

27 There may, of course, be occasions when even the killing of the innocent (perhaps in war?) is morally permissible, even without their consent.

28 There is an estimated shortfall of 1000–2000 kidney transplants alone. Of course if Transplantation Orders were to be instituted there would have to be complete confidence in the criteria for brain death and that no life support systems would be prematurely switched off.

29 Edwards and Purdy, 1981, op. cit., p. 364.

30 John Locke, *Second Treatise on Government*, Blackwell, Oxford, 1966, ch. 4, p. 14.

31 See Edwards and Purdy, 1981, op. cit., p. 362, where Trounson makes use of this very point.

32 We should note that clones may not ever be the *exact* replicas of the cell donor since some genetic material is carried in the cytoplasm.

33 Oliver Gillie, 'Microscopic Life', *Sunday Times*, 3 October 1982.

34 C. Grobstein, *From Chance to Purpose*, Addison Wesley, London, 1981.

35 Grobstein, 1982, op. cit.

36 Grobstein, 1981, op. cit., p. 130. See also Edwards and Purdy, 1981, p. 382 for information on the same possibility. We will be examining this possibility at greater length in Chapter 11.

37 F. M. Cornford, *op. cit.*, p. 23.

38 See Chapter 5 of my *Violence and Responsibility*, Routledge & Kegan Paul, London, 1980.

39 *Report Of The Committee Of Inquiry Into Human Fertilisation And Embryology*, Chairman Dame Mary Warnock DBE, London, Her Majesty's Stationery Office, 1984.

40 Ibid., p. 2, paras 4 & 5.

41 Ibid., p. 3, para. 6.

42 Ibid., see p. 46, para. 8.17.
43 Matters are morally important if they are the sort of things that tend to make a difference to whether we judge the world to be a better or a worse place.
44 Warnock, op. cit., p. 63, para. 11.17.
45 Ibid., see p. 64, para. 11.18.
46 Ibid., p. 66, para. 11.22.
47 Ibid., p. 60, para. 11.9.
48 Ibid., p. 65, para. 11.19.
49 Ibid., p. 59, para. 11.5.
50 Although the fertilised egg may develop into a hydatidiform mole and not an embryo, I would characterise this eventually as the non-actualisation of human potential rather than think of it as evidence that the potential for becoming a human being was not after all present. But either way the argument is unaffected because those who accept the potentiality argument would want to wait and see.
51 I am greatly indebted to Rodney Harris M.D., F.R.C.P., F.R.C.Path., Professor of Medical Genetics, University of Manchester, for his detailed comments and suggestions on this chapter. If any errors have none the less crept in, I am of course responsible.

Chapter 7 Whose body is it anyway?

1 *Report of The Committee Of Inquiry Into Human Fertilisation And Embryology*, Chairman Dame Mary Warnock, DBE, London, Her Majesty's Stationery Office, 1984, pp. 37–38, para. 6.8 and p. 40, paras 7.4, 7.5 and 7.6.
2 They also of course list the main points in favour, but these do not concern us here.
3 Warnock, op. cit., p. 45, para. 8.10.
4 Ibid., p. 45, para. 8.11.
5 Ibid., p. 45, para. 8.11.
6 Ibid., p. 45, para. 8.12.
7 Ibid., p. 46, 47, para. 8.18.
8 Ibid., p. 46, para. 8.17.
9 G. D. Mitchell, 'In Vitro fertilisation: The Major Issues—A Comment', *Journal of Medical Ethics*, vol. 9, 1983, pp. 196–9.
10 Ibid. See also the contributions of Peter Singer and Deane Wells in the same issue.
11 Ibid.
12 Peter Singer in his response to G. D. Mitchell, op. cit.
13 For an interestingly related argument see Jonathan Glover's discussion of Derek Parfit's 'Person affecting restriction' in *Causing Death and Saving Lives*, Penguin, Harmondsworth, 1977, p. 67. And also Gregory S. Kavka, 'The Paradox of Future Individuals', *Philosophy*

& Public Affairs vol. 11, no. 2, 1981, and Derek Parfit's reply: 'Future Generations: Further Problems' in the same place.

14 For a much more detailed discussion of problems related to genetic engineering see Jonathan Glover, *What Sort of People Should There Be?*, Pelican, Harmondsworth, 1984.

15 I'm thinking of course of the experience in China.

16 Brian Lieberman, in a symposium on the ethics of in vitro fertilisation given to the Manchester Medical Group, Manchester University, 17 October 1983.

17 See Gillian Hanscombe, 'The Right to Lesbian Parenthood', *Journal of Medical Ethics*, vol. 9, 1983, pp. 133–5.

18 See also Hanscombe, op. cit., but even if there were, the outlawing of homosexual parents would require another explanation. Many, if not most, of the people who regard homosexuality as immoral would also regard adultery in the same light, but I'm unaware of any moves to prevent adulterers from procreating. It is true that in divorce proceedings adulterers may lose custody of the children, but in most divorces where adultery is a ground for divorce or supports a claim that a marriage has irretrievably broken down, there is adultery on both sides.

19 See Hugh Lafolette 'Licensing Parents', *Philosophy & Public Affairs*, vol. 9, no. 2, 1980.

20 Roger Higgs (ed.), Case Conference: 'Making up her mind: consent, pregnancy and mental handicap', *Journal of Medical Ethics*, vol. 9, 1983, pp. 219–26.

21 Warnock., p. 18, para. 4.4. and p. 55, para. 10.9.

22 Ibid., p. 18, para. 4.4.

23 See, for example, Richard M. Titmuss, *The Gift Relationship*, Allen & Unwin, London, 1971.

Chapter 8 A woman's right to choose?

1 Judith Jarvis Thomson, 'A Defence of Abortion', in James Rachels (ed.), *Moral Problems*, Harper & Row, New York, 1975, p. 95.

2 See R. M. Dworkin, *Taking Rights Seriously*, Duckworth, London, 1977, ch. 7, p. 189.

3 The time is of course immaterial. It would still be rape if he attempted to enforce his contract in the next second or in the next decade.

4 Michael Tooley, *Abortion and Infanticide*, Oxford University Press, London, 1983.

5 Ibid., p. 45.

6 Unless of course they have a *better* concept of the person, in which case I'd be very much obliged if they would let me know.

7 This is the same point, of course, that was made in Chapter 1.

8 Janet Radcliffe Richards, *The Sceptical Feminist*, Pelican, Harmondsworth, 1982, p. 271.

9 Ibid., p. 271.

10 Of course they don't want the environment to be actually un-sterile—just not sterile looking.

11 See for example L. I. Zander, 'The Place of Confinement—A Question of Statistics or Ethics?', *Journal of Medical Ethics*, vol. 7, 1981, 125–7; and also M. Tew, 'Home Versus Hospital Confinement: The Statistics', *Update*, 1979 pp. 1317–22; and G. J. Kloosterman, 'The Dutch System of Home Births', in Kitzinger and Davis (eds.), *The Place of Birth*, Oxford University Press, London, 1978.

12 Any resemblance to existing societies and beliefs is wholly deliberate.

13 For a parallel argument see, for example, P. F. Strawson, 'Freedom and Resentment' in his collection of essays of the same name, Methuen, London, 1974.

14 I continue to use 'we' to talk about society's choices partly out of nostalgia. Of course women without men would gradually change over the generations but so will society generally even without these drastic changes. Or it will if it is allowed to last so long.

15 Given their radical feminism, it seems safe to regard this as an act of supererogation.

16 Jonathan Glover, *What Sort of People Should There be?*, Pelican, Harmondsworth, 1984.

17 I say their complacency, for while hitherto reluctance to take steps to meet and prevent the disasters to which we are prone has been fairly evenly distributed betweeen men and women, in our imagined case it is the women who are most ready to face the necessity of radical change.

18 Nor presumably would it justify forcing a woman to undergo the dangers of birth against her will.

19 Though of course they have done so from time to time.

20 And of course the same goes for all men.

Chapter 9 Sexual morality and the natural

1 Mental Health Act 1959, S.4 (5).

2 The rules relating to buggery between adults are to be found in The Sexual Offences Act 1956, S.12(1), 14(5) and 15(3). For the predicament of the handicapped see F. Menolascino, 'Sexual Problems of the Mentally Retarded', *Sexual Behaviour*, vol. 2, no. 11, 1972, pp. 39–41; Roger Harvey, 'Sexual Rights of Mentally Handicapped People', *Mental Handicap*, vol. 11, September 1983; Sue Elwood, 'Sex and the Mentally Handicapped', *Bulletin of the British Psychological Society*, vol. 34, 1981, pp. 169–71; and for a review of the literature see Judy Sebba, 'Sexuality and Mental Handicap: A Re-

view', in E. Karas (Ed.), *Current Issues in Clinical Psychology*, vol. II, Plenum, London. Forthcoming. I am indebted to Judy Sebba for pointing these out.

3 P. Devlin, *The Enforcement of Morals*, Oxford University Press, London, 1965, and H. L. A. Hart's famous rebuttal, *Law Liberty and Morality*, Oxford University Press, London, 1966.

4 *Oxford English Dictionary*.

5 See Phillippa Foot, 'Morality as a System of Hypothetical Imperatives', *Philosophical Review*, 1972.

6 Thomas Nagel, *Mortal Questions*, Cambridge University Pres, Cambridge, 1979.

7 Ibid., p. 39.

8 For example the prosecution which followed the National Theatre's production of *The Romans in Britain* by Howard Brenton, in which simulated buggery featured.

9 Nagel, op. cit., p. 49. Nagel is aware that his account has little in the way of moral content but he is more concerned with its other features.

10 Ibid., p. 47.

11 Ibid., p. 49.

12 Ibid., p. 48.

13 Sarah Ruddick, 'On Sexual Morality', in James Rachels (ed.), *Moral Problems*, Harper & Row, New York, 1975, p. 23.

14 Ibid. See p. 27.

15 Ibid., p. 24.

16 Donald Levy, 'Perversion and The Unnatural as Moral Categories', *Ethics*, vol. 90, January 1980.

17 Ibid., p. 200.

18 Ibid., p. 199.

19 Ibid.

20 Ibid., pp. 200, 201.

21 Though not perhaps in mine. This might be part of an account of what it is to *love* and perhaps the attitude to the pleasure machine is just part of what it is to be a Sybarite.

22 Levy, op. cit., p. 201.

23 Hart, op. cit.

24 Herodotus, *The Histories*, Penguin, Harmondsworth, 1968, Book 2.

25 Mary Midgley, *Beast and Man*, Methuen, London, p. 80.

26 Ruddick, op. cit., p. 33.

27 Ibid., p. 34.

28 Nagel, op. cit., p. 52.

29 Tony Honoré, *Sex Law*, Duckworth, London, 1978.

30 Ibid., p. 2.

31 Ibid., pp. 2, 3.

32 This point is elaborated by Ronald Dworkin in *Taking Rights Seriously*, Duckworth, London, 1977, ch. 10.

33 Machiavelli of course has argued eloquently the opposite case. See particularly his discussion of the case of the Venetian Admiral; see *Discourses*, III, 22.

Chapter 10 Respect for persons I

1 *Shorter Oxford English Dictionary*.
2 J. S. Mill, *On Liberty*, ch. III, in Mary Warnock (ed.), *Utilitarianism*, Fontana, London, 1972, p. 187. Mill of course had very many arguments to offer for the extreme but attractive libertarianism he defended. I have been here concerned not so much with Mill scholarship but with developing what seems to me the right account of autonomy.
3 I have been influenced here by the excellent discussions of related issues in R. M. Dworkin, *Taking Rights Seriously*, Duckworth, London, 1977, ch. 10, and by an unpublished paper of Richard Lindley called 'Paternalism and Caring' delivered to The Ethical Issues in Caring Conference, University of Manchester Institute of Science and Technology, 1983.
4 It is not possible here (or anywhere?) to give an exhaustive account of valid and invalid inference. The examples given will have to suffice.
5 Mill, in Warnock, op. cit., p. 198.
6 Ibid., p. 229.
7 And if a bystander has made a further attempt at suicide impossible or very difficult, perhaps by destroying the means of suicide, it may be that he ought to replace what he has destroyed or otherwise assist the would-be suicide.
8 Tom L. Beauchamp and James F. Childress, *Principles of Biomedical Ethics*, Oxford University Press, New York, 1979, p. 91.
9 And of course any attempt to treat a patient without a valid consent would be to treat him with scant respect and would violate his autonomy.
10 D. W. Vere, 'Problems in Controlled Trials—A Critical Response', *Journal of Medical Ethics*, vol. 9, no. 2, June 1983.
11 Ibid., p. 87.
12 I have taken these criteria from a very useful paper by M. D. Kirby, 'Informed Consent: What Does It Mean?', *Journal of Medical Ethics*, vol. 9, no. 3, June 1983. I have modified his formulation of the points slightly and made certain other changes—see next note.
13 Ibid., p. 71. I have modified point 5 and left out the sixth point which seems to me doubtful for reasons set out in this Chapter. It allows patients to waive information when giving consent to therapeutic treatment.
14 Beauchamp and Childress, op. cit., p. 162.

15 Although they seem to take the contrary view much later in the book at page 207. What their real view is I have been unable to discern.
16 Remember Chapter 5.

Chapter 11 Respect of persons II

1 J. S. Mill, *On Liberty*, in Mary Warnock (ed.), *Utilitarianism*, Fontana, London, 1972. Mill used this term to refer to peoples who in his day were thought of as primitive and so in need of that education and maturation which would render them autonomous, see pp. 135–6.
2 See my 'The Political Status of Children' in Keith Graham (ed.), *Contemporary Political Philosophy*, Cambridge University Press, Cambridge, 1982.
3 See Chapter 8.
4 Those who wish to do so should consult *inter alia*, Thomas S. Szasz, *The Myth of Mental Illness*, Delta, New York, 1961; and his *The Manufacture of Madness*, Routledge & Kegan Paul, London, 1971; Ian Kennedy, *The Unmasking of Medicine*, Paladin, London, 1983, ch. 5.
5 Mill, op. cit. in a footnote to page 198.
6 See in particular R. and S. Godlovitch and J. Harris, *Animals Men and Morals*, Gollancz, London, 1972. (The J. Harris is in this case not the present author.) Also, Peter Singer, *Animal Liberation*, Avon, New York, 1977; and Peter Singer and Tom Regan (eds.), *Animal Rights and Human Obligations*, Prentice-Hall, Englewood Cliffs, 1976; Steven Clark, *The Moral Status of Animals*, Oxford University Press, London, 1977, and Tom Regan, *The Case for Animal Rights*, Routledge & Kegan Paul, London, 1983.
7 I want to emphasise both that the injury to persons, to prevent which animals might justifiably be made to suffer, must be genuinely serious, and that trivial pain, as for example might be involved in slapping a dog in order to train it, can be justified in the way that slapping young children might also be justified.
8 We will be discussing the very problematic notion of what is involved in ceasing to be a person in the last chapter. The problem of duties to those who have not yet started to be persons is slightly different and we have already looked at it in Chapter 6.
9 Stuart Hampshire, *Morality and Pessimism*, Cambridge University Press, Cambridge, 1972.
10 Ibid., p. 32.
11 Ibid., p. 35.
12 Ibid., p. 36. He says in fact that it is 'partly because ...' But never mentions the other part or parts.
13 Ibid.
14 As taboos on sex and respect for the dead do!
15 This may of course be, strictly speaking, impossible.

16 There are many sources for the Hippocratic Oath. I am relying on the version reprinted in Beauchamp and Childress, op. cit., p. 280.
17 Ibid., 211.
18 *Tarasoff* v. *Regents of the University of California*, Supreme Court of Calif. Sup. 131, Rptr 14 (1 July 1976).
19 See Report in *British Medical Journal Supplement* no 3542 (20 March 1971), under heading 'General Medical Council: Disciplinary Committee'.
20 This case is taken from the Case Conference series in the *Journal of Medical Ethics*, vol. 7, no. 3, 1981. The case conference editor is Roger Higgs.
21 See P. J. Harper, 'A Genetic Marker for Huntington's Chorea', *British Medical Journal*, 26 November 1983, pp. 1567–8.
22 Ibid.
23 Ibid.
24 It is difficult here not to suspect sexist assumptions behind the doctor's double standard.

Chapter 12 Death is abolished

1 I believe this to be strictly true. The duties that are owed to the dead or to dead bodies in particular—duties to treat them with respect, for example, I believe are best understood as duties to the living who may be offended by or concerned about such treatment.
2 R. M. Veatch, *A Theory of Medical Ethics*, Basic Books, New York, 1981, p. 242.
3 Ibid.
4 Ibid., p. 245.
5 Ibid., p. 242.
6 Ian Kennedy, *The Unmasking of Medicine*, Paladin, London, 1983, p. 200.
7 Ibid.
8 Ibid., p. 201.
9 Ibid.
10 Ibid., p. 200.
11 Charles M. Culver and Bernard Gert, *Philosophy in Medicine*, Oxford University Press, New York, 1982, p. 182.
12 See Kennedy, op. cit. and also D. Lamb, 'Diagnosing Death', *Philosophy & Public Affairs*, vol. 7, no. 2, 1978; and Christopher Pallis, *ABC of Brain Stem Death*, British Medical Association, 1983.
13 And maybe practically as well.
14 The famous H. A. L. Computer in Stanley Kubrick's film *2001* was a graphic illustration of just such a computer-person who was eventually 'killed' by the astronauts.
15 Suppose the 2001 model were dismantled and its parts stored in different places but that it remained fully programmed with its

memories still intact though dispersed? Once re-assembled it would immediately resume personality. Would we say that this 2001 still existed let alone was still capable of consciousness?

16 David Lamb in an unpublished manuscript for a book on the definition of death. See also his 'Diagnosing Death', note 12 above.

17 See Chapter 6, n. 31.

18 I cease putting the word 'dead' in scare quotes but readers should have these ready for instant application where appropriate.

19 This might be an attractive solution to the problem of operations that were going wrong. The patient could be frozen before death and thus 'saved'. The fast freeze team would in future work in tandem with the resuscitation team, providing the one service or the other as appropriate.

20 Tom Stoppard, *Jumpers*, Faber & Faber, London, 1972, Act 1, pp. 27 and 28.

21 See again Chapter 5.

22 Nor probably is it of any relevance that they are citizens of other countries. See Chapter 3.

23 The computer might of course be itself a person making a fortune from this selfish advocacy.

24 And the chagrin of the frozen ones at being yet again passed over will go unremarked.

Suggested further reading

In addition to the reading mentioned or suggested in the separate notes to each chapter, the following texts will be useful to those interested in pursuing the subject further

I have arranged them under four headings. The first lists some of the best and most readable introductions to ethics and ethical theory generally. The second lists some texts devoted to medical ethics in particular, which approach the subject rather differently than the present work, and which the reader might like to consult for alternative ways of dealing with some of the problems considered here. The third section mentions some of the leading anthologies of essays on moral philosophy of general relevance to medical ethics, and finally I list the principal journals in which are to be found regular contributions to this debate.

General introductions to moral philosophy

Finnis, John, *Natural Law and Natural Rights*, Oxford University Press, London, 1980.

Fried, Charles, *Right and Wrong*, Harvard University Press, Cambridge, Mass., 1978.

Foot, Philippa, *Virtues and Vices*, Blackwell, Oxford, 1978.

Glover, Jonathan, *Causing Death and Saving Lives*, Pelican, Harmondsworth, 1977.

Glover, Jonathan, *What Sort of People Should There Be?* Pelican, Harmondsworth, 1984.

Mackie, John, *Ethics*, Pelican, Harmondsworth, 1977.

Midgley, Mary, *Heart and Mind*, Methuen, London, 1983.

Nagel, Tom, *Mortal Questions*, Cambridge University Press, Cambridge, 1979.

Singer, Peter, *Practical Ethics*, Cambridge University Press, Cambridge, 1979.

Tooley, Michael, *Abortion and Infanticide*, Oxford University Press, London. 1983.

Williams, Bernard, *Moral Luck*, Cambridge University Press, Cambridge, 1981.

Texts dealing with medical ethics

Beauchamp, Tom L. and Childress, James F., *Principles of Biomedical Ethics*, Oxford University Press, New York, 1983.

Campbell, Alistair V., *Moral Dilemmas in Medicine*, Churchill Livingstone, Edinburgh, 1975.

Culver, Charles and Gert, Bernard, *Philosophy in Medicine*, Oxford University Press, New York, 1982.

Downie, R.S. and Telfer, Elizabeth, *Caring and Curing*, Methuen, London, 1980.

Kennedy, Ian, *The Unmasking of Medicine*, Paladin, London, 1983.

Rosenberg, Jay F., *Thinking Clearly About Death*, Prentice-Hall, Englewood Cliffs, 1983.

Veatch, Robert M., *A Theory of Medical Ethics*, Basic Books, New York, 1981.

Collections of essays

Hampshire, Stuart, *Public and Private Morality*, Cambridge University Press, Cambridge, 1978.

Ladd, John, *Ethical Issues Relating To Life and Death*, Oxford University Press, New York, 1979.

Rachels, James, *Moral Problems*, Harper & Row, New York, 1975.

Sen, Amartya and Williams, Bernard, *Utilitarianism and Beyond*, Cambridge University Press, Cambridge, 1982.

Steinbock, Bonnie, *Killing and Letting Die*, Prentice-Hall, Englewood Cliffs, 1980.

Walters, William and Singer, Peter, *Test-Tube Babies*, Oxford University Press, Melbourne, 1982.

Journals dealing with medical ethics

By far the best is the *Journal of Medical Ethics*, which is entirely devoted to ethical issues in health care.

Philosophical journals which regularly publish papers of relevance to ethical issues in medicine and medical practice are relatively few. These are some of the most accessible:

Philosophy and Public Affairs
Philosophy
Philosophical Quarterly
Journal of Applied Philosophy
Journal of Medicine and Philosophy
Ethics in Science and Medicine

Index